SOURCE
IMAGERY

SOURCE

IMAGERY

*Releasing the Power
of Your Creativity*

SANDRA G. SHUMAN, PhD.

DOUBLEDAY
NEW YORK • LONDON • TORONTO • SYDNEY • AUCKLAND

Lines from "The Helmsman," by W. S. Merwin, from *The Compass Flower*.
Copyright © 1977 by W. S. Merwin. Reprinted with the permission of Atheneum Publishers,
an imprint of Macmillan Publishing Company.

Published by Doubleday, a division of Bantam Doubleday Dell
Publishing Group, Inc. 666 Fifth Avenue,
New York, New York 10103

Doubleday and the portrayal of an anchor with a dolphin are trademarks of Doubleday,
a division of Bantam Doubleday Dell Publishing Group, Inc.

Library of Congress Cataloging-in-Publication Data
Shuman, Sandra G.
    Source imagery : releasing the power of your creativity / Sandra G. Shuman. — 1st ed.
      p. cm.
    1. Creative ability. 2. Imagery (Psychology) I. Title.
  BF408.S452 1989
  153.3—dc19   88-26874
                                                          CIP
ISBN 0-385-24296-4
Copyright © 1989 by Sandra G. Shuman
All Rights Reserved
Printed in the United States of America
August 1989
FIRST EDITION
FG

Contents

Part Three
The Universal Language

Part Four
The Source Image

Part Five
The Magic Book

Preface

Each of us is far more creative than we realize. Over the past twenty-five years I have been developing a method for helping people to unblock and develop their creativity that I call Source Imagery. It is a technique for putting people in touch with their natural image-making process in such a way that they are empowered to express innate creative talents they sometimes did not even know they possessed.

Inside each of us, no matter what our age, dwells a delightful, imaginative being, our "child" side. When this special part of us receives love and encouragement, blocks to expressing our creativity dissolve, releasing transformative, healing energy in our lives.

In the pages immediately following you will see several samples of artwork produced by people who felt as many others do that they were not creative, or that whatever abilities they did have were "blocked." As they freed up the "child" inside themselves and began to release their creativity, not only did their artwork change but the quality of their lives and relationships was altered as well.

FIGURE 1

This is a first drawing by a client who is a businessman in his late thirties.

FIGURE 2

Three months later he is more confident and his style has evolved.

FIGURE 3

Nine months after beginning to work with me he produced this compelling drawing.

FIGURE 5
*A few months later she has started to open up
and her work shows the change.*

FIGURE 4
*A woman in her late sixties, also a therapist,
began with this simple piece.*

FIGURE 6
*Within a year her style has become much freer
and more colorful.*

FIGURE 7

When he first began to draw, this client, a businessman in his early fifties, seemed inhibited.

FIGURE 8

A year and a half later he is painting with great flair and self-expression.

FIGURE 9
*A book editor, a woman in her early thirties,
began drawing by making simple shapes.*

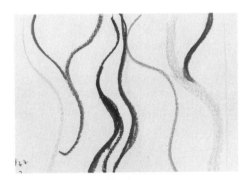

FIGURE 10
*A few months later she was beginning to loosen
up. The simple design is* moving.

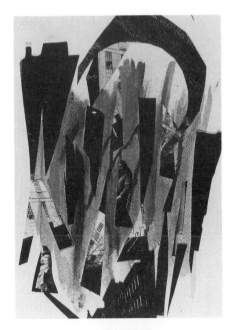

FIGURE 11
*Within two years she produced this original and
exciting piece.*

FIGURE 12
A nurse in her early thirties began with this whimsical drawing.

FIGURE 13
Two months later she created an intriguing design in bold, dramatic, colors.

The exciting changes you observe in the clients' artwork occurred spontaneously. No one had prior training in the arts or attended art classes while working with me. Moreover, the creative changes always corresponded to positive psychological changes in attitude. For example, in the first instance the client redesigned his career, and in the second, there was a late-life burgeoning of an older woman's career. In the next case, the man learned ways to balance the demands of his career with his need for recreation and relaxation, and in the fourth, the release of a client's image-making facilities helped her dissolve a long-standing writer's block. Finally, in the last instance, a woman's discovery of her artistic potential increased her capacity to communicate more effectively in all areas of her life.

These are just several examples of the kind of changes which can happen when a person's creativity is released. Although only a few people may choose to become professional artists, it is not the prerogative of just a chosen few to lead creatively fulfilling lives. Given the right stimulation and support, *we all can do it.*★

Being creative permeated every aspect of the daily lives of many people born into earlier cultures. At a recent exhibit depicting the lifestyle of the American Plains Indians I noticed that even the tents were illustrated with paintings of the battles fought by the warriors who dwelt inside them. It was not considered unusual for these men to be "artists." In fact, all of the household items as well as the people who fashioned and used them were touched by a proclivity to design, paint, weave, and embellish.

Their example can inspire us; being creative does not have to be the domain of a gifted few. Each of us has the same kind of artistic potential that our forebears did. Although we may lack the collective support the tribal environment afforded its members, we live in an age that prizes individualism and private enterprise. Today, by means of our creativity, we are each free to make a personal statement

---

★I have opted to use the personal pronoun "he" in this book, rather than the more cumbersome "he/she" form, for stylistic convenience. Perhaps because I taught grammar for so many years the pronoun "he" has a neuter or impersonal connotation for me (much like the word "on" in French or "man" in German), and I mean for it to apply to both male and female. I hope this personal preference will not offend the reader.

with our art and a unique contribution to the culture of which we are a part. In the pages ahead I'd like to introduce a time-tested process that will enable you to attain a greater degree of artistic expression on your own, in ways uniquely suited to your temperament.

At the exhibit, I was struck by the care and attention to detail taken in decorating the cradleboards. These cribs were decorated with elaborate signs, prepared months in advance of a birth. The intent was to immediately surround the new little being with symbols that carried particular import. This primitive tradition prized the creative language of images and placed a high value on the meaning it could have in the life of the individual.

Such an ancient tongue is universal and ageless, representing a legacy we are still heir to. Each night when we sleep, like one of those infants lying in its cradleboard, we are privy to special images that carry great meaning for us. We need but to become conscious of their significance in order to open doors to a magical realm of creativity inside us.

Acknowledgments

I would like to express my appreciation to the students and clients with whom I have worked during the past twenty-five years. Without their faith in my ideas I could not have developed the material presented in this book. I wish I could have included examples from all of them, but I am grateful that everyone I did ask generously agreed to contribute their artwork. Their support has been vital, and it is because of their images that the text comes alive.

Those who contributed are Margit Baldemair, Katie Barber, A. Maxwell Barnard, Sharon Bauer, Christina Hepner Brodie, Warren H. Brodie, L. J. Clave, Marjorie A. Glazer, Jean Gunn Lokensgard, Lynn Nafey, G. Michaels, Alice B. Outwater, Patricia Riley, Ann Rahimi-Assa, and others.

I am also especially grateful to my friends and associates Katie Barber and Dennis Young. Katie's understanding of the theories of Transactional Analysis made an important contribution to my thinking, and Dennis's wit, wisdom, and support inspired me. The originality of his therapeutic approach, one he has generously shared with me, has added a special dimension to the material.

I want to thank another close freind, Dr. Joe D'Amico, who read the manuscript in early draft. He helped me see things from the reader's perspective.

Thanks also to David Stephen for his sensitive rendition of the drawing for the Living Glyph and to Ann Maxwell Barnard, the artist who did the majority of the line art for the text. I feel particularly fortunate to have been able to work with someone so close to me in spirit.

Special thanks to Doe Coover, my brilliant agent and "book therapist" who brought such a wide range of talents to bear on our relationship. A skilled professional with a nurturing attitude, she has consistently been there for me. I am grateful to my editor, Sally Arteseros, who edited the text with such intelligence and precision. Her creative ability to recognize the essential has had a positive and, I hope, long-lasting effect on my writing. I also appreciate the patience of the copy editor Mary Levy and the excellent job of fine-tuning she did. I want to thank Sally's assistants, Teresa Scala and Cora Snyder, for their help.

A highlight in the production of this book was the moment when Alex Gotfyrd, art director, called to tell me he wanted to use one of my paintings for the jacket. I want to thank him for the unexpected delight this surprise brought me. I am also grateful to Susan Schwartz, who early on was so enthusiastic about the manuscript.

There are several others I'd like to thank. Two are in the distant past: Joel Dorius, a college instructor, who taught me to trust in my own ideas, and Bernhard Blume, my professor in graduate school, who taught me to see the image from many angles. Also, from the near past and the present: Mr. Douglas, the friend who gave me the gift of an IBM Selectric. Marcia Fernald, friend and professional editor, who supplied excellent last-minute hints when I was recombing the text. Barbara Dollar and her son Ben, who knew how to give me an emotional lift whenever I needed one. My brother, Morris, whose sensibilities as an artist have influenced me and who was a needed source of encouragement.

A salute to Vaska, my cello teacher, now gone, and his beautiful partner Lydia, whose love of music cast a spell on me when I was young. Their image still lingers; I see the studio filled with plants and light, with gleaming instruments; I see Lydia's glowing red hair. In that magical place I first developed some of the ideas I have about creativity.

PART ONE

The Creative Child

1

~~~~~~~~~~~~~~~~~~~~~~~~~~~~~~~~~~~

What Is Source Imagery?

A TICKET TO SUCCESS

Have you ever dreamt that you wanted to take a trip but that you couldn't locate your luggage, hail a cab or get to the airport or train station on time? Or, have you felt you had some task to accomplish but throughout the dream obstacles kept getting in your path, so that you never achieved whatever it was you set out to do? In either case you awaken feeling distracted, as if what you wanted was just beyond your grasp. And, you're frustrated because you didn't get it.

This dream experience symbolizes what it feels like to be blocked. A person knows he's got what it takes, senses it's there, but when he tries to grab hold of it, something gets in the way, preventing him from making the connection. Like the tired traveler who's missed his train, he wonders if he'll ever get where he wants to go.

Most of us have had feelings like these. Few of us are fortunate enough not to feel blocked in some area of our lives. Especially, many of us feel frustrated when it comes to being creative. We sense we have the potential, but like the person in the dream, we just can't seem to get a handle on it. Something obstructs us, whether it's a feeling of

3

inferiority, fear of failure or another anxiety. Or, our beliefs may get in the way: we think that only certain people are born "creative," that we need special training or don't have enough talent.

But, the truth is that if you ever dream, fantasize or doodle, you have all that it takes to become a far more creative person than you thought possible. The desire—and the ability—to be creative lies within each of us. But most of us haven't had the time, opportunity, or special support necessary for developing our hidden creative potential. There are many reasons why some of us have grown up believing we aren't creative at all.

Source Imagery helps dispel the idea that only a select group of people can be creative. It is a special method that I have developed for helping people learn how to tap into their natural unconscious image-making process easily, showing them how to release artistic talents and abilities. Whatever our age, we all instinctively have an urge to make images. This unconscious desire can become conscious. And to the extent that we begin to express our creativity more fully, we also begin to feel happier and more satisfied as human beings, for being creative means more than being artistic, innovative or productive; it represents a powerful healing force in the psyche. It is a universal drive that is transformative in nature and evolutionary in character.

In the series of case studies presented on pages VIII–XII you saw the exciting way in which the artwork of several clients unfolded when their creativity became unblocked. No one could predict what special form his creativity would take once it opened up. He only knew it would usher in exciting change.

What was the secret? You can learn as each of these clients did that the ticket to success lies in your own hands—in the form of fascinating images bequeathed you by the unconscious mind.

ave to find
gnificance is
y represents
reativity; it
standing the
ery and our

unblocking
heir natural,
en a person
o his creative
itive to their

activity and
it's no mere
connection of
the heart. In my experience p... hen they see
meaning in their images; the more passionate their enjoyment
of the image they produce, the more creative the form it
assumes. Source Imagery helps bring together the realms of
the real and imaginary, the physical and the spiritual, showing
how they were naturally meant to be united and why we
feel happier when they are.

The idea is simple: all images have meaning. And, if a
person is smart enough to produce the image, he's smart
enough to figure out what it means. Or, conversely, no one
ever creates an image he can't understand—all images have
meaning because they contain a spiritual element. Since the
image is child of the parent, the person who created the
image must be spiritual, also. In the realm of Source Imagery,
then, being creative is a spiritual activity, and being spiritual
is a natural part of any creative activity.

There is another important point. Everyone has a child
side. It's the part of us that likes to play, to be spontaneous.
Even if we are not as in touch with this part of ourselves as
we'd like to be, it is there. Being creative is a way of inviting
the child in us to have fun. Thus, another component of
Source Imagery is psychological, a combination of theoretical
material and practical exercises aimed at helping people
integrate this side of their personality into their lives.

To be creative, to have deep spiritual feelings, to have fun—none of these is exclusive of the other. Source Imagery as a method for unblocking creativity is also necessarily an inclusive process. It is educational in that it makes techniques for interpreting imagery universally accessible, techniques that foster a creative attitude in the mind of the person using them; and it offers enjoyable exercises that free up people's writing and drawing abilities. It also offers a psychological theory that gets at the roots of universal blocks and dispells them. Furthermore, it represents a spiritual teaching, because it explains how being creative has a healing impact on the psyche.

Source Imagery is a comprehensive, holistic approach to a complex subject. It is my hope that by reading this book and by experimenting with the exercises, you will discover new facets of your creative potential and be able to express them more fully. Certainly, Source Imagery continues to have a transformative effect on my own life and on the lives of the students and clients who have made a serious commitment to mastering the tools it offers.

This book represents the translation of a hands-on process into written form so that a wider audience might make use of it. During the years that I have been developing Source Imagery, I have made an interesting discovery. At times I have not been able to visit some of the out-of-state groups as frequently as I might like. To my delight I have found that people respond as well to the exercises I give them as do those clients whom I see more frequently at home. Group meetings have functioned as a reinforcement to the process but have evidently not been essential to it. This experience has alerted me to the fact that others can utilize the material on their own. My intention is that, in their written form, the techniques of Source Imagery will provide you with as effective a framework of support for unblocking your creativity as they have for the clients with whom I have worked directly.

While Source Imagery is a means for opening people's creativity, it also represents an original theory on the nature and function of psychic imagery in dreams and artwork. Recently, interest in the therapeutic value of imagery (e.g., guided meditation, visualization techniques, dream symbolism) has been growing into such diverse fields as medical science and the other helping professions, business, sports and even agriculture, along with, of course, the creative and performing arts. I believe that psychic images not only reflect a creative process at work within the individual, but that they can also stimulate its expression and growth. It is by knowing precisely how to tune into the creative meaning of our images that we unblock our creativity and gain access to talents and abilities inside.

Furthermore, if given the right nurturing, a person's creativity will grow as if by its own volition. The stages of growth are marked by distinct signs. They consist of certain archetypal images appearing spontaneously in dreams and artwork; these I call the universal, or "cosmic source images." At the same time, another group of images arises; these I call the "personal source images." They have characteristics unique to the individual, and they cause a person's creativity to reach maturity. Understanding the purpose of these two kinds of source images helps us to maintain a sound, healthy and more fully expressive relationship with our creativity. They are the heartbeat of the Source Imagery process; identifying their characteristics will comprise a major portion of this book.

WHAT ARE THE TOOLS OF SOURCE IMAGERY?

The theories of Source Imagery have grown out of experience; they are practical in aim. I like to encourage a healthy balance between a person's intuitive, feeling faculties and his more cognitive, reasoning ones. By combining these abilities, he learns how to consciously bring imaginative tools to bear on an unconscious, imaginative process. The effects are positive, powerful and rapid.

Since I want this book to accomplish for you what the Source Imagery workshops have accomplished for my clients, I have designed it as a how-to experience that you can implement on your own. I want to lead you to the well and show you how to build your own bucket.

Source Imagery involves a variety of tools. First, it represents a creative technique for unblocking artistic abilities, giving people access to other creative resources as well. To that end I will invite you to experiment with a series of exercises I have designed that help align your unconscious thought processes with your conscious ones, engaging your imagination and hooking your "child."

Second, it offers a self-help therapeutic approach. In that regard I explain some concepts derived from Transactional Analysis and show you how they can be applied to help free your child side. I also describe the origin of several universally prevalent blocks, helping to dispel your anxiety and to free you of the unconscious restrictions they impose.

Next, it expands the ability to communicate, accelerating the learning processes and showing you how to interpret psychic imagery on your own. You will be provided with the means not only to better grasp the significance of images as they occur in your artwork but also in your dreams and fantasies. The ability to build a meaningful rapport with your unconscious mind by tapping into dreams is essential to the Source Imagery process. Like the roots of a plant drawing water from the soil, a person draws inspiration, support and guidance for his creative endeavors by laying the groundwork for it at the source.

Finally, Source Imagery describes a holistic view of the workings of the unconscious mind, encouraging you to let go of whatever anxiety you might have about its intelligent intent. In this regard I will explain certain spiritual ideas that will enable you to better appreciate the healing nature of creativity, its transformative power and transcendent aspect. Especially I will explain "superimposition," demonstrating how images function as organizing principles in the psyche, fulfilling an essential role in a person's growth and spiritual development.

I believe that images are a key for changing our lives in many surprising ways. But we need special tools to develop our awareness of image making and to encourage our growth process.

Our first day of entering school was for many of us the last we spent in wonderland. Opening up our creativity is a way of reclaiming the lost dreams of childhood and of bringing them back to life—no matter what our age. Through the power of our imagination, we can build a bridge to join that uncommon realm with the more common one of everyday reality.

WHAT ARE THE BENEFITS?

It seems that a secret desire to be creative lies in all people. It's like the sexual urge; to deny it occasions anxiety and to repress it can eventually make someone feel "dried up," unattractive. Just as a person feels more alive when in touch with his sexuality, he tends to feel more alive when he expresses his creativity. He has more energy, hence he feels more attractive, open and interesting.

As I have mentioned, opening up one's creativity has a healthy impact on a person's life in a number of unexpected ways. Sometimes as a result of discovering creative abilities, a person identifies new career objectives or establishes more satisfying personal relationships. Often it can foster a new level of self-awareness and confidence, helping a person become more effective in his current career. If someone is already an artist, it tends to provide him with new inspiration and material to work with. Each person generates his own surprise with the material, and that is what makes Source Imagery an exciting pursuit.

I have seen people begin painting, writing, acting or pursuing some other form of creative activity; I've also seen them lose weight, quit smoking, change jobs, move, form happier relationships, go into business, get on with their children better, go back to school or leave it, and make many other positive life-changing choices.

The process of Source Imagery, which has evolved out of my experience as an educator, writer and counselor over the last twenty-five years, gives people easy access to talents and abilities they sometimes do not even suspect they possess. These creative abilities develop of their own accord, naturally. Within a remarkably short time my clients show an increase in self-confidence, imaginativeness and the ability to communicate more effectively.

The process addresses a wide variety of needs, from those of the person who feels he doesn't have a creative bone in his body to those of the artist who feels blocked. In the case of the artist, it reactivates the instinctive attraction that exists between him and his own imagery. It reinforces his autonomy, recharging him and enabling him to transcend the undermining effects criticism may have had on him in the past. It can infuse him with a new sense of confidence in his work, empowering someone who may have been reluctant to compete to strive for public recognition.

My clients have ranged in age from sixteen to seventy and have come from all walks of life. Their accomplishments using Source Imagery are dramatic. At a recent one-day workshop, for example, a woman who had never before attempted such a creative undertaking went home and began designing and making costume jewelry. That some month she sold a line of her necklaces to a large, well-known department store in New York City. Without giving up her career in television production, she discovered an avocation that enhanced the quality of her life.

Another woman, an entrepreneur, felt blocked in her career and had little confidence in her creative abilities. She decided to join a group and soon began writing—something she had always wanted to do but hadn't dared to risk. When she discovered how much she enjoyed it, she entered a short-story contest and won a trip to the Caribbean. Most important, this positive experience gave her the confidence she needed to start moving her career forward at a more accelerated pace.

Many of my clients have had no prior background in the arts. Some graphic examples of change are reflected in samples of their artwork to be found in this book. As their capacity to understand the meaning of their imagery grew and as their child side gained strength, so did their artwork, bringing positive change and healing inspiration into their lives. We can see simple lines that sometimes almost look like scribbles evolving into exciting, sophisticated designs. Or hesitant, uncertain beginnings growing into exuberant, imaginative paintings, boldly executed in bright and daring colors. And, as the artwork of my clients became more imaginative, they underwent psychological changes that gave them a freer, more positive outlook on their lives.

Along with discovering some artistic pursuit to cultivate for personal gratification, my clients also find ways in which they can redirect their careers along lines better suited to them. Their productivity increases; many find themselves asking for and receiving pay increases as a result of their greater effectiveness.

Because opening up creativity revitalizes the child in everyone, it helps people reclaim the unselfconscious delight they once took in the spontaneous expression of their imagination as children, reminding them of its uncanny ability to transform that which is dreary and everyday into something fresh and magical.

HOW DOES IT WORK?

Interestingly, a person's creative opening often follows a circuitous route. To hit the bull's-eye in creative terms sometimes means temporarily looking the other way. I've learned to trust that the shape and pace of each person's path is unique. Major roadmarks are internal, consisting as much of the occurrence of certain images as of outer activity. In fact, the changes on the outside can seem minimal at first. For example, for one client, the mother of two young children, beginning to knit and design her own sweaters represented as important a breakthrough as did creating an original piece of sculpture to another client. That step led to another; by roundabout means the unconscious mind propels a person to move forward. For this woman, taking the time to knit was a crucial act that eventually led to her finding a part-time job. While still feeling an integral part of the family unit, she established her independence outside it.

And landing the job represented reaching another plateau in an ongoing process. Source Imagery helps us first to release our creativity so that we can begin to enjoy the acts of writing, drawing, painting, and analyzing dreams. But once we have produced an image, what then? In order to stimulate the further development of our creativity, we need to learn how to respond to the image so that we feel inspired to keep moving forward. Unless we can maintain a positive response to the image, much of its power to help us advance is lost. For example, we know that in its natural state, water can be used for drinking, recreation, cleansing, irrigation and a multitude of other things. But for us to harness its electrical potential, we have to know how to direct it to run a generator. Once we have succeeded in making images, we then have to learn how to harness their power so we can use them to transform ourselves.

One of the chief aims of Source Imagery, therefore, is to help a person gain access to the creative power contained in his images. We'll investigate images from many sides, familiarizing ourselves with their special language, finding that even the simplest image has invisible layers of meaning. Like learning a second language, we'll start with simple "sentences" and then learn more complicated ones, until we feel we can grasp what our images are saying *on our own;* for, an important goal of Source Imagery is to make each person aware of his ability to interpret the images of his dreams and art by himself.

Images are intelligible, intelligent entities; they are *our* creations. Once a person has acquired the necessary tools, the images themselves have the power to lead him into deeper levels of spiritual awareness of their ever-evolving meaning.

WHAT SOURCE IMAGERY ISN'T FOR

Source Imagery does not represent a form of psychotherapy, nor is it art therapy. It is a unique method for releasing creativity and for providing people with special tools and a framework of support for developing them. Because opening up creative abilities does build confidence and self-esteem, the process has definite therapeutic side effects. In my experience you cannot remove a creative block without also removing a psychological one. In this regard being creative has a healing impact on people.

Because of its emphasis on the relationship between creativity and the well-being of the entire person, Source Imagery represents a useful adjunct to almost any psychotherapeutic enterprise. On the other hand, to enjoy the benefits resulting from the process, a person does not necessarily have to be actively engaged in any form of therapy.

Source Imagery catalyzes a unique response within each individual. The material you read should act as a formative influence on your mind, empowering you to become more creative. This book is not intended for use as a teaching manual or therapeutic aid in the hands of helping professionals whom I have not trained. But I believe that several people working in concert would benefit from using the material in the context of a leaderless self-help or study group.

The techniques I share will help people become open to their creative potential, uncontaminated by the disturbing influence of critical voices from the past. Although intended for personal use, a helping professional who does find inspiration from the material will most likely find his work informed with a higher degree of imaginativeness. I would like him to discover by using the tools directly on himself that he is his own surprising find.

IN PRAISE OF MAGIC

Not everyone will be attracted to Source Imagery. It is neither a panacea nor a miracle cure. I am reminded of a fellow I once bumped into at the airport who was sporting a brightly painted tie. I liked it, so I complimented him on it. He explained that indeed an artist had made it. We chatted for a few moments, during which I mentioned that I thought he must himself be a creative person to have chosen the tie. The vehemence of his response took me aback: "I am *not* creative, my brother is creative." "Well, then," I said apologetically, "your tie at least was a creative choice." "I am not creative," he repeated emphatically, "and nothing you could ever say or do could convince me otherwise." This reminded me that attempting to open one's creativity in the manner I prescribe won't be everyone's cup of tea. For some, no end of convincing will ever budge their resistance; and uncomfortable or not, they like it that way.

It is just because the process reawakens the child in a person that it presents a special challenge to the beginner. Like a very small child still learning to gain muscular coordination, the creative child in us feels awkward at moments. However, like a child, taking delight in his surroundings as he learns to master the use of his body, each person who patiently persists in acquiring the skills the process has to offer will experience delight with his natural successes. For although I don't believe in miracles, I can't help but think Source Imagery does contain a little magic.

A PREVIEW OF WHAT'S AHEAD

I intend to present the material here in much the same manner that I do when offering it in a workshop. After introducing you to some of the basic concepts of Transactional Analysis, I'll describe the three main blocks that may inhibit your creativity. For once you have overcome these blocks, you will more easily gain access to the resources of your unconscious mind.

Then I will show you how to interpret your imagery, pointing out the special significance of the source image, expanding your awareness of its spiritual meaning. We need to broaden our perspective on our creativity. In Source Imagery, for the image to more consciously evolve, we have to evolve ourselves. In this regard personal growth and artistic development go hand in hand.

This book also includes a practical how-to section with a variety of creative exercises. These are aimed at giving the "child" plenty of space for play. Whereas finding and unraveling the mystery of the source image will be a fascinating task, it should not be your sole aim. Rather it should be to steadily encourage the unfolding of your child side. The source image teaches us how to cherish the entire self; even though it may enliven the mind of the adult, its true purpose is to thrill the heart of the child.

2

The Power of Positive Strokes

Along with learning how to read and spell when he's in school, a person ought to learn about the most appropriate and effective way to give and receive strokes. As a client of mine excited about how Source Imagery changed her life said, "I feel like I've discovered a new element!" But this basic knowledge—of stroking, or rewarding—never seems to get transmitted to us.

Whether or not school was a positive experience for them, most people can recall aspects of being there that occasioned some measure of anxiety, or even despair. Anxiety about making a mistake, of being wrong, still lurks in the minds of most adults—especially when they have to perform or enter into a new learning situation. Fundamentally, there are only two conditions under which any form of learning can take place: a person is either alone or working in a group with others. Embarrassing memories of situations we encountered when we first entered school and started learning *in conjunction with* and *in the presence of others* can still impede us even when we decide to learn something on our own. We've internalized the critical voice of teachers to such an extent that it still operates out of our field of awareness, preventing us from feeling at ease even when we're by ourselves.

Because most of our formal learning experiences took place in school, they necessarily occurred in a social or public setting. Thus, learning and the act of performing in front of others are closely associated in our minds. At an early age we accustomed ourselves to having to perform in a competitive environment. There were ever-present pressures in the classroom. The reward, or stroke, for doing well was reflected in the kind of grade we received; to get a good grade and also to please the teacher, we had to get along with our classmates, learn to sit still, and quell the natural inclination to talk and move about at will.

Consequently, whenever we are called upon to perform, buried memories from childhood are stirred, quickening gut feelings of anxiety. We involuntarily feel as if we were in a competitive situation; we want to "make the grade" and fear we might not, are anxious to please and do whatever "it" is correctly. Either a vague or more defined sense of pressure builds internally, making it difficult to concentrate.

Sometimes the anxiety is so pervasive that it can be overwhelming. The negative feelings can impede a person from being able to perform in private; it's as if he needed a bulldozer to push the resistance away, even though he may very much want to initiate some form of creative activity. The paper is there, the pencils, the brushes, the paints, the time, the space, the ideas—but nothing happens, because he can't get his ideas on the page. Or, the anxiety can immobilize a person when he attempts to perform in public. One client, a professional musician, became dizzy every time he tried to get on stage. The irritating symptom cleared up as soon as he was able to identify and address the original source of the discomfort.

A striking experience I had in a classroom filled with college students when I was still a new instructor (I was teaching a German language course) illustrates the extent to which performance anxiety rules the minds of most adults. I had announced that when they opened their textbooks, they would notice that many more words were capitalized in German than in English. I said that was because "all German nouns are capitalized." Everyone nodded. "See?" I said, pointing to the page. "Yes," everyone nodded again in agreement.

I told them that when they were quizzed, they should be sure to capitalize every noun or I would have to take a point off for a mistake. Everyone nodded. At first I couldn't grasp why no one remembered to capitalize the nouns on the initial quiz. So, I repeated the point in a louder, more demanding tone. Nonetheless, the students still continued writing nouns with small letters.

I imagine most of them might have gone through life forgetting to capitalize German nouns but for a sudden insight I had. I then asked, "Does anyone here know what a noun is?" To my surprise, no one raised a hand. In that particular class not a single student remembered what the grammatical term meant. If someone did, certainly he didn't want to take the chance of being wrong. What amazed me was not so much the lack of knowledge but rather the force of the pressure to conform. Not one person had dared to risk losing face by admitting he didn't know what the word meant. It was as if they had all silently acted in concert, deciding as a single body not to look stupid.

I explained the meaning of "noun" along with other rules of English grammer, and it won't be a surprise to you that the students' performance improved from then on. But, it might take you a little time to remember a moment when you pretended to know something you didn't, for fear of making a mistake and losing face. Each of us has a lot invested in looking as though we have the answers by the time we become adults. And it's difficult to identify with the child inside and have to reveal our ignorance. We would much rather feel stupid as long as we look smart. But that doesn't always get us the results we want.

In Transactional Analysis the voice that dictates we'd better act smart and hide our inadequacy—the one that assumes we *are* inadequate—and, above all, maintains we'd better distrust other people is called the "Critical Parent." It always knows best. I like to think of it as the internal, infernal yenta who never quits, not even when we're asleep.

We've never done enough, we haven't done it right, we're not as smart as someone else, we'll never make it no matter how hard we try, nag, nag, nag. Its complaints are endless; it's never satisfied: a B should have been an A, an A should have been an A+. And, it's insistent: Why didn't you do it the other way? Why didn't you do it sooner? Or, You shouldn't have done it at all, I told you so.

If the consequences of listening to this voice, which continually criticizes and demeans us *out of our field of awareness,* weren't so devastating, the situation would almost be funny. I've encountered a phenomenon similar to the one in the classroom when I have counseled clients in workshops and private sessions. Invariably, upon bringing the first drawing or other piece of work to show me, the client will begin with some sort of apologetic introduction, whether he is an artist or not. This apology is, interestingly enough, not recognized to be such until I point it out.

The form can vary. The self-administered discount might be "I brought it, even though it isn't finished yet," or "I kind of like it, even though it didn't come out quite the way I wanted it to," or "I know this isn't what you expected, but . . . ," or "Except for that smudge over there . . . ," etc. I could almost record these apologies; I would only have to flick on a tape at the onset of viewing a client's work and be done with it.

On the surface it doesn't look as though there is much of a connection between being creative and our early learning experiences, but there is. Whenever we attempt to open our creativity we are simultaneously asking ourselves to perform, whether it is happening in private or in the presence of others. And the very same infernal yenta that kept the students from admitting their ignorance is the one that prevents us from freely taking a creative risk. It's difficult to perform when you're afraid of making a fool of yourself. This is why my clients are secretly abashed when they show their work, compulsively voicing their apologies. Just what punishment are they hoping to evade?

The voice of the Critical Parent is difficult to dodge, popping up unbidden and rendering us defenseless. Whether it utters a negative stroke like "you're stupid" or a discount like "that's no good," the effect is the same: one part of us constantly feels it is waging war with another. It's a distracting state of affairs.

A NEW LOOK AT THE NATIONAL DEFICIT

Stroke deprivation is a universal problem and ought to be considered part of the national deficit. You can't draw checks against an empty bank account, and it's difficult to perform efficiently if you don't get enough strokes to build self-confidence. Since everyone suffers from the same deficiency, it's unrealistic to expect to be able to bank on getting strokes regularly from an outside source. Instead it makes sense to learn how to build and maintain your own stash.

Can the Critical Parent's voice be circumvented? And by what means? Let's return to our early classroom experiences. Perhaps better than any other anecdote, the following illustrates the kind of treatment we encountered as children that had long-term detrimental effects on us. Once, a student had difficulty responding to one of the more creative assignments I had given the class, which involved drawing an image in a short story we were analyzing. No grade was involved; the point was simply to stimulate the student's visual imagination and expand his nonverbal communication skills. Try as he might, this student could not bring himself to make even the roughest of sketches.

The fellow sincerely wanted to respond but couldn't. Exasperated, unable to get beyond his block, he decided to write about it, handing in a paper instead. It was entitled "Sister Georgita." Sister Georgita had been in charge of his first-grade art class. One day, while busily coloring a picture of autumn leaves as she had instructed him to do, my student was startled out of a self-forgetful trance by the strident sound of the teacher's voice. Sister Georgita was strongly reprimanding a little girl, whose face was bright red because she had colored some of her leaves black. "Ugh," exclaimed the teacher, holding the picture up for all to see, "no one ever draws black autumn leaves! Autumn leaves aren't black. Ugh!" For unexplained reasons she decided all the students must be punished for this child's "transgression" and instructed them to put their heads on their desks for several minutes.

The student said he'd forgotten the incident until now, relegating it completely to the past, but while he wrote, it had suddenly occurred to him that, as much as he had enjoyed drawing up until that point, he'd never drawn again. That was when he was about seven; now he was in his twenties.

This unfortunate example shows the powerful effect an adult can have on a child even indirectly. It was not what had happened to him but what he had seen happen to his classmate that influenced his attitude. All of us can recall some such incident; perhaps it had to do with knowing the teacher had made a mistake but wouldn't admit it, or with our being criticized unfairly. The range is varied, the effect the same. Whenever we are called upon to perform, we tend to clench up, because we lack an inner support system to help get us over the hurdles. Feeling inadequate, we find ourselves suddenly on automatic, responding to the voice of the Critical Parent that berates us for our shortcomings, thinking it can whip us into shape through humiliation and intimidation.

Earlier I mentioned casually that I should record the apologies of my clients. In fact, the voice of the Critical Parent is like a tape. There's no rational thought involved; it's a somewhat ineffective mechanism built up over years of abuse by many generations of forebears, passed on to us unthinkingly by our parents. They hand the tape over, we make a copy, memorizing it. Having internalized it as small children, we use it throughout life to ward off any real or imagined threat to our security. Can you recall an incident from either your own or another's experience that affected you in a manner similar to my client? It's important to pinpoint it. Like a garden weed that has been pulled, once exposed to the light of day the memory is apt to dry up, wither away and cease crowding out creative inclinations you might have.

Those years in school certainly weren't all bad. But they represented a critical point in our development; as children we were sensitive in ways we have forgotten. We have buried painful memories without realizing that we did so at a cost. Like my student who simply "forgot" he liked to draw, we've forgotten many wonderful things we once enjoyed but gave up doing. It's never too late to reclaim them.

And by no means am I suggesting that all teachers were ogres. There's another story, also concerning an art teacher, whose behavior was quite different. A client's son, who was in the first grade, was very shy and had difficulty expressing himself. The teacher had instructed the children to simply play with their coloring materials, drawing anything they liked. Everyone went to town, evidently delighted by the absence of restrictions. That is, everyone but my client's little boy, who was unable to make anything other than a single black curve across a page. The teacher, who had been going around the room and pausing at each desk to comment on each child's piece, noticed the boy's discomfort. But when she arrived at his desk, try as she might to find something to say, she felt at a loss for words. She did not want him to feel excluded from the attention the others were receiving, so she withdrew to think. After a moment she returned, inspired. Placing her arm around the boy's shoulder, she asked him, "Where does that diving board go to?" The boy looked up, wondering—almost on the verge of tears—and said, "How did you know that was just what I wanted to draw?"

This teacher had empathy for and an understanding of a child's sensitivity. She responded to her bewilderment not with the voice of the Critical Parent, who always tries to gain control through derision or criticism, but with the voice of the "Nurturing Parent," who tries to guide through love and encouragement. The voice of this Parent does not operate on automatic, but on intuition.

A final story shows how finely attuned some adults are to children on this level. A friend of mine who adores her little three-year-old grandson gave him a toy stove complete with miniature utensils for Christmas. He was delighted; the grown-ups put it in the kitchen next to the big stove, whereupon he immediately set to work, pretending to cook dinner. Meanwhile, my friend sat in the living room, sewing. Suddenly the little boy came running up to her, making believe he was crying. When she looked up at him, he held his hand out for her to see: "Look, Grandmommy," he said, "I burned my hand on my stove."

My friend did not respond immediately as I might have, taking his hand to kiss the imaginary boo-boo away. Like the teacher, she sensed something was up, so she thought a moment; then it clicked. "Oh!" she exclaimed, "that's too bad. I guess Grandmommy will just have to make a little pot holder for you to put on your stove like the one she has!" "Yes," the boy cried gleefully, "yes, that's just what I want!"

In this instance the reader can observe the high degree of imagination that my friend brought to bear on the situation. Kissing the boo-boo wouldn't have been a bad response, but it does pale in comparison to the impressive way in which this lady met the challenge. The incident is important because it illustrates the similar kind of challenge that dealing with the child inside us poses for us—on a daily basis. Most of us take this side of ourselves for granted, automatically indulging it with ice-cream cones, a movie or a vacation now and then. But frequently we do not take the necessary time to listen, respond and attend sensitively to its needs, as did my friend with her grandson, or the art teacher with the severely inhibited boy. Instead, like Sister Georgita, we ignore or scold it for bothering us, and we shoo it away as if it were an irritating little pest. Just as surely as a real child brings much unexpected pleasure—along with responsibilities—into a parent's life, so does the child within us have the potential for bringing much untold enjoyment into our lives, have we but the patience and imagination to encourage it to do so.

THE NURTURING VERSUS THE CRITICAL PARENT

The Critical Parent administers negative strokes and has a demeaning influence; the Nurturing Parent administers positive strokes that are encouraging and enhancing to our self-esteem. In Transactional Analysis the self is seen as comprised of three main parts; these are the ego states, or states of consciousness, we continually shift in and out of, which correspondingly influence our actions, thoughts, and responses in characteristic ways.

When we are in the "Parent" ego state, we are concerned with setting standards and limits. This part of us should ideally consist of a nurturing, supportive side that feeds us unconditionally, and a disciplining side that prohibits, trains and requires certain kinds of actions from us. The "Adult" is the thinking part. It is like a computer; it is impartial, concerned with assessing liabilities and options. It thinks, figures and organizes. Most importantly, it provides data that helps us make choices. The "Child" is the creative center; it imagines, wants, spontaneously responds. It is also the seat of intuition.

Due to past influence—for example, inappropriate behavior our parents and teachers may have modeled for us—most of us have internalized a disciplining parental side that is oppressive, overly harsh and critical. This tyrannical manifestation of the disciplining side of the Parent is what I name the Critical Parent. To mollify its voice we tend to be either compliant or "adapted," suppressing our need for autonomy; or we are defiant and "rebellious," acting in inappropriate or self-destructive ways in order to spite it. In either case we are not responding sensitively to the needs of the natural Child. When our intent is to appease or defy the Critical Parent and not be true to the self, we lack integrity; we therefore feel as if we have been cut off from, or are not in sync with, ourselves.

By learning to strengthen the nurturing side of the Parent, we can offset the negative effects of the voice of the Critical Parent. We can't get rid of the latter; we can, however, learn to get around and defang it. Besides, the Critical Parent isn't all bad. It merely represents a judge who's gone haywire, who doesn't deserve all the authority he pretends to have. We can view him as a puppet king; without dethroning him, we conscientiously turn our attention elsewhere for support.

NURTURING THE CREATIVE CHILD

What are strokes? At their most fundamental level, strokes are units of recognition we receive from ourselves and others; they can range from a simple "good morning" to the winning of the Nobel Peace Prize. We need them to survive; they are fundamental to our sense of well-being. Essentially there are two kinds: pats on the head we get from ourselves or others for something we *did,* and pats we get for simply being who we *are.* To the first category belong statements like "Dinner was delicious!" To the second, "I like your smile!" The former is a conditional compliment; the latter, an unconditional acknowledgment. For a well-balanced sense of self-esteem, we need a combination of both kinds of strokes, administered on a daily basis.

But there is a problem. For some baffling reason, we are generally not taught how to receive strokes appropriately, let alone give them effectively. Learning how to acknowledge them is important. What good can a glass of milk do if you tip it over, spilling the milk before it can reach your mouth? Being able to recognize and internalize a stroke is a basic skill you must master to proceed with the material in this book.

Why? Strokes are the "Open Sesame" to unlocking our creative potential. Whether we're more advanced artists or beginners, we've all got that critical tape operating in our head. Its voice causes more blockage than anything else I know, when it comes to taking a creative risk. I've invented a little diagram to illustrate the subversive effect it can have upon us, as opposed to the reinforcing one the voice of the Nurturing Parent has:

This simple diagram depicts a typical internal conflict most people experience when attempting to open their creativity. Unless you can learn to give the Child part the necessary strokes not only to survive but to thrive, you won't make the positive gains you desire. The Critical Parent will see everything the Child brings forth with a critical, perfectionist, jaundiced eye. The Nurturing Parent, on the other hand, sees from a loving perspective what the Child produces; the Nurturing Parent takes pride in the Child's accomplishments and, figuratively speaking, puts all of the pictures up on the refrigerator door without throwing a single one out.

Overcoming inhibitions and the negating influence of the voice of the Critical Parent is a gradual process. Often a person undergoes a transition period in which he feels caught in limbo, somewhere between the two voices. The dilemma is best exemplified in the words of one client who, after several weeks of struggling to learn how to give herself positive strokes, came to the group with a drawing she was excited to pass around. She liked it and appeared at first to be proud of it. It was a striking picture of a fiery red serpent. "I could hardly wait to show you this," she said. "I'm so excited. It was so much fun!" She paused, and continuing in almost the same breath, she added, "Oh, but I know it's nothing to get excited about, it's just a silly snake!"

Is taking pride in our creativity sinful, a pleasure best performed in private, if at all?

My point is that the decision to give our child side a positive stroke is a *conscious choice;* it is a deliberate act of will, the intent of which is to further open our creativity.

GIVING AND RECEIVING STROKES

The best way to practice receiving strokes is to consciously acknowledge that you have received one, repeating it back to the person who gave it. For example, if a friend says, "That's a beautiful sweater you're wearing," it is not sufficient to respond by merely saying, "Thank you." You state instead, "Thanks for appreciating my taste." Or, if someone comments, "That was a good job you did," you say, "Thanks for appreciating the hard work I put into it," and so on.

It won't do to acknowledge a stroke silently. To internalize it, you must voice a response that both you and the other person can hear. At first it may seem awkward, but it gets easier with practice. For one thing, people like to receive recognition for the strokes they give. For another, as a result of this positive experience, you gradually find yourself beginning to deliver more honest, effective strokes not only to others but to yourself as well.

To achieve even more rapid results, I suggest you enlist the aid of a friend. Sit facing one another and practice giving verbal strokes and acknowledging them. You and your friend will immediately get in touch with how severe your resistance is. Like learning to pronounce the words of a foreign language correctly, generally people feel ill at ease the first few times they attempt to communicate with each other in this new tongue. But in an environment of mutual love and respect, each person can overcome the anxiety and learn to let go of these inhibitions quickly.

A stroke can be, but is not always, a compliment, because not all complimentary remarks are honest. In order to qualify as a genuine stroke, the remark must be honest. Therefore, the issue poses a challenge, often requires imagination and can't be taken lightly.

Knowing how to give the Child an effective stroke is the A in the ABC's of Source Imagery. It is a vital tool we need to master in order to coax the child inside us out into the open, where it can perform more unselfconsciously, without the fear of criticism, in the expectation of praise.

HEALING THE WOUNDED CHILD

I have explained the concepts of the Parent, Adult and Child, along with the notion of stroking, in order to highlight the importance of our learning new ways in which to treat our child side. Most of us can recall that when we were little, we frequently asked adults to watch us perform; it didn't matter what we did, whether twirling and whirling and dancing, or telling a favorite story. The main thing was that we had an opportunity to be the center of attention for a few minutes and could show off to our heart's delight.

It was also important that people clapped and demonstrated their appreciation at the end of our act. We glowed for having been entertaining. That same little performer still dwells inside each of us.

Unfortunately, because we have never learned, or have unlearned, how to encourage this part of us to perform without anxiety, it is reluctant to show its face. Unawares, we restrain it from expressing itself. We restrict it and, as a result, continue to stifle many of our natural creative impulses. It is as if we were still under the collective thumb of our early schoolteachers, waiting until someone gives us permission to go out and play. But the child in us is resilient. The wounded child, given proper attention, rebounds quickly. The sooner we learn how to attend to the needs of this side of ourselves—generously and wholeheartedly offering the strokes it deserves when it tries to perform for us—the sooner our creativity will begin to grow and flourish in unexpected ways. I've often been amazed at the quantum leaps that clients will make once this side of their personality has been revived; like a plant that has the ability to grow overnight, their creativity begins shooting off in surprising new directions.

Remember how eagerly we anticipated recess when we were children? We could hardly wait for the bell to ring. When it did, we spilled out of the classroom and ran down the corridor as one body to get outside as quickly as we could, screaming and yelling in relief. To free the creative child once and for all we've got to retrieve him from the restrictions imposed on him in the past. We have the ability to treat him differently now; we can create a loving environment for him to live in—one in which he can be free to express himself without embarrassment, without fear, without restraint, in all his bewitching grace.

3

≈≈≈≈≈≈≈≈≈≈≈≈≈≈≈≈≈≈≈≈≈≈≈≈≈≈≈≈≈≈

Claiming the Rich Territory

THE GOOD NEWS

In my experience the same factors that inhibit a person's learning abilities inhibit the development of his creative faculties. However, the good news is that once given the appropriate nurturing and support, the child in him will resuscitate, and he will see his creativity unfold almost of its own volition. It is as if there were a genetic predisposition universally present in us. For now, the question to ask ourselves is not "Do I have creative potential?", but more exactly "Why hasn't my creative potential opened up yet as fully and easily as I would like it to?"

Like an uncultivated piece of land overgrown with weeds, a person's creativity often remains dormant until he consciously decides to cultivate it. There are many reasons why it lies fallow for so long; most of them originate in the past. Again, authoritative voices we heard as children unconsciously still influence our attitudes, not to mention classroom indoctrination that overemphasized a one-dimensional approach to learning and/or religious training that may have deprecated earthly existence.

Being creative is a multidimensional experience; in order

to appreciate its complexity, we have to acknowledge that we ourselves are multidimensional, with physical, mental, emotional and spiritual components to our being. Creativity represents a special altered state of consciousness that we can easily enter into if we choose.

But as I have said, there are universal impediments that stand in the way, which are the result of movement in the past that transpired out of our field of awareness. By investigating their origin, we can free ourselves to make new choices—choices that alter our frame of reference—so that we more easily identify with our innate creative potential.

That plot of land I mentioned is not just overgrown with weeds; the soil is compacted, hard, dry. By the time we've reached adulthood, many factors beyond our control have jointly conspired to leach out our imagination. A straight life is one devoid of magic; and, by reactivating the power of the imagination, we instill our lives with a romance and spirit that have been sorely missing.

It is when we are children, growing and changing rapidly in a biological sense, that we are also the most vulnerable and sensitive to external influence. Like a seedling that needs special attention before it can become rooted and mature into a plant, our system is delicate, easily affected by outside forces.

A child's imagination is a living, growing, psychic force; but it is in a bud state, and when we are little, it needs caring. For an individual's personality to blossom and flower fully, his imagination requires the presence of certain favorable conditions.

Just as we have some painful learning experiences in common, we share other painful childhood experiences that have led us to distrust the creative side of our personality, and which cut us off from it; thus, we do not benefit from our rich imaginative resources. By involuntarily renouncing the child inside, we have—without realizing it—also relinquished the creative legacy it bears. By reowning the child, we bestow anew upon ourselves the gift of being the imaginative individuals we were meant to be. For, it is only by consciously integrating the child into our personality that we can ultimately attain our full creative potential.

EXPANDING THE DEFINITION OF ALTERED STATES

When we learn to see our child in a positive light, we find ourselves framing the creative experience from a new perspective, for the two states of awareness are intimately connected. To entertain the one is to invite the presence of the other.

In order to better create an environment conducive to the growth of creativity, we need to expand our definition of altered states. People tend to think of this as a somewhat dramatic term, one that implies either drug-induced stupors, out-of-body experiences, or religious trances.

I think of the term in a more down-to-earth sense. As a result, it's surprising that once in a while when I ask a person to meditate before doing an exercise, his response will be that he's afraid to, because something dramatic or "bad" might happen. No one has ever been able to define what "it" is; perhaps he might spontaneously enter Nirvana and never come back, or lose his grasp of reality. Meditating is a special way to relax and focus your attention; it helps you to concentrate and, paradoxically, to let go at the same time. There is not too much excitement involved, nor do you have to experience religious hallucinations while in that kind of self-induced trance. By contrast, watching television can induce a state of more dopey stupefaction than mediating ever will. So I say, if you're not afraid to watch television, please don't be afraid to meditate.

It might be useful for you to pause here and to jot down in a few phrases a brief description of various altered states of awareness that you know you have experienced (other than that of ordinary waking consciousness). You must have entered these states spontaneously, without the use of drugs: for example, the act of falling asleep and dreaming is one such state, daydreaming another.

It won't take long for you to realize that you slip in and out of different altered states or trances frequently, without effort; you'll have to deromanticize your notion that it's something out of the ordinary.

What are some of the altered states you have experienced? Here are a few that students and clients have shared with me: getting lost, being in love, being depressed, being extremely bored, feeling the euphoria that can accompany childbirth, having an athletic "high," experiencing rage, being at war, being in a rush, driving in a racing car, having hypochondria, and being half-awake and half-asleep at the same time (I call this in-between state the "mezzanine floor" of consciousness).

Driving under exceedingly heavy traffic conditions induces a negative state of mind to which almost everyone can relate. So does standing in a long line that is moving slowly when you are in a hurry. You involuntarily begin to feel trapped and impatient, and can become unreasonably hostile. Even the state of mind precipitated by working hard at a pleasant task can bring on an altered state; you tend to lose track of time, forget to eat, can even forget pain or discomfort. On the other hand, if you don't like the job, you become restless; think about food; daydream; feel bored, sick or cranky; and wish time would move faster. In both instances you have entered an altered state; in the former, everything but the task at hand fades into the background; in the latter, you wish the task itself would disappear.

We perceive that a shift in consciousness influences how we might view reality. It colors our emotional responses. Some trances cause us to feel at ease, satisfied, in sync with ourselves and others, whereas other trances cause the opposite effect. I believe a person should try to enter as many naturally pleasant states or comfortable, joyful trances as possible.

Going on vacation represents another interesting altered state. When vacationing, a person gives himself permission to "get away" from responsibilities, to immerse himself in the fleeting enjoyment of the moment. By letting go of the familiar, he hopes to recharge and return home rejuvenated. The feeling of being renewed will cast things in a fresh light, affording him a clear perspective. As with a pile of mail that he has accumulated and neglected to sort through, when he comes back, he finds that the passage of time has made matters easier to prioritize; problems that loomed as large and pressing have diminished. Thus he can discriminate more easily between the important and the unimportant.

What's changed here is not the situation but the person's perception of it. We see that in order for us to change anything, we need to change our consciousness first, because it is our consciousness of things that most often changes them.

A CHANGE IN CONSCIOUSNESS

There aren't any "wrong" altered states any more than there are "wrong" emotions. The intrinsic value of a state of awareness is relative; it either helps you have the experience you want or it doesn't. To enter a desired trance, you need to make the appropriate adjustment. If the thought of being creative induces a sense of anxiety, it won't do any good to "think positive" about it. To affirm that you are creative, that you can enjoy creativity, doesn't accomplish very much.

I think of the unfortunate student who encountered Sister Georgita in his first-grade art class. He was snapped out of his creative trance with her vociferous "ugh!" Involuntarily, he associated losing himself in pleasure with the pain of receiving an unpleasant emotional jolt. When I asked him to draw, I could have stood in front of the door of his mind all day, asking the key to turn by voicing all manner of pleasantries. It wouldn't have worked, try as hard as we both might to get him unstuck and into a new position.

To get a new result, he would have to make a new choice. An affirmation is not a decision, although you can make affirmative decisions. Long ago the boy had made up his mind that it was scary to draw; the decision was firmly set, and then he forgot he had made it. With time the old choice faded until eventually he came to believe "I *can't* draw." His act of will was transformed, changing into what appeared to be a physiological given instead.

Why did he make that choice? Young and defenseless, he probably saw no other alternative. Within the context in which he was operating, his choice made sense—because he couldn't fire Sister Georgita or tell her she was a jerk.

The thought of drawing now induced a negative trance in this person, one that immobilized him and threw him into a state of panic and dread. To draw a picture was not merely to take a simple risk with his creativity: it was synonymous with *risking humiliation*.

The unconscious intent of the trance he put himself into was to avoid humiliation at all cost. So, even though on a conscious level he wanted to draw, and spent a lot of time trying to talk himself into it, he couldn't get the desired result. He was going to have to alter his frame of reference to get a new perspective. He would have to replace one trance, whose intent was to avoid pain, with another—whose purpose was to bring pleasure.

In order to change your intent, or to redirect the energy of your will, you must make a new choice; it's the best way to turn the key to entering a new state of awareness. It won't happen by itself. In order to enjoy the refreshment of a vacation, for example, a person who habitually avoids going away would have to rethink his position and choose to take a trip.

Suppose for a moment that you have decided to buy a new coat. You have a specific style in mind, but can't find what you like at the first store. You have a choice. You can either stay there and get depressed or continue your quest elsewhere. It would be folly for you to think you could never find the appropriate coat because of that one experience. Being a smart shopper and a determined person, you decide instead to actively keep looking rather than to passively bemoan your state. By framing the situation in this positive light, you optimize your chances for getting the outcome you want.

Every altered state a person enters is the result of a choice he has made to entertain it; it has an influence on how he frames his perspective of reality.

You might inquire, What if I, like that little boy in first grade, were dragged along against my will, that is, What if I were taken on a trip and did not choose to go? How could I be faulted for having an experience I did not wish to have?

True. But the choice the boy made about how to frame the situation was his alone. It is likely there were students sitting in that room who, in response to the same set of circumstances, decided nothing was ever going to keep them from drawing. I have met such people.

In order to reframe our perspective on the creative experience, we have to be willing to *choose* to reframe it. The inhibited student would have to be willing to change his mind and decide that it might be possible for him to draw. He would have to decide to try out a new position, or *switch his frame.* Because of an early negative experience, he associated pain with the act of being creative. Such a choice encourages a depressing, immobilized state of mind.

He could choose to stop trying so hard to avoid being humiliated, and instead look forward to the surprise of discovery, the joy of achievement. He would not feel he had to assume guard duty when attempting to draw, but would behave more like a loving parent, someone who anticipates a challenge and greets it responsively. This choice would encourage a productive frame of mind and most likely lead to a positive outcome.

A person might just as well associate the act of being creative with entering an altered state that relieves stress as associate it with one that induces it. He is in the same old boat, but definitely headed in a new direction. As with someone who looks forward to making love as a means for releasing sexual tension, the student might find himself displacing the old intent to avoid the pain of embarrassment with the more optimistic one of finding an outlet for his feelings. In this context, creativity represents an altered state that's exciting to be in because of the pleasure it engenders.

The following story illustrates what can happen when a person decides to change his mind and reframe his perspective. I was attracted to buying the big old house I live in partially because of its large yard. When the former owner handed me the keys, however, he mentioned with a dour smile that I was going to find the yard a pain to take care of. I nodded in agreement, didn't think much about it and forgot the incident. Years later, after much renovating, I stood looking at the yard and wondered why it was so neglected and overgrown with weeds. A close friend pointed out its potential, piquing my dormant interest in gardening.

Suddenly I remembered my old choice that the yard was going to be nothing but a problem for me. Now I faced the consequences of having made that decision. I changed my mind—giving up a negative, unproductive frame, and switching it for a more enlightened one.

Instead of viewing the yard as if it were impossible to care for, I saw the advantage that owning such a piece of land represented, and I began to perceive the outline of the invisible garden it contained. As a result of my new choice, the place was gradually transformed and became a refuge where I could recharge and find peace of mind. First I did have to hire someone to cut down the weeds with a chain saw, because some of them had grown so thick. But now I am instinctively attracted to being there.

I hope you will be able to affirm your creativity in the same way that I can affirm my pleasure in gardening. To look forward to such an outcome, you must first be willing to change your mind, deciding you possess a rich and exciting territory within you that, as the fallow land adjacent to my house, just awaits the touch of a loving hand to burst into bloom.

4

Retrieving the Child

THE FEAR OF LETTING GO

In order to begin gardening, I had to feel like it first. Once I had made a choice that helped me frame things in a healthier light, my experience of the yard changed. While I may not be able to help you figure out what choices you have made that are preventing you from appreciating the full range of your creative potential, I am nevertheless in a position to help you remake one major decision, through a process called "redecisioning."* Changing how you view your child side can help to create a dramatic new frame, inviting favorable results.

I have pointed out the causes of the performance anxiety we all tend to experience. Once we are in that state of mind, it is difficult to acknowledge a positive stroke. When teaching, I was often struck by my students' attitude in this regard. "Where are the red marks?" they would ask impatiently. Some were indignant. "I don't want to know what I'm doing that's *right!* I want to know what's *wrong.* Where are the criticisms?" The implication was that unless I inflicted pain, they weren't learning anything.

Similarly, people tend to disparage their creative output

* This valuable concept is described in *Changing Lives Through Redecision Therapy,* by Mary and Robert Goulding (New York: Grove Press, 1982).

36

and are reluctant to acknowledge positive strokes regarding its value. For example, the lady who was excited by her painting of the fiery snake but then decided it was silly had difficulty accepting the fact that other members of the group liked the piece. She was not just discounting the picture; she was actually discounting the possibility of her originality. And this tendency to belittle her potential for being original is one she shares with many other people.

Why is the fear so prevalent? What is its cause? The need to deprecate our originality, to tear down what we have made in our own and others' eyes, is almost compulsive. It's as if we must steadfastly keep something hidden from view, something bad and disgusting that being creative exposes to the public eye. What is this negative feeling or projection all about?

It is connected to feelings we have about our child side. Being creative involves spontaneity, imaginativeness, playfulness and expressiveness. These are attributes of the child which, taken at face value, seem desirable and attractive to us. However, most of us have memories of being helpless and vulnerable when we were little, not only by virtue of our size, but by our extreme dependency. In most instances we have suppressed these memories; but each time we attempt to enter a creative frame of mind, we feel inexplicably anxious and, like the student, are temporarily immobilized by the unconscious block. We long to be like a child again, and yet we have a tremendous distrust of expressing this side.

Long before we were subject to the dictating voices of our early teachers, we became accustomed to the sounds of our parents' voices, without whose diligent advice we might never have learned how to put our pants on right or tie our shoelaces correctly. It is the combined sound of this entire chorus of grown-up authority figures that goes on in our head every time we take the risk to express our creativity.

A whole battery of silent questions is raised concerning who's going to be in charge of the show. And is there any question really about who's running it? To the invisible parent holding court in our brain, we address all manner of ingratiating inquiries: Can I do it? Do you like it? Can I enjoy myself as much as I like? If I promise you I'll be good at this, will you let me do it again? Will you approve of it? Do you *approve of me?*

Very rarely, if ever, did we get to run the show as kids, even if we were the center attraction. Our parents were in control. To be a child meant *not to be in control, to be out of control, to lose control,* or to have to *learn control.*

Being creative is about letting go of what's inside. To engage the child in the creative act conjures up ghosts of sphincters past; in deciding to let go and release the child side, we wince with anxiety. If we make a blotch, we haven't just made a mistake, we've *soiled ourselves* in public.

At some point most of us decided that it was better to keep the child in check than to lose control and have unnecessary cause for embarrassment. In order to feel better about being creative, we need to reframe our attitude toward the child. Our compulsion to hide our originality lies in the hidden contempt we have about the child's not being okay in this regard.

THE TRADITION OF SUPPRESSING THE CHILD

In discounting our originality we are actually discounting the value of the talented child inside. Instead of appreciating its winsome, lovable qualities, we mistrust it. To release our creativity we need to free ourselves of this anxiety.

It is significant that at some critical point in each of our young lives, we were humiliated in the presence of others. This public violation had deep consequences. It negatively reinforced, by powerful means, the unconscious idea that being a child also meant being victimized by circumstances beyond our control. If prior to this experience we had merely felt defenseless, now we were stripped of dignity. I suppose in a well-meaning but perverse manner, we adults imagine we're doing children a favor when we force their spirit to go underground by publicly humiliating them.

I've already described the classroom episode in which the innocent girl's loss of face was to have such a damaging impact on a classmate who witnessed her disgrace. The episode appears to be nondescript, but it had a harmful, unconscious effect. Such an event may transpire at home, in school, in church or elsewhere. And, there must be an audience at hand, usually composed of one's peers and a grown-up. Rather than being considered an aberrant occurrence, it is accorded no great significance; it is internalized as something ordinary, to be expected by the child—just an inescapable part of the humdrum stuff that makes up everyday life.

The effect is to put the child's pride in being a child and the unselfconscious pleasure he takes in being himself in chains. All at once, like the girl in the following story that a client related, we are shorn of some of our natural spontaneity.

The client told me that when she was four or five years old, her mother gave a birthday party for her and a group of her friends on the back porch. It was summer and very warm. At the last minute, just before cutting the cake, the child suddenly decided to run upstairs to change her clothes. When she came rushing back, eager to sit down again and eat some cake, her mother, angered that she'd left without permission, abruptly called her over. She reprimanded her sharply, inexplicably demanding to know if she'd remembered to put her pants on. Then, in plain sight of the guests, she lifted the girl's skirt up to check. Mortified, the girl slunk into her chair as she was bid, her spirits deflated as a dead balloon. Whatever pride she'd felt at her party had vanished without anyone taking particular notice of it.

And was it fair? What possible harm could it have done anyone if the girl, who indeed had her panties on, hadn't? The only crime being committed was an unconscious one, and it was on the part of the busybody parent.

Her insensitive behavior reflected a tacit social agreement which assumes that every child must be guilty by nature. But of what? Her innocence? Most adults can remember being violated in a similar manner when they were little, or of witnessing someone else's humiliation. The stories differ only in detail. The experience serves no useful function, cutting the free spirit right out of the child, leaving in its place a willingness to conform, and a fear of taking risks.

The form that the incident took is irrelevant; the mere fact that we were humiliated in this fashion is what is of primary concern. Any psychoanalytic meaning we might attribute to it now is a secondary concern. Like the senseless tradition of cruel hazing rites in college fraternities, the violation of the child in a social setting is a cultural tradition, part of an indoctrination process passed down through the generations, representing a rite of initiation; we've all experienced it, whatever its degree of intensity.

Generally the blow comes without warning, taking a person off guard, causing a permanent loss of balance. Because we were children lacking the reasoning capacity of adults, and because we had become accustomed to the wear and tear of our daily interaction with them, we did not think to ask whether the treatment we were receiving was appropriate. It was our unquestioning lot to adjust to whatever grown-ups did, whenever they did it, *to survive.* We might make believe we'd run away, but we never did.

Is it surprising, then, that on some level we associate being a child with being the fool? Through this icy brush with grown-up reality, we learn it's better to belong by playing it safe than to continue to playfully enjoy being our own person.

But this idea of being our own person must become part of the new decision we must make in order to open our creativity and enjoy it. As adults we are in a position to protect our right to privacy and to express our individuality. Since we ourselves have the authority to take responsibility for the outcome, we can reframe our attitude toward what it means to be like a child again.

No one escapes the invisible guillotine that society drops on the unsuspecting child. By axing the child's pride in himself, we end up throwing the baby out with the bathwater, prematurely cutting the person off from his propensity for being imaginative. In one fell swoop we decide to leave the joys of childhood behind, along with the pain. In our hearts and minds it truly become never-never, never-again land.

By reframing how we view the child, we invite ourselves to once again take pleasure in our imaginativeness. We can reclaim the creative promise we had as children.

It is indeed frightening to identify with our child side. We fear that instead of rebirthing it, we are simply reopening a wound that hasn't healed. The unconscious memory of what has gone before inhibits us. In this regard, to take a risk in expressing our creativity definitely means to go against the norm, tradition, the urge to conform. It means we opt to move out of the comfortable, reliable easy chair for a chance to take flight on a brand-new magic carpet of our own making.

We can use the Adult's ability to make intelligent choices to launch us into a new reality.

BECAUSE WE DIDN'T KNOW ANY BETTER

I once lived in a little seaside house. I'd moved in before the owner had finished rebuilding it. There was still some work to be done on the exterior; the roof especially needed further repairing. One day the back doorbell rang. I went to answer it and was startled to see a neighbor's little boy standing there.

He was about three or four and must have wandered out of his backyard and into mine without anyone realizing it. He was grinning from ear to ear, paying me an unexpected visit for no apparent reason other than to share with me his delight in making a new discovery.

He'd found a half-filled pail of tar and a brush standing next to the back porch, and had evidently been using them to paint a design all over the shingles and himself. He'd been quiet about it until now, hence his creative activity had gone undetected. One look told all. I pitied his mother; the black pitch covered his blond curls, his face, his neck, his clothing. His bright blue eyes twinkled with glee; pleased with himself, he was happily unaware of the mess.

I barely had time to figure out how to get him home without getting tar over myself before I heard his mother shouting for him. She came running up the stairs, horrified. She apologized, then yanked the child off the porch. Surprised, he protested. Probably he'd intended to continue painting and couldn't understand why everyone was so upset. Having emptied the proverbial bucket, he must have decided to ring at the well to get more, and now he couldn't understand his unfriendly reception. Of course his crying did no good; he was ignominiously dragged home. I could only imagine the kind of fun that would begin once his mother tried to invent ways to clean him off.

In his innocence, perhaps the boy thought we'd be as pleased as he was with his handiwork. He didn't realize what a headache he was creating. I've often thought of that little boy when people deliver their perfunctory apologies about their work to me. Like the child, they've been innocently enjoying themselves, taking pleasure in exploring uncharted domains. But all the while they've been stirring up old memories and anxieties, whose shadow casts a pall over everything, black as pitch itself.

Do they think I might hit them if I don't like the image, or tell them to get lost, or keep them locked in their rooms just to teach them a lesson?

Every psychological block is comprised of compound elements, and the urge to suppress the child in us is made up of the fear of loss of control, the aversion to feeling defenseless, and finally the wish to avoid hurting ourselves while having fun.

Often, the creative act involves spending time playing by ourselves, creating all manner of interesting messes along with their unexpected outcomes. And, once before, when we innocently partook of the pleasure of exploring such options, we lived to regret it. At times we were severely rebuked. Otherwise we might hurt ourselves or others. I remember my three-year-old brother's dismay when he learned the consequences of feeding the guppies with Spic & Span. The young inventor thought he was giving them a treat and killed them instead.

Such early experiments were all part of reality testing when we were growing up; to be reprimanded for those that fell short of the mark helped teach us what the limits were and how they were set. Unfortunately, we've unconsciously turned those early limits into an unfriendly NO TRESPASSING sign. It takes ingenuity, determination and willpower to get around the self-imposed, self-protective barrier to our creativity.

Luckily for us it isn't impermeable. And it's not the work of a foreign miscreant. The block I'm speaking of is more like a callus, a protective covering of scar tissue that grew out of our response to abrasive conditions in the environment. It began to take shape at a time when we didn't know how to avoid getting irritated. Now we are in control and know how to handle the child better than we did before.

The overview we have regarding the child side helps us grasp why we often end up in a bad mood at the thought of being creative. Though we might be primed for action, we're equally as much on the defensive; thus, our desire to express ourselves never reaches the light of day.

Trying to overcome the resistance without assistance is difficult. It's tough to let go, to trust the child and believe there will be a positive outcome. We'd desperately like to recapture the spontaneity of childhood, but we instinctively recoil—feeling the price we'd have to pay would be too high. Because we equate being little with finding ourselves in a helpless position—with being exposed and inadequate—we stick to the status quo, dissatisfying as it is. Better to enjoy the illusion of feeling superior than to discover that we are inferior—an attitude which reflects an uncreative, unproductive frame of mind. The desire to be creative and the simultaneous tendency to squelch it are part of a vicious circle that is difficult to break.

A person can have entertained negative feelings about his child side for so long that even if he decides to have a change of heart, the feelings can't dissipate overnight. Like a person accustomed to driving in a heavily congested area who suddenly finds himself in the country, it takes him a while to relax and get used to the idea that he doesn't have to be so nervous all the time.

Inevitably it will take time for someone to adjust to the new emotional climate once he's made up his mind to change his attitude. He has to alter some habits of thinking and acting. Depending on the intensity of the particular "trip" he's been on, he may only be able to chance expressing himself in gradual doses.

To some extent we are all victims of an early depression that engendered the current problems we're dealing with. The decisions we made then in order to cope with the situation still exert a powerful influence on us. Unless we consciously make new choices and alter our frame of reference, they can adversely affect us all our lives.

Rarely do we appreciate the power of those early decisions regarding our creativity. We responded instinctively to the pressures we were under, forming strategies to cope that worked for us then, perhaps, but have no relevance now. In a sense the block I'm discussing is impersonal in origin, in that it was socially imposed and encountered to some degree by all children; similarly, the choices we made as children have a common denominator. Separately, but en masse, we decided that to be like a child was definitely *risky business*.

PLAY IT AGAIN, SAM

Because of the child's intuitive gifts, I liken the child to a "little wizard." Indeed, the fertile territory we want to cultivate lies in the hands of this small, magical and enigmatic personage. He owns all the toys we want to play with. Because we have learned to distrust this part of ourselves, however, that which should represent a never-ending rich adventure of the soul—exploring the outermost reaches of our inner creative imagination—has become synonymous with fooling around with something dangerous and taboo.

It's amazing how our unconscious assumptions can shape reality. A client who wanted to paint and felt blocked related a story about her father. She had long ago given up playing the cello and had left it in her parents' home for safekeeping. Her father became interested in playing it himself and decided to take up music lessons at the age of sixty-nine. His daughter, a teacher, urged him to shop around and carefully select a sensitive instructor. Impatient to begin, he quickly settled on someone who was conveniently located in the neighborhood. She was an older person herself, and so he thought they would be compatible. The man started practicing, quickly advanced and before long was sawing off tunes which his wife was only too happy to accompany on the piano.

The aging couple had unexpectedly discovered a new pursuit together that was adding fun to their lives. At this crucial point, however, the man ran into a block. He began to feel frustrated with his progress and wanted to move faster. Instead, he'd bumble. Thus, he began to lose interest in practicing. Discouraged, he asked his teacher what he might do to remotivate himself, because he really enjoyed what he was learning.

The woman glared at him and said impatiently, "Well, what do you expect! You're too old to begin learning to play an instrument now!"

The nature of both that woman's ancient unconscious choice and the man's surfaced to coincide at precisely that moment: no one ought to take too great a risk with his creativity at any point in his life. If before the man hadn't taken a risk because he was too young and busy, now he knew for certain he couldn't, because it was too late!

It's no surprise that he laid the instrument away and never took another lesson, either with that teacher or any other. Instead of playing on, he decided to play it safe forever. The decisive factor was not just the teacher's reaction to his dilemma. It was the power of his unconscious choice. To keep on pursuing his new goal, to break through his limits, he needed special support. Voices outside his field of awareness were telling him that at his age, it was too risky to try something new. He was secretly hoping for criticism so he wouldn't have to give up a favorite position and could stick to an old prejudice.

A person may not like the outcome of a choice he made in the past, but at the same time is almost always reluctant to make a new one.

STICKING TO YOUR GUNS

I wish the man had stuck to his guns and persisted in playing. What he probably needed when he went to his teacher for advice was someone to give him a hug and tell him about strokes. Had he learned how to stroke himself appropriately for (1) his courage in taking lessons in the first place, (2) the progress he had already made, (3) the lift the new pastime was giving his marriage, and (4) his intelligence and talent, he might have felt renewed and equipped to take up the challenge the temporary block represented.

He also would have needed to make a new choice and to reframe his perspective on the child. He probably had decided long ago that he was a sensible, responsible grown-up. But being in touch with the child part of oneself does not preclude also being able to fulfill one's responsibilities as an adult. The child never dies and is forever young. To own the child and take pride in it empowers one to live with more heart, verve and integrity. The man's attitude toward his child side constituted a block. And that's what was preventing him from going on the next level, not his age or any other imagined inadequacy. But the necessary support he needed to make that kind of breakthrough was missing.

How can you, operating alone, chart a safe course through some of the inevitable obstacles once you have made a new choice? I hope that this book will help you stick to your guns after you've decided to take the chance of opening your creativity. Contrary to the woman who told the old man to give up his attempts at learning something new, I'd like to urge you to keep up the good work.

NOT MISSING THE CLUES

Later in this book you will have the opportunity to observe a client's source image evolve from a simple into a more complex manifestation of itself. Many of the people I have worked with had no prior exposure to the arts or formal training, and that's what makes observing their creative process all the more exciting. It is as if there were some kind of superior creative intelligence at work that we can all tap into.

I've emphasized the importance of cultivating a positive relationship to our child side. This we begin by first familiarizing ourselves with the power of positive stroking, and next by remaking old decisions regarding our attitude toward the creative potential of the child.

Because it is the child we are trying to reawaken, and because it is that side of ourselves we must learn to trust anew, many of our initial attempts at being creative—in any medium—might at first appear childlike to us.

An axiom to keep in mind is this: Nothing is too simple to appreciate or to keep.

Often my clients who are parents find that, as they begin to do artwork, it inspires responses in their children. One parent, the mother of two young boys, brought in a piece her three-year-old had drawn for me. He had asked her to title it "Some Lines," and had instructed her to give it to me as a present. It looked like this:

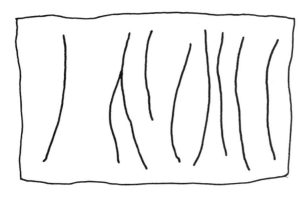

FIGURE 15
A copy of the child's original piece, which he drew with Crayolas.

You will recall the simple V-shaped line that the woman drew (Figure 9). I see little difference between these two drawings. The major one is that in the former instance the creative seed will take many years to mature; in the latter it will occur quite quickly, because it is being consciously cultivated. Both represent powerful outcroppings of the unconscious mind in seminal form. One appears crude because it is the work of a child; the other seems simple because it is the work of an adult.

The child's rendering and the woman's, both drawn with Crayolas, are equally valuable and special. I hung each of them on the wall. The child's drawing especially reminded me to trust the creative process at work in those clients who were, like him, just beginning, acquainting themselves—however awkward their initial attempts might look—with the workings of their imagination.

You must *expect* a tendency to view your first experiments with a critical eye. And when you do, go on the *alert*. The misfortune of one client who didn't have such fair warning comes to mind. If only his brain had flashed him an all-systems alert signal, he might still be writing today instead of just trying to start where he left off many years ago, in junior high school. Since he didn't have the necessary tools, the shocking message he received sent him into a "warp" he's had difficulty exiting from ever since.

He was accustomed to receiving little attention from his parents and teachers, but he had an inexplicable hankering to write from an early age. In his early teens he decided to enter a citywide writing contest for the fun of it. Like entering the lottery, he did it for a lark, never thinking he would win.

He usually sat in the back of the room. He was shy and did not speak up often in class; moreover, he believed the teacher disliked him, so he tried to avoid getting called on as much as possible. The announcement of the contest winner arrived in a sealed envelope. The teacher opened it and read his name aloud. He couldn't believe his ears; he was dumbfounded. So was she. Raising her eyes, she looked straight at him, angrily stating, "I don't believe it. There must be some mistake!"

He at least deserved a handshake. Or perhaps a friendly nod. Since neither was forthcoming, he decided the whole thing was a mistake and never tried writing again. This fellow didn't have a clue as to how to protect his beginnings from assault, nor did he have any inkling as to how valuable they were, contest-winning or not.

Every creative gesture is part of the movement of a larger, unseen body within. But to make contact with it, we must overcome one other hurdle. Even more distressing than those blocks concerned with inhibiting the child is the one that concerns the disruption in the relationship to the unconscious mind. It is between the conscious and unconscious selves that society has striven to drive the most uncomfortable wedge, upsetting the balance in the most intimate of all possible connections. In the next chapter we'll discuss the implications of this and try to right the balance.

5

<hr>

Understanding the Unconscious Mind

THE SPECIAL BRIDGE

Children can be naughty, difficult, even hurtful, but now we know that we have nothing to fear from the child side of ourselves. We also have nothing to fear from our unconscious mind. I'm designating it "our unconscious mind" rather than simply "the unconscious," because from my perspective what we refer to as "unconscious" is neither unconscious nor simple; the term "unconscious mind" pertains to super- or transpersonal awareness—that which is still beyond awareness, embodying all that is *not yet conscious*. It also implies a universal as much as a personal intelligence, and includes future as well as past and present knowing. And, even as it reveals its secrets, it always remains in part a mystery, beyond the grasp of the conscious mind.

It was surprising to me as a teacher to learn that many adults have a fear of their own unconscious mind. In the writing courses I gave at the university I often included a series of creative assignments, among them one in which I asked the students to write about a favorite daydream. I was attempting to familiarize them with their image-making process in this way. Already accustomed to unusual assignments, the students ought not to have been surprised. Yet they were, for more than half of them could not remember a daydream, and some drew a blank because they didn't know what one was. Many of the students couldn't grasp its function.

After I described the nature of daydreams, they were relieved, and some remembered that they often had such waking fantasies. None of them attributed much significance to the phenomenon, considering it a random wandering of the mind rather than an intrinsic and necessary part of their creative process—as essential to their well-being as entering the dream state.

Others had more difficulty remembering, but eventually everyone could identify and describe at least one daydream. It helped the students to learn that they quite instinctively formed pictures of their daily comings and goings before living them out; that daydreaming, as an extension of this natural activity, is the state we enter to form pictures in the mind for sheer entertainment. We're all born dramatists when it comes to amusing ourselves in this fashion; and, generally, we have no real intention of enacting the fantasy. The pleasure lies in the act of imaging itself.

Describing daydreams gave rise to many a fascinating paper, eventually helping to loosen the literary tongue of a surprisingly large number of students. In most instances it's fun to have a daydream, so those students who usually dreaded writing also discovered it could be fun.

In discussing their initial difficulty with the assignment, the students explained that while in school, they were accustomed to repressing completely the fact that they daydreamed; consequently they tended to forget the daydreaming occurred all the time, as a matter of course. It was an automatic reflex, one offering them sure relief from boredom.

Students tended to deny they daydreamed because school was a place where they knew they were supposed to stay alert and not let their minds wander. Unfortunately, the truth is that from an early age, we learn to think primarily utilizing one side of the brain only—the left, rational, linear side. In an atmosphere of such one-sided emphasis, students gradually come to associate intelligence itself with the capacity to use just one side of the brain adroitly. It's a lopsided state of affairs. No one would assume dexterity means wielding only one hand with ease. It's no wonder most students were haunted by the feeling they were dealing with only half a deck.

Just as the indoctrination we received from teachers, parents, and clerics has cut us off from a long-lasting, healthy relationship to our child, so has it had long-term effects on how we view the unconscious mind. By the time we have reached college age, we assume that to imagine, to dream, to wonder, to intuit, is to be absentminded—absent from the mind, dumb. We take for granted that being intelligent has to do with forcing our attention continually outward to find the answers, and we erroneously suppose it has little to do with turning the attention inward to fathom the solution.

To be in control as a student meant to squelch the natural urge to daydream. But that assumption is as illogical as supposing that we are in control of our sexuality merely because we are not in a sexual relationship. If this is the case, we might rather consider the possibility we are out of touch, rather than in charge.

The separation of mental functions and the elevating of the status of one side of the brain to the detriment of the other has a devastating effect, limiting rather than enhancing our reasoning capacities. Without realizing it, in order to cope with the artificial stresses of a classroom environment, we've had to divide ourselves into pieces, surreptitiously hiding some, dutifully revealing others.

What an impoverished state of affairs! The mind thinks in pictures. To rob it of its favorite métier is to handicap it. I believe that learning and the ability to create dreams go hand in hand. In fact, the closer we get to the unconscious mind, the easier it is for us to concentrate and learn something new, because our whole self is involved, not just one part of it.

Furthermore, each of us knows through experience that often we do our best thinking when we can get our conscious mind off an issue. We don't put our cognitive faculties to sleep, we merely set them aside, and presto! The solution presents itself as soon as we stop trying so desperately hard to figure it out. Each of us has different ploys to quiet the mind; for example, I may get up from my chair, go down to the garden and weed. Another person might take a walk, go shopping, do some task about the house.

I'm not suggesting that students shouldn't pay attention.

In fact, I have pulled many an unconventional stunt to keep my students' attention. But people learn more easily when they are having fun. And, one of the ways for a person to have fun when he's learning is to simultaneously be learning something about himself, not just the subject at hand.

Such a natural coalescing of inner desire and outer aim takes place when an individual can learn to integrate unconscious thought processes with the more conscious ones. No one would suppose that the leaf constitutes the complete plant; the flower represents the culminating of an entire larger process of growth, of which the leaf is but a part.

Similarly, the conscious mind is but one aspect of a larger intelligent process at work within each of us. What's missing in most classrooms is the same thing that's missing from our lives when we leave childhood to enter the realm of grown-ups—a bridge. Instead of learning how to take our imagination along with us on the trip, we're forced to leave it behind; instead of learning how to think with heart, we forget we have one. And, it goes without saying that a lot of fun goes out of life, not to mention inspiration, when we don't have permission to imagine or to trust our feelings. Our parents and teachers ordered us to pack up and move. In the rush to get to the new place, we forgot our playthings.

As with our child side, we need to learn to trust the unconscious mind. To build a bridge between the imagination and everyday reality, between the outer realm of the conscious mind and the mysterious inner one of the unconscious mind, we need to master but one trick—the art of image making. Psychic images produced spontaneously in fantasies, dreams, and art are the stuff the "bridge" is built of. They are Legos of the mind; we're free to create what we like, but we do it best in the spirit of play. And, in the act of figuring out how the pieces fit together, we keep discovering new ways to join them. Best of all, these Legos don't cost a cent, we've all got a plentiful supply, and we can invent any new parts we need whenever we want.

LOSS OF HEART

In discussing the bridge we need to build to the child and to the unconscious mind, I equated the repression of the unconscious mind with that of suppressing our feelings, drawing an analogy between the intuition and the heart. There is a powerful connection between the capacity to feel and have empathy, and the ability to be intuitive and have a hunch.

Because of our conditioning to use just one side of the brain, we've overloaded some circuits, while others have gotten rusty with disuse. We've all had the experience of picking up the phone to call a friend and being startled to hear his or her voice on the other end of the line before we've even had a chance to dial. Or, we'll find ourselves thinking about an acquaintance only to bump into him or her suddenly, as if by accident. We usually don't think much about these everyday occurrences, absentmindedly stuffing them into the same back closet in which we keep our child side, along with the other parts of ourselves we deem unacceptable.

Such impulses, or so-called psychic experiences, arise from feelings deep inside, beyond the conscious field of our awareness. It's as if the heart were a forgotten brain. Sometimes it gets so entrusted with neglect that when we attempt to stimulate it into action, we find it only resonates dully.

Our resistance to the unconscious mind is the by-product of a culturally ingrained prejudice, and it can be removed. The denial, rejection and misunderstanding of our inner processes has hurt our hearts. We have felt the loss without realizing it. Vague but everpresent feelings of anxiety, the plaguing sense that there's more to life than we have experienced or that life has no meaning at all, the use of artificial stimulants to keep going—all these are symptoms that a major psychic joint is painfully out of place.

The situation can be remedied. The more we are willing to entertain a loving relationship to the unconscious mind, the more open we become to learning to speak its special language, the lighter our hearts become. Because, in our hearts we know this is how it was really meant to be.

Like a child who fears the loss of family unity when his parents divorce, we have suffered greatly from the effects of the divorce between the two sides of the brain and between the mind and the heart. When we were growing up, there was little we could do to prevent their growing apart. Now we are in a position to bring back together that which has always belonged together.

MENDING THE SPLIT

The combination of social pressures that acted upon us when we were growing up had a great impact, shaping our view of reality and our relationship to others in ways that were to have lasting and damaging effects. It's as if in order to take our place in society, we unwittingly went through a pruning process. In relationship to the unconscious mind and the imaginative powers of the child, we're like a plant cutting— clipped at the roots, forced to nourish ourselves artificially rather than being able to draw needed sustenance from the well, at *the source*.

Yet, we have memories of what used to be and inklings of what can be again. Just as we once swam fearlessly in the embryotic fluids of the womb, we can again learn to swim fearlessly in the waters of the unconscious mind. It is our natural habitat, attractive and as fascinating to us as the sea. Secretly we long to coexist in harmony with it, wishing to restore the ecological balance that Mother Nature has destined.

But we tend not to trust the workings of the unconscious mind. This mistrust gradually erodes our ability to maintain a healthy sense of our own center, of wholeness and spiritual integrity. We furtively hide mystical inclinations and childlike wonder at the magic of the universe from ourselves and those around us, lest we appear naive or, worse yet, unbalanced.

Being creative is a spiritual antipollutant, helping us regain our psychic equilibrium, bringing about peace of mind, renewing our faith in the sanctity of the universe itself. It quite naturally precipitates altered states of consciousness that reveal to us metaphysical knowledge about aspects of our being and the source from which our being springs.

RESTORING REVERENCE

We can appreciate the power and strength of the unconscious mind without fearing its dark side. When I stand at the ocean's edge I am drawn to it; although I enjoy swimming, I experience anxiety under certain conditions. For example, before I dive in, I like to know the whereabouts of undercurrents, large outcroppings of rocks, and so forth. Whereas I may approach an unknown area with a certain degree of caution, I never think of the water itself as something bad or harmful. On the contrary, it is a natural force for which I have the greatest respect.

The unconscious mind is also a natural force. Like the ocean, it operates according to predictable, preordained laws, representing principled energy in action, a cyclical phenomenon, life-giving and life-sustaining in essence.

When viewing a breathtaking seascape, we take in the beauty and vastness of the scene, appreciating the might of the water. We're awed by the sense of its infinite majesty. Even when the surface appears rough, churning wildly in the wind, we never think, "Gee, the water looks disorganized, it might be crazy and out of control." Similarly, the unconscious mind is not disorganized, nor does it represent a wild and crazy force. What can get out of whack is our perspective. As a society, we are beginning to perceive the cumulative, destructive effect our exploitative attitude has had on the physical environment, realizing it is not nature herself that is out of control but we who are out of hand.

The same destructive tendencies are reflected in the relationship we have chosen to entertain with the unconscious mind. Like children at the zoo, we poke aggravating theories at it, provoking unwelcome responses because of the ignoble, unfeeling manner in which we are handling it.

There are a variety of ways in which we can attempt to gain access to our creativity and unlock the resources of the unconscious mind. One of the most effective comes as naturally to us as the desire to dance or sing. We like to make images, we do it all the time, when asleep and when awake. We don't need to work at creating them, they bob about in consciousness, ripe for the taking.

In the spirit of play we can reach out to grab and hold onto them, elusive as they are. As we more closely examine what we have discovered, our delight naturally changes to awe; like a treasure we've found while beachcombing, in their outlines we catch glimpses of the mighty forces that have brought even the humblest of them into being. Having emerged from the vastness of the not-yet-conscious mind, they bear traces of its mind-altering, life-transformative essence. More than mere symbols, they are comprised of healing substances and are charged with special energy; messengers of the soul, they are transmitters of consciousness itself, and as such are potent agents of change.

THE SURPRISING FIND

More than once I've sought to relax and refresh myself by walking on the beach. The rhythmic movement of the waves, the undulating patterns in the sand, the sun and air are uplifting and give me peace of mind. I sense the intelligence of nature at work and feel myself to be inextricably part of the flow. The same ordering principles that give rise to the shape of the landscape must reflect, I think, an ordering principle at work within me, shaping my awareness, changing my consciousness. It is there and active whether I will it to be so or not. Lying in the sand, feeling myself let go of anxiety, I feel a connection to the life process itself and know I can trust it.

In reclaiming the child, in opening our hearts to the unconscious mind, we find that blocks to expressing our creativity are removed; without great effort they've silently started to wash away. For, like the waters changing the sands of the shore, there is a force ever in motion within us, organized, intelligent and powerful. Just as we do not need to will ourselves to be part of nature, we do not need to will ourselves to be creative. It is an instinctive drive. As nature's children we are all artistic; our fingers, like her hands, are potential agents of transformation.

Indeed, it's as if we possessed her creative intelligence in the depths of our very genes. Once unblocked, we find images that rise to the surface of consciousness, seemingly posited there by a higher intelligence. Like cells, they possess their own life cycle. Our minds and hearts are the perfect receptacle in which to place them, a natural petri dish providing them with the life-support system they need.

Once stimulated into activity, these image-seeds grow of their own volition, rapidly undergoing one transmutation after another. Just as seeds planted in a garden change the landscape, so do these psychic ones have the power to change the contours of our reality. They precipitate the growth and development of artistic capacities in each individual, bringing about creative transformation in his personality and environment.

It is a growth process that has its own momentum. Once the force of this creative energy has been released in a person's psyche, we know that in time his life must also change its form. The surprising thing is that he will no more need a guide to draw him an outline of how these events should proceed than nature needs a teacher to direct her handiwork. A natural beautifying principle, intrinsic to the larger scheme of things and to the human condition itself, directs the show.

It is difficult for people to let go and trust an internal process when they have been conditioned to think that what they need to master a new skill lies outside them in some academic syllabus. At least in this one instance there is no school we have to attend to begin advancing in the right direction. In fact, it might even behoove us to avoid such technical input until a later time. Otherwise we might find our talents have been tampered with at the roots. Regarding the cultivating of our creativity, we are our own best experts.

Accustomed as we are to developing almost all of our mental faculties using only one side of the brain, the culture we live in is often not the most appropriate "culture" for inducing the kind of mitotic but mystical event I'm speaking of. The necessary ingredients for turning on the reproductive machinery in the imagistic cells we've inherited are within everyone's immediate reach. In the first stages of their growth cycle, a warm and loving environment is more essential to their unfolding than a traditional classroom setting. So the only door to open is the door to your own heart.

Look at the bright side: it's cheaper to cultivate your own creativity, and *there are no grades.* You can freely squish your fingers through your art supplies unimpeded by restrictions; like going to the beach and squishing your toes in the sand, the process can be a delight, bringing relief from the woes of tension rather than inducing them.

TRUSTING THE PROCESS, TAPPING THE SOURCE

The natural attraction that exists between a person and his unconscious mind, and between him and his images, reminds me of the power and intelligence of the sexual drive. No one ever really teaches us how to get excited; at a certain age such feelings arise of their own accord. The urge to touch, embrace, and make love is programmed in the genes. Left to their own devices, people naturally tend to mate; it's instinctive.

Similarly, the urge to connect with our creativity is instinctive. It's not the drive that is the issue, it's how we handle it. Because of social conditioning, most of us do not enjoy as full and free a relationship to this side of ourselves as we might like to. Once we change our attitude, however, we find that dynamic changes begin to occur, and that they do so with instinctive insistence, in orderly stages.

In the case studies presented in the Preface and in Part Four, you will note that there is an unfolding to each person's artistic side. His ability opens up naturally. Each client moved at his own pace, yet the progressive movement transpired in a certain sequence; it almost *was to be predicted.* This unfolding was supported by an internal movement in the client's psyche, reflected in the spontaneous appearance of certain images in his dreams and artwork.

I want to emphasize that, once activated and given adequate stimulation and nurturing, an individual's creativity will begin to grow and develop an independent life of its own. Just as we know a baby will go through a preordained sequence of developmental transitions, we know that there will be an intelligent, sequential development to the unfolding of a person's creative faculties. In the case studies following, you will perceive a fascinating progression of events. You will observe how, as a person's imagery undergoes a series of natural transmutations, his artistic abilities gain in sophistication and character.

The pace of unfolding varies from individual to individual, depending on matters of environment and personal circumstance. Whereas the stages of change are predictable, the ultimate outcome of the process is not, for a person's creativity necessarily bears the mark of his unique nature. Since the original source of his imagery never dries up, neither will his capacity to fashion that which is original out of it.

I am astounded at the infinite variety of forms contained within the relatively small warehouse of the human brain. But over the years what intrigues me even more is an interesting discovery I have stumbled across while observing the creative imagery in the work of students, clients and friends.

THE SOURCE IMAGE

With consistency I have noticed the occurrence of two major kinds of images. One type I call the "cosmic [or universal or generic] source image," the other is simply the "personal source image." Both of these signal growth and stages of development in the creative life cycle. During the sexual act our hormones react to stimulation, which signals that the body is spontaneously undergoing a chain of preordained responses to touching. Similarly, once stimulated in a specific manner, our "creative hormones" are aroused and begin to respond in a predictable fashion. Those images that universally arise upon receiving this stimulation I call the cosmic source images. Their occurrence in dreams and/or artwork heralds the awakening of latent capacities within each human being. Interestingly, each of those images has ancient and mysterious roots. They are associated with prehistoric mother goddess worship, and among them are snakes, dragons and other serpentine shapes; the egg; the spiral; the crescent; breasts; the circle; the triangle; the bull; the cow.

Opening our creativity, therefore, seems to be related, at its most fundamental level, to opening up a universal spiritual predilection to worship the earth in all its wondrous—and sexual—manifestations. At the same time that these images occur, another kind arises. Its shape varies from individual to individual, and it is highly arbitrary in both form and content, varying in contour from the delineation of a specific thing, like a calla lily, to a more highly abstract image, like a Figure 8. Whereas the appearance of a cosmic source image indicates that a person has begun to tap into his creativity, the personal source image has a somewhat more complex function. Identifying the presence of the former means that a person has located the fuel; identifying the latter means he's at work building the rig necessary to reach it.

Cosmic source images reflect the growth of creative inclinations universally present in people. The personal source images encourage the unique direction these inclinations will take once they are opened up. A special organizing principle intrinsic to the species seems to ensure that there will be continual creative expansion without repetition.

Let us suppose a person wants to design his own clothes. To do so he will have to familiarize himself with, among other things, the principles of dress patterning. Once he knows how to make a pattern and once he has the ability to draw sketches of his ideas, he can create any kind of line he wants. Thus, the purpose of the cosmic source image is to awaken the impulse to make creative patterns. The personal source image shows us how we can create a unique design out of the material at hand.

The cosmic source images operate as a *formative influence* on the psyche; the personal source images have a *motivating force*. Because motivation is the purpose of personal source images, they never dry up but keep evolving, changing their shape and meaning, prompting a person continually forward, provoking him to take further risks with his creativity. Like Tantalus reaching for the grapes, he never completely grasps the meaning of his personal source image; the desire to more fully understand and possess it stimulates him, however, to reach ever harder for it, tempting him into renewed creative activity.

By extending himself in this way, a person finds he is automatically making corresponding changes in his environment to support the growth process. Both the personal and cosmic source images act as catalysts inspiring orderly change and growth. The transformation does not induce chaos but the gradual emergence of a harmonious new design in his artwork and life. The changes it effects, like the alchemical ones described in books of yore, infuse the everyday with the glow of the wondrous, turning mundane dross into something fantastical.

The major ingredient that sets the whole cycle into motion is less intellectual than it is emotional and spiritual; a person merely gives in to his natural desire to enjoy playing with the images he creates. Whereas this choice is simple, actualizing it is not. It is challenging to learn how to attend to our images to keep the process going. Like seeds we have planted in the garden but then neglect to water, unless we can learn to maintain a loving relationship to our images, they dry and wither.

It's akin to parenting. Our children reflect the kind of care and attention we give them. Images have the capacity to effect change and bring creative transformation into our lives. Unless we are willing to love them, they will not grow to reach full stature and fulfill their potential.

CARING FOR OUR IMAGES

Extrinsic forces have interrupted the natural flow of energy between the individual and his imagery. His feeling of attraction toward it has been inhibited. We might think of these forces acting like stubborn weeds that need to be removed so that light and nutrients might reach the hidden, fledgling plants.

Once a person sets to work consciously unblocking and reactivating his creative energies, there is a built-in internal support system, a psychic superstructure that assists him in achieving his goals. How does it work?

First of all, we see the principle reflected in the nature of the source images themselves. These appear to be coded with intelligent messages: just as the biological coding system determines the universal characteristics of the species and designates the specific ones of the individual, so do the cosmic and personal source images determine what the creative components will consist of in a person's work.

In the human body each cell contains cytoplasm, a special material through which nutrients pass into the cell from the surrounding environment, and out of the cell into the body. It's a creative medium of exchange essential to the healthy working not just of the single cell but of the entire organism.

The source images are not accidental; like the living cell, they have not arisen from a vacuum. Each cell, an entity in itself, is equally an intrinsic expression of a larger, intelligent whole. So are psychic images part of a systemic network of intelligent connecting points joined to a larger entity, which is also growing and evolving.

The same organizing principles we see at work under the microscope are at work under the painter's brush, the sculptor's fingertips. No aesthetic phenomenon is an isolated event. God has left no loopholes, nor have we been left existentially in the lurch. Should we decide to explore the many facets of our creative nature, we'll find we're neither lost in a void nor stranded on a deserted psychic isle; rather, we'll see there are myriad means of internal support for furthering our investigation.

Just as a researcher has the technical means to isolate and examine a single cell, so, too, do we all have the faculties for isolating and examining a single image. Yet, else we distort our perspective of its ultimate meaning, we must never lose sight of the fact the single entity is part of a larger whole.

An aspect of caring for our images involves learning to trust the creative process ever at work in our consciousness. We trust the flow of blood through our veins and the natural movement of our breathing, and we don't think about these until we get sick; we know the body knows how to take care of itself. To be creative represents the human manifestation of an organizing principle at work in a larger body of intelligent life, of which we and our images are a part.

As we gain a healthier appreciation of the workings of the unconscious mind, we will begin to rely on its functioning in our spiritual behalf the same way we know we can count on our body to be a reliable vehicle for fulfilling all our physical needs. Might we not even consider the possibility that in its very invisibility, or *immateriality,* the unconscious mind represents nature's divine, not her aberrant, aspect, becoming manifest through us? And might we not furthermore suppose that each creative gesture we make is an attempt on *her* part to make this aspect more intelligible to us?

6

≈≈≈≈≈≈≈≈≈≈≈≈≈≈≈≈≈≈≈≈≈≈≈≈≈≈≈≈≈

The Invisible Whole

DRAWING CLOSER TO THE SOURCE

Images are a manifestation of the unconscious mind, from which all our creative impulses derive. Like a bee attracted to honey, we are drawn to images—they have magnetic power. Just as the petals of a flower lure the bee to its center, so does an image, as an enchanting extension of the unconscious mind, entice us toward the center, the inner self.

But, to draw closer to the source means to approach an aspect of our being that appears to lie beyond the realm of the ordinary senses. As intangible as a dream, as far away as the legendary Isle of Avalon, it coexists with our everyday reality while seeming set apart from it. I can run into my garden for refuge whenever I like; I know it lies near the base of the stairway in the backyard. I have but to make up my mind to go there to reach it. There's no mystery about what route will take me there; it's all in plain sight.

It's not so easy to set up a meeting with the unconscious mind or to find sanctuary in the inner aspect of the self. What path will take us there? And when we arrive, how do we know it? Developing a closer relationship with the unconscious mind requires patience.

When we plant a bulb in the garden, we realize that it will take several weeks to see signs of growth. We trust the

63

natural laws of the cosmos in this regard, and try to operate in cooperation with them by, for example, planting seeds at the appropriate time and keeping the ground moist rather than letting it become dry.

As we cultivate a garden by using our physical senses and logical reasoning abilities, we cultivate the path to the center of the self by means of the inner senses and with the aid of intuition.

Because such a large part of the creative stuff of which images are made originates in the unconscious mind, much of this material remains invisible at first to the naked eye. In order to appreciate its significance, we have to practice using inner senses of sight, hearing and touch. To garner the gifts of the soul, a person needs to learn how to cultivate them as much in a spiritual as a physical sense; then, like the blossom that suddenly bursts forth from the well-cared-for bulb, his creativity bursts forth in all its vigor, surprising him with the vitality and strength of its color and size. That which was invisible becomes visible, that which was sensed as an intangible reality becomes real in front of his eyes.

WHERE DO WE START?

It irritates me when I can't find my glasses and a client politely points out I have them on. I have been *looking right through them*. All I needed to do in this embarrassing instance was to acknowledge that I already had what I was seeking. A change in perspective, an oblique glance at my nose, told me I had what I wanted.

I'd like you to treat the rest of this book as if it were a travel guide, as if you've already got your ticket, reservations for a place to stay, and your own personal, if mysterious, itinerary. A chief purpose of this book is to provide you with the necessary vocabularies for finding your way around, and to feel comfortable about your stay.

Learning to speak the language of the unconscious mind is definitely akin to learning a new tongue. Most adults are hesitant when they try to master a new idiom. What's interesting is that we consistently speak in the language of the unconscious mind without realizing it. Just as I had my glasses on but didn't see them, we talk in images without hearing what we're saying.

In the Preface you noted that the first drawing of one woman consisted of a line merely resembling the letter V. Yet that V shape also could just as well depict a triangle, or it could be an abstract, symbolic representation of a vagina. Whatever her conscious intent, there are several layers of meaning we could attach to the apparently childlike rendering.

Similarly, when trying to depict a snake, I might inadvertently draw this shape:

At the same time that I have realized my conscious intent to make a snake, I have unintentially produced a figure eight and the letter S. Suddenly the picture is no longer simply about a "snake." To the extent that I tapped into my conscious memories of what a snake looks like to produce the drawing, you see the intelligence of the conscious mind at work in the piece; but to the degree that I have unwittingly produced an intriguing combination of *unintentional* forms, you can also perceive the intelligence of the unconscious mind at work.

By means of these examples, I'd like you to deduce that there is no such thing as a simple image; even doodles, as well as our dreams and more complex artistic images, have meaning. It is by learning to appreciate what is *already there* but not noticeable to us at first glance that we will discover the key to opening our creativity. For it is in the "found" form, the unintended shape, that we find a secret message of significance, a clue that leads us to the source, the center of the self.

WHICH COMES FIRST, THE CHICKEN OR THE EGG?

Understanding the origin of our performance anxiety and learning how to circumvent it, trusting in the child and being open to the workings of the unconscious mind, are prerequisites for releasing our creativity. Since we live in an age in which we seem to place more trust in technical aids and machinery than in ourselves, we find it difficult to regain our trust in that which is organic; to some extent we've lost our *feel* for being in sync with nature. I'm not suggesting we switch allegiances, or give up machines; rather, I'm emphasizing that we need to reawaken our faith in the forces of nature to see how they might be of assistance to us.

To open our creativity using the means I'm describing requires that we acknowledge the limits of the human condition itself, giving up the culturally ingrained expectation that we can control everything that happens to us through technical intervention, and that it is desirable to alter the flow of an organic process whenever we so desire.

The other day I noticed two young men at a car wash diligently cleaning a spanking new Thunderbird. It was a coin-op operation; even with the aid of mechanical devices to speed things up, I'll bet the job lasted over half an hour. Yet, these fellows didn't mind spending the time they needed to keep the car bright and shining.

On the other hand, I notice TV ads for fast-food chains promoting the idea that customers who are hungry can get their needs instantly gratified.

This overreliance on technical assistance to get results as quickly as possible has an interesting side-effect on the mind. Even as we utilize the machine to reduce the sense of pressure in our lives, a terrific sense of pressure builds; we become ever greater victims of Our Schedule. We expect to be able to jam more and more into a day; we expect to be on time and get upset if we aren't.

But time is a contrary force. Most of us feel we haven't got enough time to do the things we really want to do. And it's true, we've scheduled time for *just being* out of the picture. The wristwatch dictates our movements day and night. We're goose-stepping through life in rhythm to its commands. Like news announcers, we have no time to digest events; there's a feeling of having to rush, as if experience itself were being squeezed into a box the size of a cue card.

I notice that my clients reflect an ambivalent attitude toward the use of "their" time. On the one hand, many people initially have difficulty scheduling, into a life already crammed with obligations, fifteen minutes for doing just a bit of artwork, which is all that's required at first to initiate the process of change. On the other hand, they're disappointed that once things get going, they can't make them move faster.

The ingredients you are being introduced to in this book will help you gain a greater understanding of your creative imagery quite rapidly. However, they aren't the equivalent of an instant mix. They will sensitize you instead to a process that, like everything else in nature, has its own tempo.

Often a person who begins working with the Source Imagery material—and this is true of both men and women— dreams of himself or of someone close to him becoming pregnant. At first I took the dream experience at face value, sending female clients, at least, for a pregnancy test. With time I came to realize the meaning behind the event, which is that *the psyche registers every creative act as a birth*. The image is, therefore, a symbolic announcement and forecast. Something is germinating, is in its initial stage of development, and will, like a baby, make itself manifest in time and on time.

The image of birthing is an apt one for the creative process. Just as the possibility of the complete person is contained in the fertilized egg, so is the future image contained in its initial manifestations. It is an important principle to bear in mind, for any breakthrough piece of art, writing, or dream experience has had its forerunners in the many less dramatic, more tentative imagistic experiments that preceded it. No matter how quickly the "big" dream or "big" art piece seemed to spring into being, before reaching this flowering point it was germinating in nascent form within its apparently less important predecessors.

Thus we can only begin to appreciate the significance of an image when we take a long-term view of it. We need to keep track of all our images and not discount the ones that seem insignificant at first; eventually we will realize that any image is always more than itself, is part of a larger whole coming into being. Like the cell growing in the womb, it carries its own future within itself. Indeed, at each new stage it is suffused with the potential for what it is intended to become at the next stage.

THE META–IMAGE

I have observed that my clients not only tend to pooh-pooh the results of any of their initial attempts to be creative; they also discount the idea that a mysterious force in the psyche, always at hand but out of their immediate control, is at work supporting and furthering the process. Because of this skepticism, I ask them to hold on to all of their responses to the exercises I give them.

Why? Because it is only with hindsight that a person can see the intelligence of the unconscious mind at work, can see that an enigmatic shape like this:

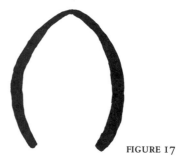

FIGURE 17

is in reality the seed-beginning of one like this:

FIGURE 18

It is by means of an overview that we perceive the larger thing that consistently seeks to actualize itself within the presence of the smaller. Just as we realize when viewing the adult human body that it grew out of a single cell, so with time will we recognize that a complex body of artwork grows out of modest beginnings. The horseshoe shape in Figure 17 was, in its first manifestation, already part of the invisible whole of the flower it was destined to become.

This idea has certain ramifications. For example, any meaning we might attribute to an image must take into account that what we presently see of it is but a partial manifestation of something else. It is a never-ending story—every conclusion is a new beginning. When we begin to interact with our images from the point of view of Source Imagery, we will avoid jumping to conclusions about their significance. We'll neither assume that our first attempts at being creative are simple and foolish—and therefore contain no meaning—nor will we swing to the other extreme and rush prematurely to guess at their meaning.

Instead, we have to keep an open mind toward the future even as we purvey the present and the past. Each of our creative images is part of a "meta-image" slowly taking shape in consciousness, gradually manifesting itself in time. The presence of the meta-image, like that of a blueprint in a builder's hand, acts as a helpful guide, determining that each of our images possesses an evolutionary quality. When we see the framework of a house under construction, we assume it is being built according to plan and that it will evolve into something more complete. As one aspect of a master plan emerging, every image we encounter is but a new side of the meta-image actualizing itself. It's a metaphysical paradox: on some timeless level of awareness the meta-image *already exists* in its entirety; on a temporal level of experience, however, it manifests itself piecemeal.

We are limited in our capacity to define what any one image means because it is just a partial representation of the meta-image. We may correctly assume that any recurrent shape in our imagery reflects our present perspective of this more inclusive entity taking shape in the mind. Like someone who has a set of binoculars trained on a single point in the distance, we have our inner eye cast on a single facet of the meta-image. It exists in the future, but we live in the present, fleshing out its elusive outline one step at a time, by means of imagistic flashes coming one after the other.

Our images have a metaphysical component or transcendent quality that lends them a mystical air. Because some of their components are invisible, studying an image is different from studying human anatomy. Yet, to illustrate the nature of the relationship between the meta-image and its parts, it serves to draw an analogy.

If a student were studying anatomical pictures of the human body in order to see what the heart looks like, he'd simultaneously have to look at front, top, side and bottom views of the organ. Similarly, any one occurrence of a creative image represents but a single impression of the meta-image. The difference between the picture of the physical organ and the psychic image consists in the relation each bears to time. It requires far less time to perceive the dimensions of the physical object than those of an imaginary one.

If we stick to this analogy we'll see why it is important to keep track of our images, not discarding those we deem too simple or unsatisfactory, for everything leads in a meaningful direction.

A TRUSTING EXCHANGE

The best way for you to overcome your resistance to the unconscious mind is by learning how to look at it from the inside out instead of the other way around. The rest of this book is designed, therefore, to assist you in gaining this special inner perspective on its workings. In Part Two and Part Three we'll acquaint ourselves with the fundamental components of the language of imagery. The more creative our grasp of the message the image transmits, the more creative its influence on our lives.

We need several kinds of support for achieving the release and development of unconscious artistic abilities. Some I have already mentioned; another is the need for a special creativity support group. Fortunately, there is one handy, though it is also one whose presence might go unnoticed because it is comprised of an invisible membership.

Each of the images used as examples in this book, from the simplest to the most complex, touched deep and personal places in my clients. First they were willing to share them with me and, also, if participating in a workshop, with the other members of the group. In revealing their feelings via their imagery, these clients demonstrated the same kind of trust toward others that they are showing now by extending the boundaries of the group invited to join their audience. Although they know they are unlikely to personally interact with the readership whom their images are intended to inspire, they hope that they can, by means of their invisible presence in the images, lend silent encouragement to people willing to risk opening their creativity.

The images they produced, like the friendly spectators who cheer runners on from the sidelines during a marathon, are essential to the process, offering silent guidance and companionship.

JUMPING IN

I'm intrigued that people often dream of diving into a swimming pool or lake when beginning the Source Imagery process. I particularly liked one version of this symbolic experience; a skeptical young person dreamt the entire group formed a circle near a body of water. Everyone started jumping in and swimming around but him. He lingered near the edge, deciding to proceed inch by inch, just letting his toes get wet first.

I took this dream as an excellent hint. Why should anyone have the feeling he's getting in over his head too fast? How about a series of creative exercises that lead in only gradually?

It isn't easy to break down a spiritual experience into various components without losing sight of the whole picture. And, having once studied the parts, we have to remember to fuse them together again. To accomplish this we'll need all kinds of intellectual paraphernalia, which like a wet suit once donned, will have to be shed in order to get at the bare truth. For, in the final analysis, to reach the basic heart of the matter we have to become vulnerable again.

Just as frequently as they dream of a pool, clients also dream of appearing naked in public at critical points during the process. It's as if they know they must let go of an outworn sense of identity—stripping off and discarding unconscious limitations and inhibitions before they can let the artist in them surface, permitting themselves to project this unconventional side of their personality into the open, where it can be appreciated by others. A feeling of being exposed and vulnerable is almost inevitable, reflecting a sensitive state of affairs.

Utilizing the Source Imagery material will not only help you overcome the immobilizing effects of the blocks I've described but will also help you overcome the anxieties that arise when you begin working with your creativity. Once you've jumped in, you'll find plenty to keep you afloat. Parts Two and Three will provide you with a grasp of the whole principle. Like pointers on a map, the ideas in these sections will help orient you in the direction of the larger picture, the more comprehensive goal toward which you are striving. You can internalize the ideas, practice using them a little and then forget them with your conscious mind if you like. Once you have begun to explore the territory on your own, using the exercises in Part Five, you can refer back to Parts Two and Three whenever you need to.

THE BLOCKBUSTERS

Images are the blockbusters of the psyche. They have force and power, not only slicing through a person's resistance to growth and change, but cutting through time itself. What gives them their fine, sharp edge? Even the dullest-looking of them has a scimitar-like quality. Against which surface of the mind do they undergo abrasion in order to attain their special polish?

Imagine a room full of mirrors. A single lamp, strategically placed, lights up the entire space. It is illumination by reflection. It is not the lamp itself that is so powerful; it is the interplay of all the elements within the space that effects the remarkable result.

It is by means of the creative interaction of several different elements that the power of a single image is enhanced.

Think of the brain as a room; inside it the ideas of past, present and future hang on the walls like mirrors, casting their reflections on the mind. When we focus on an image and try to understand it, we find that by virtue of the special position it enjoys in consciousness, it has the capacity to light up this inner realm for us in a powerful way, giving us a glimpse of ourselves as we are evolving in time. But here in this uncommon room, time exists more as a concept than as an actual sequential phenomenon. We can play with possibilities unfettered by the restraints of everyday reality.

It is fascinating that many authors state that their work provides them with an arena in which they can play out unfulfilled aspects of themselves. For example, in writing about his book *The Magic Mountain,* Thomas Mann said that had he not invented a hero who sought retreat from life by holing up in a Swiss sanatorium for several years, he might have had to enter one himself. Writers recognize the importance of the fictional self. As an extension of the personality, it can cut through the limits of time and space in ways the physical self cannot. Thanks to Hans Castorp, Thomas Mann was able to speed up the outcome of a possible course of action, deciding not to take it for himself after all. By means of this adroit maneuver he saved himself time, money and effort, augmenting his erstwhile fortune as a writer even as he creatively reflected—by means of a fictitious account—on what would happen to him should he flee the scene, temporarily giving up all his writing responsibilities.

We might conclude that the story Thomas Mann imagined helped him circumvent the possibility of encountering writer's block. Whether this is true or not, certainly it prevented him from immobilizing himself in other ways he wanted to avoid. Moreover, like an ingenious time machine, the imagery in his work transported him toward an actual future that he wanted, in which he intended to enjoy public acknowledgment for his growing literary accomplishments. And, it enabled him to rather painlessly shed an immature aspect of his personality; positing it between the pages of his novel in the form of the inept Castorp, he made it a useful part of his experience. As an example of the author's power of self-transformation, his fictional hero not only did Thomas Mann much good but an untold number of readers as well.

I'd like you to image again that room of mirrors in

which the single lamp stands shining. In your mind's eye I'd like you to reduce the entire scene to the size of a postage stamp. The whole thing thus miniaturized now looks quite different. The mirrors surround the lamp like a shade. The bulb, glowing against their composite surface, emits a powerful, incandescent light. Now imagine this multifaceted object standing once again in a room full of large mirrors. The means for intensifying the effect of the light has greatly increased.

With this picture in mind, I'd like you to think over a few of the ideas about the nature of imagery. Remember that every image reflects aspects of an individual's personality, as Hans Castorp's did Thomas Mann's. Because every image is also free of time's restraints, it has the power, like the lamp, to transcend its own boundaries, to reflect more than itself while it remains itself. In this regard, Thomas Mann's hero helped him get beyond his own limits at a time when he felt his existence threatened by them. While Hans Castorp played out his fate, Thomas Mann grappled with his future destiny as a more fully realized and successful writer.

An image reflects the varying aspects of the self as these potentially have evolved, are evolving and could evolve over time. Like the single lamp, an image is economically conceived, eliminating the need for an unnecessary expenditure of energy even while it serves to expand energy.

In its capacity to reflect so many differing aspects of our being, the image is multifaceted; in its power to connect the past and present with the future, and the future with the past and present, the image is multidimensional. Does it puzzle you still that you cannot grasp the meaning of a dream or other creative image all at once? You would have to be a fortune teller gazing into a crystal ball to surmise the untold dimensions a single image possesses.

The rest of this book is devoted to casting light on those parts of the image that you don't see as well as those that you do. You'll be delighted to discover that, like quixotic leprechauns, your creative images accomplish most of their unique magic when you're looking the other way and least expect it. In that spirit I invite you to look more closely at your images while showing you how not to look at them at all.

PART TWO

The Living Glyph

7

‾‾‾‾‾‾‾‾‾‾‾‾‾‾‾‾‾‾‾‾‾‾‾‾‾‾‾‾‾‾‾‾‾‾

Why Images?

THE TICKER TAPE

Have you ever asked yourself why, when you fall asleep and dream, you see images instead of words? The brain is an efficient, multifaceted organ. You might just as well close your eyes and read a ticker tape recapping the day's events. Imagine reading several colorless pages worth of information about yourself, one elongated paragraph of black and white following another with predictable regularity and in precise detail, with constant revisions, rewrites, never reaching the end, one endless draft after the other. If given the choice I would much prefer to watch a moving picture show!

By means of a few beginning exercises, I want to lay the groundwork for your understanding of the nature of images. The following one will help clarify why you unconsciously communicate with yourself at night predominantly via images rather than words. First, I'd like you to close your eyes and relax by concentrating for several moments on the even motion of your breathing. Then, I'd like you to begin thinking about the particular mood or feeling state you are in, identifying its characteristics in a few written phrases.

Now I'd like you to compare your description with those of some clients attending their first meeting:

1. I'm tired, a little anxious. I want to get on with it and am impatient to begin.
2. I'm skeptical and fascinated. I want to be here but wonder what's going to happen next.
3. I feel happy. I'm also confused, eager and excited.

After you have compared your response to those in the text, I'd like you to close your eyes again, taking a few moments to relax and concentrate on your breathing. This time I'd like you to breathe in and out a little more slowly than you ordinarily do, consciously focusing on the motion of your breathing to help you relax more deeply. Then you should suggest to yourself that you want to picture how you're feeling in terms of an image rather than words, letting one pop into mind. Once you've got it, I'd like you to jot it down and compare it to the following ones:

1. A door opening.
2. A racehorse nervously stomping at the starting gate.
3. A small stream with rapids.
4. A volcano.
5. The last abandoned car in an empty railroad yard.
6. A mass of fresh dough.
7. A child's pinwheel, spinning.

I think you will agree that, whereas both modes of communicating provide graphic descriptions, the one in pictures generally is more striking. It has a powerful, immediate impact on you. Why?

For one thing, it's more fun and easier to respond to an image. It hits the senses directly, bypassing the intellect, evoking strong feelings. Words predominantly occupy the head. An image travels as if on a trajectory aimed directly toward the heart—the emotional center—as well as toward the mind, intrinsically commanding more of our attention than mere words can.

Long before it was discovered to be fact, the German thinker Nietzsche imagined that Greek drama was a multi-media event, composed of words, dance and music. He thought the record we had of the tragedies in written form was but a naked fragment of a more totally engrossing creative experience.

I've often postulated how sensational it would be if I could transmit to a client how I was feeling by means of a hologram rather than mere words. Imagine instead of saying, "Good morning! I feel eager to begin working with you today," I might convey my intent by means of an all-encompassing three-dimensional image. The client would see opening before him an expanse of sea, a stretch of bright sand, a blue sky overhead. He'd see white gulls flying, hear the surf pounding, feel the warm rays of the sun on his back. In the background there would be dramatic strains of music, perhaps a symphony by Sibelius.

Clearly he'd get the message. And more than one. He'd not only grasp that I was feeling fine but that I wanted him to feel good also. The image would imply that I intended him to be refreshed by his experience with me.

Images put us more immediately in touch with our senses and feelings. In this regard they fulfill a primary function in the psyche. By reminding us of the depth and complexity of our emotional nature, they help to bring the mind and heart, and the intellect and the intuition, into alignment.

When we sleep, it is not just the body that is suspended in a state of repair; it is the whole self striving to regain a balance among its many contrasting parts. Just as we seek moments of rest in the midst of a hectic day by some pleasurable physical distraction, we often unconsciously seek spiritual respite from life's worries by some pleasurable creative distraction like fantasizing, drawing, singing, listening to music, reading or writing. It is as if a person must be engaged in creative activity of some sort in order to recharge. And, if he neglects to do so consciously, the psyche rights the balance by providing him with creative, imagistic activity at night.

BUT, I DON'T REMEMBER MY DREAMS!

Because a person doesn't remember his dreams doesn't mean he doesn't have them. It's mostly a matter of practice. For example, I don't remember all the classes I took in high school, but I do know I attended them. I don't even remember—at least not on a conscious level of awareness— what I did last Thursday at 4:35 P.M. I'd have to check my calendar to remind myself of what it was.

Moreover, I tend to remember things in highlights, not in specific details. Or is it the highlights that help me remember the details? For example, I do recall that I bought a new dress last week. And, once I start thinking about it, I remember when, where, and the conversation I had with the sales clerk.

Remembering our dreams is an art that can be cultivated over a period of time. Dreaming is an important aspect of our image-making process, but it is not the only one. There are specific drawing and writing exercises that can kick off a whole string of imagistic events, including activating our ability to remember dreams. Interestingly, it is often the person who in the beginning has the most difficulty remembering dreams who ends up recalling not just the fragments but entire odysseys of dream experience.

We want to strike a balance between the conscious and unconscious mind, between the reasoning side of the brain and the intuitive side of the psyche—not cultivate one to the detriment of the other.

To that end, it's important for you to acknowledge that images are powerful because of the feeling response they evoke in you. They transmit nonverbal messages whose logic you can register and appreciate even if the meaning eludes you at first. They hit all of the senses simultaneously, stimulating intense and deep responses against which you have few intellectual defenses.

You spontaneously engage in image-making activity when dreaming, whether you consciously will doing so or not, and whether you remember it or not. By virtue of its own momentum, your growing interest in images is bound one day to evoke spontaneously the memory of some night-time fragment. You will see how whole stories can be recounted from such tiny seeds as these.

I am asking you to become curious about your ability to dream; I don't ask that you keep an encyclopedic dream journal. At this point it is not necessary for you to record your dreams with deliberate intent. Many clients who have at first had difficulty recalling dreams have derived as much insight, stimulation and healing from others' dreams as from their own. You also can benefit from thinking about the dreams discussed in the text.

DON'T WORRY

I can imagine that there is one of you who worries that he alone, among millions of others, may be the one person who not only can't recall dreams but *never will*. This is the voice of the Darth Vader of the brain interfering with your creative risk-taking abilities again.

As a counselor I've sometimes noticed how eager a client appears to be to cancel an appointment when I've asked him to reschedule it. Invariably I get this response when he is at the verge of a big change. Under the guise of cooperation, he hides his resistance to give up the old ways of thinking.

Similarly, you may find that you are all too willing to believe you have some kind of organic defect and might as well bow out of the process while you're still ahead. Like the client eager to cancel an appointment, you may be only too eager to give up the quest to open your creativity.

But the psyche is no fool. There are backup devices. Should your dream recall be poor, there are plenty of other imagistic resources at your fingertips, springing from the same creative wellspring within the unconscious mind. For now, I just want you to recognize the power of images and to realize that image making is a natural proclivity. Dreaming is but one aspect of this universal activity. Our attraction to the creative process is instinctive, spontaneous and innate; we make images and respond to them because *we have to*. Images appeal to us, they exert an irresistible influence, reminding us that *we are what we feel and not just what we think*.

To reiterate: Images are more powerful than words because they engage the whole, not just a part of the self.

FROG CONSCIOUSNESS

"Experiments on the optic nerves of frogs have shown that only a tiny fraction of the rich world available to our sight ever gets past the retina of the frog's eye. The frog can see a small dark object moving towards its eye but cannot see it if it is moving away. A leafy tree, unmoving, simply does not exist for the frog. A lovely sunset makes not a ripple in frog consciousness."

This interesting observation was made by George Leonard in a *Harper's Magazine* article entitled "Language and Reality" (November 1974). It was Leonard's contention that our use of language restricts our capacity to view things from a multidimensional perspective, just as the frog's eye limits his capacity to appreciate things from a three-dimensional perspective. He writes, "For a long time, words have been used to block the way towards transformation. Now the situation is so urgent that we would be unworthy of our own insights if we stepped aside from the task of seeking words for a new world, no matter how difficult or embarrassing the effort may be. Perhaps our knowledge that transformation is possible comes from the realm of no-words. But we will need words to let it happen."

I am going to ask you to participate in a special exercise, one that represents a crucial stepping-stone in the Source Imagery process. It will help you bridge the gap between the realm of symbolic, intuitive experience and that of words, of rational, linear experience. It will begin to activate unconscious responses that will help expand your creativity.

I am limited in my capacity to convey to you how magical and mystifying it is to get in touch with your creativity. The relationship between us is necessarily restricted by the use of words. For us to bridge the gap between words and no-words, to be able to talk in images with each other, I need you to take a big leap, leaving froglike convention behind.

This exercise, a drawing one, will open the door to the right side of your brain, setting into motion a series of events that will further the creative process. The tools may be mine, but the laboratory is yours.

MAGIC MARKERS

I'd like you to glance back at the diagram depicting the Nurturing and Critical parents in Chapter Two (Figure 14, page 24) in order to remind yourself of the power of positive strokes. You should remember that you'll need to encourage yourself to give things a try, especially if you think you can't draw. At this point it doesn't matter whether you like what you produce; the only thing that counts is that you produce something. What is going to be important is the content of the picture. It is of no concern whatsoever how well it is drawn. Anything you make is fine.

To begin the process, it helps to have some interesting materials around to use: a few Crayolas, Magic Markers, some pastels or watercolor pencils, some glue, different shades of glitter, a large pad of drawing paper. These supplies can be found at an art-supply store, a children's toy store, or even the local supermarket. The child inside us is attracted to shiny, bright things and enjoys having options, so the greater the range of materials you have to chose from, the more likely you are to have fun doing the exercise.

Once at a nude beach I saw a little boy jumping around trying to get out of his tiny trunks and into his birthday suit as rapidly as possible. "I want to be free, too!" he cried. But his pleas were to no avail. His parents, firmly entrenched on the other side of an invisible line dividing us, had no intention of heeding his innocent plea.

If the reader is keeping his child inside a place that says "restricted," let him cross over the invisible line to the other side. It's the Critical Parent who's afraid to let him come out into the open and be free.

THE TREE, THE SEED, THE STAR

Once you have some coloring materials handy, I'd like you to attempt this simple drawing exercise:

> Relax, using the meditation technique I've intro-
> duced you to. When you're quiet, with your eyes
> closed, imagine a tree. It can be any shape, size or

color. It's your tree and there are no rules about
how it should look. Let the image go and then
imagine a seed, and finally a star. Now relax again.
Using your imagination, recall your images and see
them joining or touching each other, creating a
picture together. Relax again. When you're ready,
come out of this meditation and draw your picture.

It's really not important for you to try to produce exactly
what you saw when meditating. In fact, you can add
something new or anything surprising you'd like. The idea
is to use the meditation as a jumping off point. There is no
right way to do this exercise. The drawing can be simple,
childlike. You can use stick figures or abstract, impressionistic
forms. Embellishing the piece with glitter or other sparkling
things adds fun to the activity. It is more important to enjoy
the process of creating the thing itself than to be concerned
with how well it matches the picture in the mind's eye. The
main idea is that when you are finished, the shapes of the
tree, seed and star are distinguishable from one another;
you'll shortly recognize why.

When you're finished, I'd like you to take a few minutes
to pat yourself on the back for completing the exercise and
to think about what elements in your drawing please you. If
you're lucky, you might find you like the piece. However,
I want to emphasize again that it is the shape of the image,
not how it is drawn, that counts. A person doesn't have to
especially like the piece; he just needs to be curious about
what meaning it might contain.

SO, WHAT'S SO SPECIAL ABOUT MINE?

After you've looked your drawing over and taken time to
appreciate some aspect of it, I'd like you to compare it with
color plates 1 through 4. As you look at the drawings, I'd
like you first to pick out the obvious similarities between
your own and those in the illustrations, and then to determine
what the differences consist of.

Every picture depicts, of course, a tree, a seed and a

star. Although some are more abstract than others, all the drawings have those three elements in common. Beyond that, however, they share few other similarities: some people clearly depict the roots on their tree, others don't; sometimes the star appears overhead, sometimes not; the branches of the tree can be full or bare; the seed may or may not resemble an actual seed.

For years I have introduced people to the Source Imagery material via this initial exercise and therefore have seen innumerable examples of these drawings. Isn't it remarkable that no two have been identical! If a person should do the exercise more than once, he also would notice he never draws the same version twice.

What makes your drawing special is that it is *yours*. Only you could have produced that particular rendition of a tree, a seed and a star at this time. As simple and unprepossessing as the drawing might appear, it must be appreciated for the characteristics that make it unique.

Whether a person likes his drawing is secondary to the fact that he is capable of producing one; he must experience firsthand that however simple they might appear, his images are different from everyone else's. It is their individuality that makes them special.

WHAT MAKES THE IMAGE SING?

There is no such thing as a simple image, because the simplest we can imagine is made up of both a universal and a personal component. These two aspects of the image—the universal of the thing and our idea of the thing—are always inextricably interwoven. It is out of the creative juxtaposition of the one against the other that the image begins to sing and we can hear its message.

The man who produced the illustration on Plate 1, in the color insert, was surprised to find out how much he enjoyed drawing it. Although he wanted to open up his creativity, prior to doing the exercise he was convinced he had absolutely no visual imagination. Now, however, he was becoming sensitive to the fact that his images were special. On the next page is the piece he produced:

FIGURE 19
The client produced this interesting image in response to the mirror exercise.

It's as if doing the first exercise had split open his block. Now he realizes that he not only can make images but that they have great significance as well. Because he had the courage to still the strident voice of the Critical Parent and take a risk, he now has access to a harmonious flow of creative ideas. His images, like musical notes, are arranged according to a special ordering principle, one that connects him to the genius of the inner self. In the next chapter we will explore the special connection our images have to this larger self, whose mysterious voice sings to us in a language of mystical glyphs.

8

The Living Glyph

In musical sign language the ⸙ signifies a rest stop. When it appears in a line of music, the player instantly knows he must rest for the value of a quarter note before continuing. The ⸙ is a glyph, that is, a symbol transmitting nonverbal information to the musician in the same way that a directional arrow on a road sign conveys information to the motorist. One might say that images are not only more powerful than words but that they convey a message more rapidly, too. Although the conscious mind cannot always interpret their content as quickly as the musician grasps the meaning of the rest sign or the driver that of a pointing arrow, we sense their significance nonetheless.

Images generally stand for a complex of feelings and ideas. In this regard they are metaphors: they represent something else as well as themselves. Literary language abounds with such devices: for example, "the woman is like a rose," etc. But images are also glyphs: they function like directional signals in the psyche. They comprise a sign language that provides special guidance to the viewer.

Like the pictorial language of the ancients, they are complex ciphers, hieroglyphs whose meaning we do not easily discern. Reading an image is like cracking a code. Just as we can best understand the meaning of the hieroglyph within the context of the culture in which it arose, we can best grasp the significance of an image by understanding the special context in which it arose.

As a result of doing the tree, seed and star exercise, you gained an increased awareness that you possess a personal repository of images special to you. Fantasy is not random; your dreams, your drawings and artwork, contain representations of your version of the thing, as well as standing for the thing itself; anyone might dream of a house, for example, but each dream house is unique. In order to understand the function of the house or any other of your images, you must become sensitive to those forces in your psyche that have left their imprint upon you. Like the hieroglyphs that our ancestors left behind as visible markings of their intelligence, images are the visible markings of an ever-present intelligence operating within the psyche.

As we proceed, I will explain on two levels the special psychic code being described. First, I will describe the special context in which an individual's imagery arises; next, I will help you grasp the syntax of this unique language. Once you have gained perspective on the context and can understand the basic components of the language, you will know how to read the messages your images communicate—how to crack the code and come to see your images as carriers of a great, civilizing, creative influence.

THINGS AREN'T WHAT THEY SEEM

As I have said, many clients present their drawings of the tree, seed and star with an apologetic air. Through experience I've learned to ask that they please bring in whatever they draw and not throw it in the trash basket. It is often only with hindsight that a person can truly appreciate that his modest beginner's attempts represent creative seeds extending their first mysterious shoots into the conscious mind. In the realm of imagery, things are never what they appear to be at first glance, and we need patience to proceed.

I encourage you to go ahead and glance at the exercises listed in Part Five: there are interesting materials you can begin to collect, and there are directives for beginning to keep a magic book or source book, both special forms of a creative journal. The sooner you begin cultivating a private space in which to let your images take shape, the sooner you will benefit from the rest of the ideas presented in the text.

The concept that an individual needs hindsight in order to appreciate the significance of a particular image is an important one. It is fascinating to observe how images undergo change, continually evolving. It is similar to the pleasure we derive from looking through a photo album; putting the collection together one picture at a time is time-consuming; what is most enjoyable is to be able to get a pictorial overview of the events in our lives at a single sitting.

We gain a new perspective on our origins from the vantage point of the present. But we tend to think we have moved from the past to the present as if on a straight line:

A ___1942____1963____1972____1976____1981____1989___ Z

Point A represents the moment of birth; in the album there will be baby pictures. Between that starting point and point Z, which represents the inevitable moment of our physical demise, there is a large collection, lined up chron-ologically, of other pictures marking various events of greater and lesser consequence.

The neat album coincides with the idea that time moves in a straight line and that we can leave the past conveniently behind as we move forward toward point Z. But if that is the case, why bother remembering the past at all? Why celebrate the notion of our origins? Why should we be curious to have this overview? Even if we wanted to leave the past behind, we couldn't; it is impossible to forget everything. Memories have an annoying way of popping into conscious-ness unbidden.

The notion of the past is a convenient deceit we use to keep things organized in the mind. Insofar as the past can never be repeated, it represents a fait accompli; inasmuch as we can recall the past at will at any point in the present, the past represents an influence that always *is*.

Similarly, although we can never know with certainty exactly when we will die, realizing only that the event lies somewhere up ahead, the knowledge that we must die follows us incessantly through life. Death is a seed in our consciousness as surely as the egg was in our mother's womb; it is an ever-present eventuality, whether we choose to think about it or not.

In terms of psychic reality, we cannot reduce the totality of life's experience to the simple concept of a straight line. The picture is defined by a greater complexity, looking more like this:

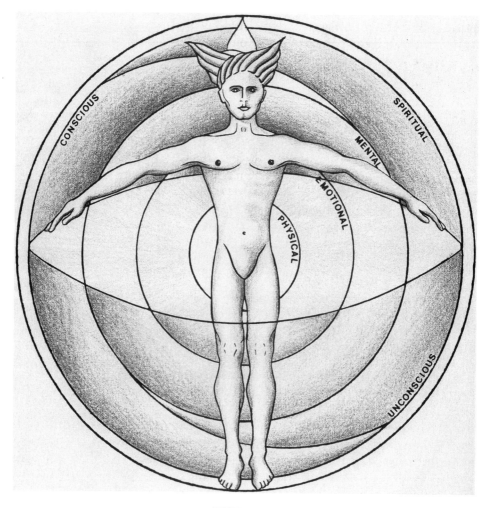

FIGURE 20

The Living Glyph, *drawing by David Stephen after design by author.*

The conscious record we keep of the events in our lives marks but one aspect of them. As we journey forward in time, moving steadily toward point Z, we also keep an unconscious record of what transpires. Thus, those conscious experiences marked off on the straight line depicted on page 89 each have their unconscious corollary; it is as if each were a mirror reflection of the other. Sometimes a person's unconscious reaction to an event will pop into conscious awareness via a dream. For example, students studying for exams often dream of being notified at the last minute that they are responsible for taking one in a course they didn't know they were enrolled in. On a conscious level, the students think they are diligently preparing to be tested; on an unconscious level, because of extreme pressure, they feel as though they will never be well-enough prepared. Whether they are pleasant or unpleasant, we systematically register our unconscious reactions to events in our lives.

Thus, the photographic record but skims the surface of things. Although we may not see clearly what is taking place beneath the surface of the voyage, we sense the mysterious presence of the inner self. W. S. Merwin has given voice to this idea in his poem "The Helmsmen":

The navigator of day
plots his way by a few
daytime stars
which he never sees
except as black calculations
on white paper
worked out to the present
and even beyond
on a single plane
while on the same breathing voyage
the other navigator steers only
by what he sees
and he names for the visions of day
what he makes out in the dark void
over his head
he names for what he has never seen
what he will never see
and he never sees
the other

the earth itself is always between them
yet he leaves messages
concerning celestial bodies
as though he were telling of his own life
and in turn he finds
messages concerning
unseen motions of celestial bodies
movements of days of a life
and both navigators call out
passing the same places as the sunrise
and the sunset
waking and sleeping they call
but can't be sure whether they hear
increasingly they imagine echoes
year after year they
try to meet
thinking of each other constantly
and of the rumors of resemblances between them★

Each of us dwells in two realities—the "seen" of the outer, external world, and the "unseen," or sensed, of the inner one. To the poet one realm is necessarily a vital but invisible extension of the other. To the dreaming self, conscious reality is a blur; to the waking self, unconscious reality dwells elusively in the shadows. Bound together on the selfsame quest, these two parts of the self feel far apart, yet are mutually desirous of closer exchange.

Figure 20 depicts the concept that life is not lived on a single but rather a multidimensional plane. The images we create combine conscious choice with unconscious intent. Thus, they represent a perfect vehicle for transmitting many levels of information about ourselves to us and to others who see them. In Figure 19 the client deliberately drew a boxlike shape with bars of music emanating from it. The two-dimensional drawing conveys that the man is becoming aware of the multidimensional quality of the image, which—like music—affects many levels of his being at once.

★ W. S. Merwin, *The Compass Flower* (New York: Atheneum, 1977), pp. 30–31.

THE MULTIDIMENSIONAL SELF

A client, a professional artist in her early fifties, came to work with me in order to learn how to enrich the understanding of her own imagery. She hoped that by so doing, she could expand her horizons not only professionally but also personally. Sensing that her imagery had special significance, she wanted to learn how to decipher its messages. She felt the inspiration she would gain would empower her to take risks in new directions both as an artist and as a woman.

Though eager to advance her career, she did not want to do so at the cost of losing the satisfaction she derived from the act of painting itself. She wanted her art to remain a vehicle for self-expression as well as to become a means for acquiring public recognition. The image of the woman's jacket composed of a light and a dark side suggests the artist's desire to integrate her inner quest for significance with the outer one for success.

FIGURE 21
Because the artist used various kinds of glitter and shiny pieces of fabric the jacket appears iridescent.

It is as if the canvas itself represented a kind of suitcase into which the artist had packed hard-won insight. Like the navigators of day and of night, two apparently separate aspects of the self, the conscious and unconscious parts of the personality are striving to unite in this piece. This is no ordinary garment. It is made for a special ritualistic event, perhaps a marriage.

It does not represent a wedding between two separate people, however; it is the celebration of a *wedding of intent* within the personality itself. The jacket is composed of many disparate parts—fragments of ribbons, netting, decorative paper, glitter, binding, sundry remnants of fabric, lace, feathers and jewels. The artist's paintbrush, like the seamstress's needle, has the capacity to weave its own special order, making sense out of the stuff of life. Although it can't be worn on her physical body, the image reveals an important awareness the artist now carries in consciousness; her imagery has more than one side to it; it is comprised as much of invisible meaning as of visible content.

A marriage signifies the forging of a lifelong commitment; perhaps the painting, like the photo in the album, marks an important turning point. As she grows older, the woman recognizes that her integrity as an artist increasingly consists of her capacity to integrate the needs of her heart with those of her mind. She is making a lasting commitment to view her work not so much as a commodity but as a vital expression of her multidimensional being.

SUITCASES OF THE ZODIAC

Images are powerful because they pack so much information into such a small amount of space. I call them the "suitcases of the zodiac" because we are able to compress great intelligence about ourselves and our life's experience into these highly pliable, lightweight forms, and we can take them with us wherever we go.

But what is the nature of this intelligence? What can we learn about ourselves by understanding our images?

You will notice that the figure depicted in the middle of

the diagram of the Living Glyph, (Figure 20, page 90), is divided into four distinct parts, each representing a major aspect of human nature. As animals we have bodily needs, as feeling creatures we have emotional ones, as thinking beings we have mental proclivities, and as creative individuals with imaginative capacities we have metaphysical inclinations; that is, we instinctively strive to *satisfy hungers of the soul and spirit* as well as of the mind, heart and body.

Thus, while we appear to journey through life on a horizontal axis, we are simultaneously responding to life's events as though oscillating on a vertical one; like the outstretched limbs of a tree, we extend our arms to grasp life even as the sap of life circulates up and down our veins.

A photo album ultimately presents a paltry, surface replica of a life. The stuff it is really made of, the record of the heartbreak and joy, the successes and failures, the disillusionment suffered, the vision gained—in short, the entire *felt journey* we have traversed—cannot be depicted within the two-dimensional circumference of such a collection. We cannot pass through space and time as if moving on a horizontal line; the past, present and future are not static concepts but rather fluid experiences. We move up and down, in and out, back and forth. The earth is not flat. Is it not folly to journey toward an edge we can never reach?

On the round face of the world there are no sides, it is a spherical plane whose surface is comprised of an infinite continuum with neither an end nor a beginning. And such are we, spherical creatures whose finite edges are an illusion; we, too, represent a continuum of experience without beginning or end. The brain is no cul-de-sac, it's a doorway to infinity.

Thus, as we traverse reality "on the single plane," we do not move simply along a horizontal, two-dimensional axis from birth toward death. We move in and out of the shadows (the sphere of the unconscious mind) and the light (the realm of the conscious mind); and as we do so, every level of our being is influenced by our experience. If we had special X-ray vision, we might be able to see through the surface of the pictures in the album into the heart and soul of the person whose life is being traced. And we would perceive what kind of relationship he entertained to his body, what kind of feelings, thoughts, and values he had. We would see where he might be stuck, where he was evolving.

But no one really has this kind of vision, at least not on a conscious level of awareness. Caught in the everyday world of waking reality, no one ever sees the whole picture at once; we tend to calculate utilizing two-dimensional tools. It is only by using imaginative multidimensional tools that we can reflect the complexity of our nature. Each of us, like the woman who created the magical jacket, has the power to wield imaginative psychic tools. We too can create images that, like hers, are packed with vital information, rendering spiritual insight into tangible form, transforming the everyday into something exciting and transcendent.

THE NEED TO SURVIVE

If we were able to examine the original painting of the jacket closely, we would observe a series of pictures illustrating the heads of wolves collaged along the top and left-hand edge of the canvas. The half-hidden faces of these animals peer out at the viewer with unswerving intent; their gaze is both stealthy and eerie, compelling and majestic.

The presence of these animals, of animals in general, reminds us of the unremitting urge we have to survive as biological entities, taking care of our physical needs on a minute-to-minute basis as long as we live. Animal intelligence, like the eyes of the creatures in the painting, has its own integrity. We cannot escape the knowledge that life is finite; to be true to ourselves means to be true to our animal instincts. Like animals we are powerful, yet like them we also have distinct limits.

Sometimes we forget or do not recognize these limits and blindly run up against them. Childhood especially is a time for familiarizing ourselves with our biological limits. The amusing fate of a friend of mine who as a little boy desperately wanted to fly illustrates what I mean. He climbed up on the roof of a neighbor's house while his mother was visiting a friend, his father's black umbrella in his hand. Just as his mother was about to take a sip of tea, she glanced up to see his little figure helplessly plummeting past the window, umbrella dauntlessly upraised, into the bushes, which fortunately for him were thick and sturdy enough to break his fall.

Although he was disappointed to learn that, indeed, he couldn't fly—even with the aid of Daddy's big umbrella—he, like his mother, was relieved he survived the experience unscathed except for a bruise or two. Throughout life, try as we might, none of us can ever forget we are animal beings, with all their incredible strengths and great weaknesses.

The artist who made that jacket was a smart person with a good head on her shoulders. She recognized her limits. She knew she couldn't survive without success, but also that her success depended on her learning new ways to survive. For, wisely, she sensed she did not merely want to satisfy her human hunger for greater recognition but wanted to satisfy her need to deprive spiritual satisfaction from what she was doing as well.

Just as we have a biological need to survive, we have a spiritual one to thrive. The wolf is an animal that eats and partially digests the kill, regurgitating and storing it in a secret hiding place for later use. In other words, it eats the same thing *twice* in order to sustain itself.

We could easily say, Let's leave art to artists and desist from this discussion. What right have I, if I'm not an artist, to live off my own images? Well, there's more than one way to look at this issue. If it is the quality of our life we are seeking to improve rather than the level of our fame, we have every right to expect to live off our images. We don't need to own a farm to be able to grow the vegetables we eat.

The physical fact of our existence is not all there is to life. The urge to create images, the fact that we must create them, grows out of a spiritual need to survive. We want, we must find meaning in what we do, or a vital part of us withers and dies. We must eat twice of the stuff of the world, once to feed the body, once to feed the spirit, or we cannot thrive. There is more than one mouth to feed in the psyche; there are many hungers to be stilled. Like the sly wolf, we too can make a secret lair, and erect a special storage place in the mind.

The jacket in Figure 21 sparkles magically. Comprised

of found objects, everyday detritus, it shines as if embellished with costly and precious things. Once we have learned to consciously wield the power of the imagination, each of us can derive new pleasure and unexpected satisfaction from ordinary experiences. We can gorge on our own creations to our heart's content, making a feast of insight, growing strong on the fat of the palette. To have spiritual integrity means to acknowledge this need we have to sustain the transcendent side of our nature, to continually harvest the food of experience in a form the whole self can enjoy.

9

~~~~~~

The Whole Experience

THE CART BEFORE THE HORSE

The idea that creative expression is a means for transporting ourselves into a realm that is out of the ordinary yet necessary for survival is reflected in the following collage made by a woman who had no prior training in the arts. A book editor who had some practical experience in overseeing layouts, she longed to become a creative writer; skeptical about her artistic abilities, she reluctantly participated in the initial exercises. Shortly thereafter she found to her surprise that she possessed a powerful visual imagination. This piece was the second in a fascinating series of collages she produced. She decided to set aside her interest in writing for a while to concentrate on speaking this new, intriguing language.

FIGURE 22

The client has a great sense for combining images. She creates surprising juxtapositions.

Like the jacket that seemed to be floating upward from the bottom of the canvas and appeared to have sprung onto the canvas and out of the artist's mind with the whimsy of a jack-in-the-box, the woman in the picture has appeared out of nowhere riding in the giant, four-wheeled red cart of a child. The cart itself is in a room located apparently on the top floor of a modern high-rise apartment building.

Is the cart standing in front of the horse? Or, is the horse before the cart? And just what metaphorical cart and horse are we talking about?

The exercises have opened up the client's child side, giving her access to its wit and imagination. Still distracted by the duties of her career, she has begun to set aside time for creative activity. The Source Imagery material, with its emphasis on gaining access both to creative and spiritual resources of the unconscious mind, has had a disquieting effect. At the same time, it has set things into motion.

Her sensitivity to the needs of the child and her growing awareness of the power of the unconscious mind have precipitated a rearranging of priorities. Instead of writing, she wants to make images; instead of using a technical approach, she is activating her creative drive first. Rather than saying she needs to learn how to draw in order to be creative, she's saying she needs to be creative before she can learn to draw. Thus, she is, at least according to tradition, putting a new cart in front of an old horse. But to the extent that she recognizes her need to rely on her creative process and her unconscious mind to guide her, that she does in fact require the presence of a "teacher," she is also placing a new horse in front of an old cart.

In which direction is she traveling? Are things moving forward or backward?

Because the client has become conscious of the multi-faceted nature of her imagery, she is also aware that things aren't always what they seem. Like the figure in the diagram of the Living Glyph, the person seems to be moving on a horizontal axis; though the scene transpires within the top-most level of a vertical edifice. The client has realized that her images transport her through time and space away from the past toward the future, and from the future back into the past. She recognizes that she is an entity with both finite limits and infinite spiritual capacities.

A rectangular shape in the ceiling looks like a skylight. It suggests that within the narrow space where she temporarily dwells, she can have access to limitless realms. And, rows of neatly stacked books are lined up along one side of the room in a bookcase that opens up in the wall like a window. The client realizes that her images give her access to knowledge readily available but located in a special space, which she can only reach by unusual means. Not an artist in the traditional sense, she has the capacity to use the same set of creative keys to unlock the door to this secret hideaway that the professional painter did to open hers.

WHAT IS THE WHOLE EXPERIENCE?

On the one hand, our psychic images arise in response to our reactions to the outer world, showing us how forces extrinsic to us affect us. On the other, they also arise in response to unconscious forces operating within us, revealing the different kinds of internal needs we must satisfy in order to feel well-integrated.

Images help to establish a connection between our outer and inner worlds, our conscious and unconscious selves. Notice in Figure 22 that the lady, although comfortably ensconced on a bed of pillows, is precariously perched half in and half out of the cart. Like each of us, she seeks to strike a balance between that which lies outside her and that which is inside.

There is a definite note of yearning in Merwin's poem about the daytime and nighttime navigators. Like two parts of one self, each senses the reality of the other and longs to unite with him; without this union the picture is never complete, and there is a feeling of void. Each of us is secretly attracted to the realm of images, for it provides us with a magical space in which to bring about a meeting between these two sides of ourselves.

Creative images help us to dissolve the barrier between the inner and outer selves. Even more important, they represent an alternative aspect to our everyday life experience. If we were to isolate a specific moment in our life that lay in the past—for example, that of becoming a parent—what moment would we define as that in which we felt ourselves to have become a parent? Was it when we decided to become one? When the baby was conceived? At the birth? During the baby's childhood? Later? Or was it the whole thing—the entire experience of parenting, past, present, and future? Moreover, our experience of parenting is comprised of our feelings and thoughts about it as much as of actual interactions with the child.

Suppose we feel we have made mistakes at parenting. To the extent that we can assess them and base future decisions on a new line of action, the past—along with its mistakes—no longer represents a fait accompli. The old relationship, instead of being a burden, can become a teacher. As we look back toward the past from the healing perspective of a present in which we have made more creative choices about our behavior, we realize the past represents but a moment in time; it is but a fraction of *the whole thing* taking place on a continuum we call the parenting experience.

In this regard, time represents a fluid force. Every

decision we make has a ripple effect backward and forward. Creative images act like psychic transistors. Learning to listen to them with sensitivity enables us to make new sense of our lives. We reinterpret what has gone before in the light of what we would like to see take place ahead.

Some images we encounter are pleasant, some are not. All of them provide us with information that can help us make choices for our benefit. In terms of the language of imagery, being creative refers to the capacity we each have to draw on unconscious resources to help us move in a direction best suited for growth.

One client dreamt that she approached herself dressed in a favorite outfit she often wore to work. Just as the two selves were to meet, the self in the familiar garb, surrounded by a glowing light, began to smile and wave good-bye in a friendly manner. Upon waking, the client felt troubled, and decided she'd continue wearing the outfit. Ironically, she never thought it fit quite right or looked as good again. Gradually she changed her style. This dream stirred the woman's awareness that she was undergoing a change in identity. She was considering a career shift, one that would affect her outer appearance as well as her inner state. Although disquieting, the image was prompting her to look at herself from a fresh perspective, reinforcing her desire to move in a new direction.

To make room for the future, the client was going to have to let go of the past, and it made her afraid. What the dream helped her realize is that all she needed to shed was an outer shell, because her essential self, her core, was undergoing transformation, not annihilation.

LIKE A JEWEL

When we make images we are participating in a transformational process, one that encourages growth on all levels of the psyche at once. Any image extrapolated from dreams and artwork can have an impact similar to the one just described. An actual physical event, like the act of becoming a parent, cannot be limited to an isolated point in time, nor can its influence transpire on just one level of reality or affect only one aspect of our being at a time. What the entire event has been, what it has become, what it still can evolve into is *the whole experience*.

And our images, with their potential to evoke transformation, are a vital part of the whole experience. Only when we see that images are not static but organic entities can we appreciate that they are an intrinsic part of a dynamic interaction between the conscious and unconscious mind, between objective and subjective reality. Images tend to integrate one mode of perception with another, providing us with information about our spiritual, mental, physical and emotional states of being. As such they are mixed messengers of the zodiac, conveying special intelligence about both *movement and events* that take place in our lives above and below the threshold of consciousness.

Working with an image, therefore, is like making an archeological find. It presents the viewer with a complicated history of activity, revealing a cross-section of the psyche. To derive the greatest benefit we need to cultivate the habit of looking at images from several angles at once. Then we discover how they can become an impetus for spiritual growth as well as artistic development.

Like a faceted gem, the more of its angles our mind comes to rest on, the more the image shines in our consciousness:

FIGURE 23

We call the faceted gem a jewel. But what does the "jewel" we see here really consist of? Does the past in which it lay beneath the ground in raw form no longer exist? Has its essential nature as a crystal been lost or rather transformed by the process of change? For the jewel to be what it is now, it has to have been—and still include—all that it was before. At the same time, is it no less a jewel for the fact that it has not yet been placed in a setting? And what might the setting consist of? Will the jeweler make it into a ring, a necklace, a pin? How many people will own the piece, and what will it come to represent to each of them?

The jewel, like each of us and each of the images we create, is part of an ongoing process. No single image ever represents the complete picture; in it we see reflected glimpses of the past, inklings of what is to come. To be creative means to consciously cooperate with those forces in the psyche that will our spiritual evolution as well as our creative growth.

WHAT IS THE INSIDE AND WHERE IS THE OUTSIDE?

In Chapter Six I used the term "meta-image" to describe how our images evolve in an artistic sense, emphasizing that we need to value everything, even the simplest image we make, because it is an intrinsic expression of a more complex entity gradually taking shape.

"Meta-" can mean "supra-" and refer to a more highly organized form of the thing represented, a greater and transcending order. It also implies "metaphysical," referring to a more transcendent or spiritual manifestation of the thing represented. We are careful in our waking life to distinguish the inner, subjective world from the outer, objective one, sometimes creating a needlessly painful dividing line between them. But as we endeavor to bring forth the creativity within us, we will find that making such fine distinctions is not always in our best interest.

The German poet Rainer Maria Rilke concluded that the ultimate manifestation of a thing was not the physical thing at all but the version of it that his creative imagination brought forth. The finite boundaries of the physical thing were impermanent on two counts; first, the material object is destined to decay, and second, it can undergo transformation by means of our interaction with it. In this regard, physical reality is transmutable and highly changeable, susceptible to the creative touch of the human imagination. He suggests that all distinctions we make between the outer and inner worlds are moot, as the piece on the next page illustrates.

> One space permeates all being,
> The world of inner space.
> Birds fly right through us, languidly.
> Oh, how I want to grow.
> As I look outside,
> The tree grows inside me.★

The creative imagination has a transformational effect upon reality:

> Space extends outward from inside us, changing the shape of things. To successfully harness the existence of the tree, consciously wrap inner space around it, composed of the space that once existed within you. Let it add dimension to the tree which itself cannot set limits. The tree is first actualized when cast into form through your act of relinquishing.†

What we need to relinquish is a tight, unimaginative grip on reality. We need to invite our whole self to the party, to let that which is invisible be part of the show. To Rilke there was no such thing as an outside objective world that could be differentiated from an inside, subjective one; there was rather only one reality, composed of the stuff of both realms. His poetic heart rejoiced at all the infinite connections there were to make between them, and so can we.

Like a fruit that ripens on the vine and decays if not eaten, our creativity if held in check and not gladly "relinquished" can begin to cause us pain. In her book about a lesser-known version of the New Testament, entitled *The Gnostic Gospels* (Random House, New York, 1979), Elaine Pagels translates a saying attributed to Jesus:

> If you bring forth what is within you, what you bring forth will save you. If you do not bring forth what is within you, what you do not bring forth will destroy you.

★ Rainer Maria Rilke, *Sämtliche Werke,* Volume II (Frankfurt am Mein: Insel Verlag, 1966), p. 93, *my translation.*

† Ibid., p. 168.

This Jesus also had an interesting, unorthodox view of heaven. It represented not a place but a special state of mind:

> When you make the two one, and when you make the outside like the inside, and the above like the below, . . . then you enter [the Kingdom].

All we need to do to get in touch with a more transcendent order of reality is to better understand the power of our creativity. Like chameleons we can change from one form to another, utilizing our images to show us the way to a more complete experience of our whole being.

THE SLEEPING BEAR

There is more discomfort in keeping our images locked inside us than in letting them out so they can breathe and enjoy the light of day. Sometimes the "heavy" feeling we have about life is not so much related to the bad things happening outside as to the burden of carrying around the good things we keep stifled inside.

One client, a woman in her late twenties who underestimated her creative potential, suffered from chronic depression. She dreamt of finding herself in a strange building, dripping with moisture, the atmosphere dank, stifling and oppressive. Plants, vines and other growing things were climbing over the walls and hanging down from the ceiling. Her creative impulses, like plants struggling for survival in an overgrown terrarium, needed an outlet. As she gained confidence in and received permission to express her creativity, her depression lifted. Consequently, she felt and looked better. She then risked making new, exciting personal connections and exploring more satisfying career options.

We need to release the force for creativity inside us, trusting its innate goodness and its capacity to provide us with guidance. Like a hibernating bear, our creative drive has been lying in hiding for safekeeping. Once the climate is right, *it wakes up* all by itself.

We know that, much as we consciously measure time

by means of an hour hand, we are subject to a biological clock; it is as if the body measured time by its own instincts. There is yet another kind of mechanism for measuring time based on our spiritual needs. A good teacher or therapist is familiar with this kind of timing, withholding information from a student or client until the "time" is right. A message delivered too soon can fall on deaf ears.

Our creativity can be a slumbering giant. A whole string of events is set into motion once it has been awakened. It has its own rhythm. It is best that a person fall into sync with this aspect of his nature, not bully or try to *control* it.

We are dealing with a special kind of time frame, one unique to the unconscious mind, requiring patience and an attitude of expectant attentiveness on our part. That's all that is needed. Our creativity itself is powerful enough to get the job done if we are but willing to learn how to live cooperatively with it.

The whole idea is to enjoy the prospect of finding out more about what lies ahead—or rather inside—on this unique quest.

There is no need to worry about how we are going to get "there." Each of us possesses a guide map of our own, composed of special images to lead us along the best-suited route. Like the woman who dreamt of the building overgrown with plants, many of us have had a desire to become more creative that has been building for a long time. Now that we are ready, the psyche will assist us in realizing our intent.

WE ARE SUCH STUFF AS DREAMS ARE MADE OF

The meta-image has another meaning—that all psychic images, whether occurring in our dreams, fantasies, or art, are interconnected. The drawings in Figures 17 and 18 illustrated how a simple line becomes a complex shape; but there I primarily focused on how this evolution takes place within the context of a person's artistic development.

No psychic event is an isolated occurrence. The meta-image is a term, therefore, implying that every image we create interfaces with every other. Whether we dream or paint it first makes no difference—we tap into the same unconscious reservoir. The two modes of awareness represent two different routes to the same source. Tapping into one realm of creative activity gives us access to the other. Every line we draw is potentially—and inadvertently—part of a larger subconscious image coming into focus. Conversely, what we dream has the potential for attaining conscious form in a work of art.

In the dynamic world of the unconscious mind, *everything* is grist for the mill. There are no good or bad images, there is only *becoming*. Each of our images is connected to all the many different parts of us. As they unfold, we unfold; as we unfold, they do, too.

When we deal with an image, we are dealing with more than one dimension of reality. Thus, opening our creativity will change our experience of reality because we begin to perceive life in all its manifestations from a less limited, multidimensional perspective.

We need to be less concerned with judging ourselves and our images, and more concerned with being delighted that they exist at all. Our dreams are an entryway to heaven; let's not tarry at the gate.

INTENT

At this point, you may find it helpful to think about what you hope to gain from opening your creativity. Use the following exercise to help you identify specific goals: Take a few moments to relax, using the simple breathing exercise I described in Chapter Seven. When you feel quiet, think about some of the creative changes you'd like to achieve within the next six months. What are some new feelings you'd like to have about yourself? And what are some concrete, practical changes you'd like to see? When you're ready, jot your impressions down, dividing the list into two sections, one describing the inner changes, the other the outer ones.

Setting goals, like planning an itinerary, is an important part of any process of change because it orients you toward specific action. Unless you can point to the spot you'd like to reach, having a map is an interesting but hardly useful device for getting you where you want to go. On the other hand, you can have the best time traveling when you keep an open mind and are flexible about the unexpected turns of events that can lie ahead.

Thus, although I suggest that clients utilize this exercise to outline their goals, I also emphasize that they can never predict the exact outcome of the process; often a person who has wanted to write discovers he can paint instead or vice versa, or someone who wanted a job change is delighted to get a challenging promotion.

Defining your intent as clearly as possible helps you get the desired results. And, differentiating the feeling you would like to have from your actual goal helps you get down to specifics. But, even as you set about identifying exactly where it is you want to go utilizing the Source Imagery method, you've always got to be ready to change tacks according to nature's whim.

10

Images Are Organizing Principles

WHAT IS AN ORGANIZING PRINCIPLE?

It is easier to grasp an abstract idea if we think of it in concrete terms first. When building a wooden frame house, for example, a person basically organizes its shape around the idea of a rectangle or square. Even if some interesting curves and arches are incorporated into the design, the idea of a square will predominate in the layout. A few doors away from my house is an interesting old building called "the round house," whose design was conceived around the idea of a different organizing principle. An historical oddity, it is built in the shape of a circle. No one lives there; unfortunately it is boarded up, and the eccentric who owns it lets no one peek inside.

I've been told that even the heating system is round, with ducts radiating out from the center like the spokes of a big wheel. I've speculated about how the interior is laid out. I imagine the rooms might be wedge-shaped, like pieces of a pie, or oval or round. Although I knocked down walls and made radical alterations in my old house, I really couldn't change the basic rectangular shape around which the design was originally conceived into a circular one. One way or another, "squarishness" is reflected throughout the entire space just as "roundness" must be in the other place.

An organizing principle, then, is first that which determines a thing will have *consistency of design* throughout all its parts.

Thus, it refers to the design of a thing in the sense of its actual physical form. But, "design" also signifies intent, as for example, in the expression "the young man has designs on that young woman." No architectural design is ever laid out without a specific intent in mind. In the case of the house, the purpose of the structure is to provide adequate living space for its inhabitants. Even if well built and appealing to the eye, unless it fulfills this function the building has fallen short of the mark, and consequently is poorly designed.

Next, therefore, an organizing principle also ensures that a thing will have *consistency of design and intent* throughout all its parts. For only if the thing has both structural and functional integrity can it fulfill its ultimate purpose. If a house is poorly constructed, if the roof leaks in bad weather or the cellar floods and the house does not function as efficiently as it might, as long as it provides shelter to the inhabitants it does possess integrity; leaky roof or not, it still has the potential for becoming that intangible something it was meant to become, a place called "home." In this regard, a half-finished or empty house is of no use, devoid of meaning.

In order to fulfill the rather ineffable function of helping people feel they're "at home," the finished house must, in fact, stand in some kind of ongoing relationship to the people who dwell inside it. So an organizing principle also necessarily implies *a way of ordering the relationships* between parts of things to each other so that they will exist in harmonious correspondence not only to themselves but to the things immediately surrounding them. The organizing principle ensures that the potential of the thing, in this case the blueprint of the house, is actualized, and the completed structure becomes a home.

"Organizing principle" is a term, therefore, that describes not only the structural and functional relationships of the parts to each other, but also refers to the relationship the whole thing entertains to a complex larger set of coordinates. In the case of the house it describes the relationship of the building to its inhabitants and of the building to its surroundings. A large six-story tenement would look out of place next to a row of one-story bungalows clustered on the waterfront.

Thus, an organizing principle implies consistency of design and intent, and an intrinsic *harmony of order*. The organizing principle does its ordering first in a logical temporal sequence; that is, a house takes shape initially on the drafting board in the form of a blueprint, next as a structure on a particular plot of ground, finally as a "home" in someone's life at a special point in time. Then it just as consistently orders a nontemporal set of relationships: that of the parts of the house to each other, the house to its occupants, and that of the house with its occupants to the rest of the neighborhood.

The organizing principle is not static, it is fluid and responsive in that *it defines relationship as well as design.*

ABSTRACT ORGANIZING PRINCIPLES

Just as a concrete thing like a house reflects the presence of an organizing principle, so can an abstract thing like an idea have such influence and force. Ideas, like houses, have structure and purpose, are either poorly or well conceived in "design." It is not difficult to understand a "well-designed" idea; its "shape" is that of a clearly articulated message, its intent to occupy the mind of the listener, its ultimate purpose to make a point. If it doesn't, like the poorly constructed house, it can't bear much weight and falls easily apart in the mind of the listener.

As long as an idea consists of an intelligible message, hits home with a receptive audience and makes a point, it is well designed and can stand the test of time. Even if the premise is faulty it will help to define a person's mental space with predictable consistency.

Certain psychological ideas operate as organizing principles in the mind, especially ones voiced by our parents when we were young. The comments "Shut up!" "Be quiet and get out of the way—can't you see I'm busy!" constitute, if often repeated, a powerful message that the sensitive child interprets as a signal to "get lost!" The message makes a lasting and disheartening point over time: "I want you to be invisible." This idea, which has an undermining effect on the child's sense of well-being, becomes a building block of his self-image. Although "full of holes," it perseveres.

Many people with outstanding creative potential never risk showing it. Over the years it remains stashed on the back shelf of the closet they've built out of the ideas their parents unwittingly transmitted to them. In fact, their entire mental home is sometimes constructed out of such ill-conceived points, handed down from generation to generation.

Precisely because they have withstood the test of time, these "holey" ideas have become scared to their possessors, even if debilitating in effect. Like the house in need of repair, they need fixing, because they inhibit a person's ability to function efficiently, causing him to feel out of sync with critical parts of his environment. Although such ideas are supposed to help him create a sense of order in his life, he feels off-balance, nagged by the feeling that something is profoundly "out of order."

IMAGES ARE ORGANIZING PRINCIPLES

An organizing principle, whether physical or mental, helps order experience. Images also have this power; they, too, function as organizing principles, operating, however, on both a concrete and abstract level. Like the architectural blueprint, they have a tangible physical outline; their contours can be traced in a drawing, a piece of sculpture or in writing. But, like the verbal utterance, they are abstract, containing a message. They provide the special means by which the psyche helps us organize our inner and outer experiences in meaningful sequence.

Images promote integration between various parts of the self, aligning our conscious perception of it with a larger, more all-inclusive unconscious one. Through them a person's awareness of himself as a biological organism operating within a physical field of energy is brought into balance with an awareness of the self as a psychic entity evolving within a nonphysical field of energy. Images help us perceive the connection between these realities, showing us how they interrelate. They invite us to acknowledge how these alternate aspects of existence are dependent on one another, for each without the other is like a house standing empty, waiting for occupants to make it a home.

The messages that our images contain, unlike the arbitrary and sometimes destructive ones we heard as children, always make a positive point. The point any single image, cluster or series of images is trying to make concerns the nature of the ongoing relationship between the inner and outer selves, our physical and spiritual being. No matter how negative it might appear, any image is attempting to establish intelligible communication between these parts of the self, and is simultaneously providing us with guidelines for nurturing and furthering it.

The image is the parent of the creative relationship between the inner and outer selves and of the self with its environment. It signals to the attentive listener changes he can make to promote growth and well-being on all levels of the personality and in all areas of life.

THE NEED FOR LOGIC

The organizing principle promotes consistency. To be functional any house must incorporate its components into itself in a logical fashion; if it doesn't, chaos ensues and the place just won't work. Stairways and corridors must lead from one space into another. A ceiling has to rest on supports, a door must have two sides, walls must rise vertically, floors lie horizontally, etc. An organizing principle then, *promotes logical alignment,* for it is the logical ordering of the parts that determines the sense of the whole thing.

It's precisely the same with language. The organizing principles that determine the order of the parts of an English sentence are familiar to anyone reading this page. Each ordering principle, like the differing bodies of grammer in foreign languages, has *its own logic.* Should we compare the grammatical ordering principles of the German language with those of English, we'd find a striking contrast. In German it is not so much where the word is placed in the sentence that determines its function (i.e., signifies whether it is acting as the subject or object) but rather, the particular ending affixed to it. Because the language is inflected, that is, there are special endings to place on words to signify their function, a person can determine, by analyzing the endings, which word is the subject and which is the object, no matter where they appear in the sentence. Thus, the simple combinations of the words "the man throws the ball" and "the ball throws the man" are both declarative statements identical in meaning. Neither version is illogical; as long as the endings are correct the statement has coherence.

This method of ordering words in a sentence is logical to the German mind but often makes little sense to an American learning the language. Accustomed to ordering sentences by the rules of English logic, he can't grasp that Germans not only like to vary word order, but—given their frame of reference—they must. Thus, at first he unconsciously rejects the German logic, opting for his own, getting irritated when German sentences aren't written "like they're supposed to be." As he becomes better acquainted with the German way of ordering words and comes to appreciate its inherent logic, it gets easier for him to speak and understand the language.

Every organizing principle, then, has its own logic. Without this logical ordering there would be no coherence, and without coherence there could be no meaning.

THE LOGIC OF THE PSYCHE

Just as both English- and German-speaking people have their own ways of ordering sentences, so does the psyche have its unique means for ordering experience. And, just as a person can adamantly cling to his old, familiar expectations about what makes grammatical sense, disregarding his need to grasp the new order of things, so can he cling to an inappropriate form of logic when attempting to gain an understanding of his dreams and images.

The unconscious mind speaks in images, we talk in

words. And these two modes of communicating are structured according to quite different ordering principles. To understand the language of the psyche, we must be willing to make adjustments similar to those we would when traveling. There is more than one level to experience. Like a person who can speak several languages, those of us who gain the ability to speak intelligently about our images feel at ease in a wide variety of challenging situations. Our increased facility opens doors that might otherwise have remained closed.

From time to time I used to let my cat Alexander outside to play in the yard. When I would call him to come in, he'd run and hide in a corner under the eaves beneath the porch that was impossible for me to reach. No amount of cajoling would work; despite cries of "pretty boy, pretty, pretty boy," he wouldn't budge, staring at me with those incredibly appealing and luminous but implacable eyes. At that moment, gazing into them, I thought he might be smarter than I. But when I would open a can of his favorite food and place it between us, he'd instantly come bounding out; in one effortless flash, balance in the relationship would be restored.

I was thinking with animal logic and therefore got better results. I had another cat once; she also was smart—and imaginative, to boot. She liked catnip. Despite the fact that it was tightly stored in a glass jar, she figured out where it was kept. However, I didn't realize she had. One night, because I heard her meowing, I came into the kitchen to find her standing in front of the cabinet in question, inexplicably whining. I couldn't figure out what she wanted. She kept walking back and forth, crying continually while I stared at her uncomprehendingly. Suddenly she got a bright idea. Locking her eyes with mine, she began rolling over on the floor, making precisely the same series of sinuous movements she did whenever she got high on catnip. Of course I got it. How could I deny her the treat she wanted? She'd stretched her cat brain in order to communicate with me, utilizing my kind of human logic with feline ingenuity and winning grace.

THE MEANINGFUL GESTURE

In order for me and my animals to communicate effectively, we were each required to appreciate the other's special kind of logic. To the degree we were able to do this, we were more quickly able to evoke a cooperative response, get the desired result. I used the example of wordless "talking" with my pets because there was a gap between us no words could bridge.

I think sadly of Alexander. For months before he died, he cried for long periods of time for inexplicable reasons. He didn't appear to be sick and therefore I would get irritated with him. Because of his incessant whining and my lack of understanding, we sometimes didn't get on well.

All at once he did get sick and I took him to the vet. It was too late to save him; overnight the quality of his life went downhill, and when his demise was imminent I decided to put him to sleep. The doctor explained that cats often mask symptoms; she herself had lost her own pet in a similar fashion.

Nevertheless, I wished I had understood earlier what that gentle creature's crying was all about. If only I could have interpreted his meowing—perhaps I might have saved him.

Alexander was part of my life, he wasn't part of me. How much more important it is for each of us to establish an intelligent rapport with our own psyche, the part of us that does not speak in words but creates pictures instead. Images, like the sinuous movements of the cat on the floor, are soundless but meaningful; they are the wordless gestures made by one part of the self when attempting to communicate its needs sensibly to the conscious personality. Unlike my cats, the unconscious mind does not, however, embody a lower form of intelligence but rather a superior and more advanced one. Just as my pet had to stretch the limits of her mind to communicate her desire for the catnip, so does each of us have to stretch the limits of the conscious mind to establish rapport with this greater aspect of the self.

Each of us remembers having said, "I just can't put that into words." That's where images come in. Just as a body is shaped around a skeleton, so the experience of the psyche is shaped around images. We naturally tend to translate emotional experience into image; it's the silent work of the artist functioning within us. We all unconsciously "draw" imagistic equivalents of our life's experience in our dreams, fantasies, artwork and writing.

Images are "life organizers," helping create order out of internal experience much as a daily calendar both records and organizes our outer one. As with that calendar, certain images provide an overview of the events in our lives, only in this instance they are psychic in nature.

Images are uniquely suited to fulfill this function; plastic and malleable, they more easily conform to the differing "shape" and shades of feeling than words do. Like a great potter at the wheel, the unconscious mind continually creates receptacles into which we can cast experience, and gather the essence of a lifetime.

THE FLUID MEDIUM

Why are images more fluid than words? First of all, we can't assign as specific a meaning to an image as we can to a word. Words by nature tend to distinguish among things, and can with time change their meaning but *not their form*. Images, on the other hand, tend to blend the distinctions among things, combining this unexpected thing with that unlikely one, each time changing their meaning *as well as their form*.

The English word "fix," for example, assumes several different meanings depending on the context in which it occurs. Whereas there are several varying connotations a person might affix to this word, their number is necessarily limited or "fixed" in his mind, determined by the list of definitions in a standard dictionary.

There is no standard dictionary for images, and any book that presumes to list such definitions is missing the point. Images defy neat categorization. When it comes to trying to identify their equivalent in sound, they are more closely related to the musical notes in a scale than to letters in the alphabet. The unconscious mind thinks like a composer, not a pedantic scholar.

Although words may have multiple definitions, their

function is to define the exact meaning of things. If we fail to pronounce or write a word correctly, confusion can ensue. We especially notice the need for precision when speaking a foreign language. I inadvertently offended my landlady once when living in Germany. I thought she told me—for inexplicable reasons—that her brother's home was a "mess." Since she'd used a colloquialism (the word "pigsty") to describe it, I thought she meant the house itself might literally be falling down or that his marriage was falling apart. Shocked, I offered her my sympathies. At first she looked taken aback. I had the bright idea of checking to see if I'd heard her correctly: "Your brother's house is a pigsty?" She burst into laughter. She had said, "Schreinerei," which means "carpentry shop," not "Schweinerei," which meant something else entirely.

One letter made all the difference. Because I had misheard the pronunciation of a word, I'd made a false connection. Words assist us in making the right connections between things by delineating the differences between them. Images, however, help us make connections by pointing out hidden affinities between dissimilar things, upsetting the apple cart of the conscious mind by dissolving the boundaries and blurring the edges between them. Words help us to focus, to narrow something down. Images expand our vision, enlarging our perspective by creating connections where formerly there were none. And, whereas words have to appear in consecutive order to be logical, images cluster in patterns that can appear jumbled and chaotic. But, these unusual patterns possess their own logic and have as coherent a design as any sentence composed of words.

If, for example, the exchange I described with my landlady happened while I was dreaming, I might suppose that how I misheard the word was the way I was *supposed* to hear it—that, in fact, although the woman's brother was a contractor, his life was indeed a mess. The unconscious mind never sets up unlikely connections without a reason. Like a body of water bridging the gap between landmasses, it joins disparate pieces of information to create order and sense out of them, and does so in ways we might not have suspected— or yet dreamt—were possible.

WITHIN TIME'S FLOW

As a child I loved going to watch cartoons at the movies. Saturday mornings our parents would deposit us at the door and flee until the show was over and it was time to pick us up. Every cartoon closed with the familiar caption "That's all, folks!" To the noisy audience that meant that—at least for the next hour and a half—another cartoon would soon follow. Although familiar characters appeared in most of the episodes, each one was a distinct entity, not part of a series. "That's all, folks" meant the end of a book, not a chapter.

When it comes to psychic images there is no convenient "That's all, folks"; there is only a "To be continued." Both words and images entertain a relationship to time, changing and accruing new meaning through usage. Yet only in rare instances do words alter their shape to accommodate the new content. Images are less static, altering their form when their content changes. Thus, all definitions of images are working definitions; any meaning we ascribe to an image must necessarily allow room for the inevitable alterations that will take place. Like plans for a house constructed out of modular units, reflecting the built-in idea of future additions, the image needs room in which to grow. Events in the future will add new dimension to it, enhancing its overall significance.

Our present grasp of an image is, therefore, limited. The idea that the image intrinsically bears a connection to the future, that it represents a bridge linking one aspect of our experience in time with another, is vital. When seeking to interpret an image, we always have to leave a door open in the mind, one which might lead into an as yet undefined space.

THE TIME-RELEASE CAPSULE

I have said that there are verbal messages which we heard as children that still have an influence upon our reality, often configuring experiences we would like to change. These messages, uttered unthinkingly by adults, do not necessarily make any sense.

I question whether some of the messages we heard as children ever had a useful purpose. I recall the frustrating experience of one client who never derived satisfaction from any of her accomplishments. No matter how hard she worked, she was plagued by the idea that she was "lazy" in contrast to her older sister, who was "smart" and the achiever.

The message, perhaps relevant when she was a child, was of no logical consequence now. However, like a tape programmed in her brain, the client kept playing it in her mind; it wielded an unconscious and restricting influence upon her actions in the present. Like a time bomb, the full impact of the words didn't hit her when she was five; they were set to go off in consciousness as she grew older. As long as the client believed she was lazy, she was forever held captive within an old frame of reference.

The present was a repeat of the past, holding no window onto a future in which she might ever see herself as an industrious sort of person. Her imagined good-for-nothing-ness acted as a powerful organizing principle, limiting her possibilities and draining her energies.

Images also wield an unconscious influence upon us. But, unlike some of the damaging messages we heard as children, they open a window onto the future. The intent of the image is to free us from the limitations of the past, disclosing our creative potentialities to us. Like a time-release capsule, the meaning of an image reveals itself gradually. Although we can arrive at a partial interpretation of an image in the present, some of its significance remains shrouded in mystery, unveiling itself only in a future we have yet to attain. In that the verbal message represents a self-fulfilling prophecy, it can prohibit the hope for change. In that the image is an ambiguous pictorial event, containing a prophecy of self-fulfillment, it encourages change and therefore hope.

The image is a powerful nonverbal organizing principle that orders experience according to a special relationship to time. Whereas the value of outworn unconscious beliefs restricting our growth depreciates with time, that of the image appreciates, one day becoming part of the very meaning we then attach to the image.

11

$\approx\approx\approx\approx\approx\approx\approx\approx\approx\approx\approx\approx\approx\approx$

Images Make Sense

THINKING ASSOCIATIVELY

When we use words as the medium of exchange, we generally form sentences by combining nouns and verbs. Nouns strung together in a series without any verbs between them don't easily entertain a clearly definable set of relationships. Similarly, when communicating by means of psychic images, there is an essential element that helps them make sense. This essential element is our ability to *think associatively*. Unless we consciously bring our imagination to bear on the subject, we just won't see why certain things appear together or are connected in a dream, painting or poem.

The more we bring our creative imagination to bear on understanding an image, the more creative its impact upon us. Thinking associatively is itself part of a creative process, and it comes naturally if we let our imagination have free rein.

A client recently inherited a large fortune from her mother, who died a very old lady. Although she had known her mother was well-off, the woman had no real inkling as to the extent of her mother's wealth, and it came as a great surprise. In our sessions we no longer discussed how she would make ends meet should she switch jobs but how she would spend her money if she didn't work at all. Thanks to her mother's thrift—which bordered on outright miserliness when she was alive—many of the woman's worries were over, at least from a materialistic point of view. Unfortunately, old as the mother became, she had never enjoyed spending any of the money on herself; she couldn't see the difference between playing with and squandering it. As a result, she'd never freely dipped into her own resources, probably feeling that to let herself go in this regard would be a waste of time and energy. It's a pity, because even if she had done so there would still have been plenty left.

At first the client worried inordinately about wasting the money, spending sleepless nights thinking about how she might "save" it. Then she decided she would learn from her mother's mistake and enjoy the money while she was alive. She invested a large sum in savings and with the remainder bought a loft. She also gave up a steady job to begin her free-lancing career. Thus she utilized the money as an incentive to increase, not to diminish, her risk-taking abilities.

It is important not to be a miser with our creative imagination, but to let it flow. If one idea doesn't work when we analyze an image, another will; with patience, our ability to indulge our fantasy in the interpretive process pays large dividends.

DREAM INTELLIGENCE

The advantage of thinking by association is that we need not reach outward to find the meaning of the image. Instead, we use our own imagination and intelligence to figure out the connection.

A client, a man in his mid-thirties, was considering a career change. He had been working in the food service division of a nursing home for many years and then as a supervisor in its recreational activities department. Now he felt frustrated; he wanted to set out in a new direction but was confused about what his next step should be. Feelings of inferiority had often hampered him in the past from going after the things he really wanted. Among his many outside pursuits he was particularly interested in fitness and health care.

One night he related a brief dream in our workshop. He was back once again in the cafeteria of the high school he'd attended as a teenager. A dog race was going on there. That's all there was to this interesting fragment of the dream, but it cast revealing light on his situation. The juxtaposition of the school cafeteria and the dog race was surprising. Dogs do not logically belong in this setting; they usually run outside and if they race, it is at a track. By a process of association, however, we can see why the images of the dog race and the cafeteria are joined.

Children in a cafeteria compete in line to get food; dogs appear in a lineup to compete against each other in a race. When the race is over, some are winners, some are losers, and the group in the middle, those who slipped by and got through, are also-rans. These are the ones who, like those students who consistently receive a mark of C, distinguish themselves neither in a good nor bad sense but simply manage to survive the competition unscathed.

All of us hunger for the bone of recognition. Rather early in life we make decisions about our competence and how we measure up to others in terms of our performance abilities. These decisions are based in part on realistic and in part on unrealistic assumptions concerning our potential. Often our experience in school reinforces either a positive or negative self-image. We arbitrarily make up our minds about how we measure up in comparison with other people. Grades tend to substantiate the internal choice we've made.

By a process of association we can see the logic of the unconscious mind at work in the dream sequence. The images of the cafeteria and the dog race have the theme of competition in common; the connection is beginning to make sense, and we can surmise why these two disparate things might occur together in the man's mind.

Once again the client found himself, as he did when he was a child, at a formative stage of development. He was getting ready to assess his potential and determine where he stood in the lineup, but this time from a healthier and more well-informed standpoint. As a result of his work in the group he had begun to demonstrate to himself and others the extent of his creative potential. His responses to the drawing and writing exercises had a catalytic effect on his sense of self-worth, helping him to appreciate his unique proclivities. He therefore no longer considered himself a "loser" or an "also-ran" but wanted to be a "winner," striving for excellence in the field of his choice. He might not know precisely what step to take next, but he was definitely readying himself to go for it.

The "it" he was hungry for was no longer the bone of recognition; it had to do with a feeling of satisfaction that he derived from exercising his own unique talents. In reality he had just begun to realize he was a person well suited for outstanding performance in the field of sports management and training. Like a child eager to eat or an animal to run, this fellow wanted to let go and follow his gut instincts. What were they? By association we perceive a link between the institutional setting in which he currently operated and that of the old school cafeteria. Neither "space" provided him with suitable legroom in which to stretch out. He was going to have to break free to become the winner he secretly longed to be.

Via the image, or the juxtaposition of disparate elements in the dream, the unconscious mind had provided the man with useful information. We ascertained its significance by thinking associatively on two counts. First, we figured out how the two images could logically relate to one another *within the context of the dream experience.* Next, we reasoned how the symbolic event, a competitive activity, could connect to *an actual event in the man's life,* a job change.

Once we perceived the reason for the connection between them, we were better able to comprehend the bearing these images might have on the client's current situation. The strange juxtaposition implied he was ready to graduate, not from a school complex but from an inferiority complex. He wanted to get rid of the old impediment to getting ahead, an ancient dread of competing based on a negative self-image. The dream encouraged the man to aspire to new goals without being "hounded" by the fear of failure, confirming that he not only thought better about himself, but that he felt better, too.

The unconscious mind had used its own language to register a change transpiring in the man that was difficult for him to identify. Whereas on one level the dream imagery reflected an actual physical occurrence about to take place in the man's reality—a shift in career—on another level it also reflected a spiritual occurrence taking place in the psyche, that of a change of heart. Thus, the dream recorded a multileveled occurrence which could not be registered in physical terms alone but which sought expression by means of the image itself. By economic means the unconscious mind devised a way to bring what the man consciously knew about himself into alignment with what he subconsciously sensed. A new feeling, not immediately discernible through the physical senses, had emerged. Although intangible, the change of heart was becoming a reality.

By using the imagination, by thinking associatively when dealing with dream imagery, we have begun to interweave the logic of two realities, creating a bridge between them. As we do so, a new order emerges in the mind, one which combines subjective and intuitive awareness with cognitive and rational insight, encouraging a holistic perspective of the events in a person's life.

FEELING ASSOCIATIVELY: INTEGRITY

When trying to arrive at an understanding of the connection between the images in the dream, we were not only thinking associatively but also comparing feelings the man had about himself in the past with those he had in the present. In practice, then, to deal imaginatively with an image implies that we must be able to reason on more than one front at a time and to process the image by thinking and feeling associatively.

Feelings, like colors, are difficult to define, especially quantitatively. We can say, "That's a deep, overpowering or loud red," but not "that's a big or very large red." Or, we can say, "I'm angry or furious" but not "he has an overweight anger" or "a very wide fury."

When dealing with feelings, it is almost impossible to outline their contours in words. It can be frustrating if we don't use our imagination. Poets and artists have long evoked the power of metaphor to describe the quality of a particular feeling. Just as the painter must reach to the palette and keep mixing colors until he gets the perfect salmon-colored hue for a sunset, so the unconscious mind reaches into the realm of images to approximate just the right hue of feeling. In this manner it transmits the qualitative—and even the quantitative—aspect of a particular feeling.

The conscious mind, dealing predominantly with words to define its reality, can hide feelings from itself, opting at convenience to lie about them, suppress or rationalize them away. The unconscious mind, operating in harmony with the realm of instinct and intuition, however, remains in closer touch with feelings, attempting to communicate what it knows to the conscious mind, striving to help a person maintain a balance between his outer and inner experience.

It is a challenge. How can the unconscious mind get the concept of an angry red across to someone, for example, who in conscious reality insists on wearing rose-colored glasses?

It is by means of the image that the unconscious mind penetrates our armor of defense, which is built of words and rationales. Through metaphor and by association, it familiarizes us brilliantly with the reality of feelings we may find it difficult to admit having. The case of a nurse married for many years to an alcoholic illustrates how this process can work. Despite the pain her husband's irrational behavior caused her, she insisted on thinking of the bright side: the children, the occasional good times together, the years of shared history, the great sex. In order to preserve the marriage she suppressed her frustration, denying she was angry and afraid. Resolutely she viewed things through rose-colored glasses, hoping the pain would disappear and the problem would go away.

She thought she could withstand the toll physically and emotionally. She feared that to allow herself to see red, to give vent to the rage, would mean she'd explode. She opted instead to hide the uncomfortable feelings; meanwhile, a crisis was building internally. She suffered from chronic backaches, high blood pressure and bouts of severe depression.

When asleep and dreaming, she naturally fell into closer rapport with the unconscious mind. Her defenses down, one night she literally did see red. She dreamt she couldn't put the proper label on the blood-sample bottles in her charge. The numbers kept falling off and getting lost. And one of the vials changed into a plastic bag that swelled and filled with blood almost to the bursting point. Distressed by the feeling of anxiety the image aroused in her, the client wanted to discuss it.

When interpreting the dream about the school cafeteria and the dog race, I had wanted to show the logical connection between things that look as if they don't belong together; here, however, I wanted to point out how by a process of association a dream image can bring important information to the surface, calling it to the attention of the conscious mind. The client had seen something disturbing and couldn't rest quietly in the old place; unpleasant as the image was, it was causing her to get up and move, *fast*.

What's interesting is that the red she saw in the dream was not specifically the red of anger. Had she, for example, dreamt of having an argument with her husband and seen her face flushed with rage, she might have wiped the memory away. I think the unconscious mind played a trick on her because it knew so well how she operated. This person was very proud to be a nurse and enjoyed her work. The red in the dream image was that of blood, and was associated with feelings of satisfaction she derived from her professional life and the independence it afforded her.

Yet in the dream a crisis—depicted in red—had reached extreme proportions. Even though the woman was attending to her responsibilities, things were out of control, her competence was in question. Try as she might, she couldn't keep the labels on the bottles; the numbers fell off, i.e., the count was off. In reality her blood pressure had been rising, i.e., *her* blood count was off. Whereas she might deny the distress this information had caused her on one level, on another she couldn't. That which she would not acknowledge as a wife she had to admit to herself as a nurse. The bursting bag signified that something wasn't right, had reached the boiling point and was ready to explode.

There was an urgency to the situation, one that reminded the person of feelings she had had in waking reality but had shoved aside. Thinking about the image began to evoke emotions she had been suppressing: being a caretaker was getting on her nerves, fulfilling the role of the dutiful wife was making her mad, viewing things through rose-colored glasses was starting to make her sick. Just as she would sit up and take notice of symptoms in a patient, she had to sit up and take notice of signs of ill health in her own person.

Whereas the client prized her autonomy as a nurse, she despised her dependence as a wife. Through a process of association the image brought a professional sense of duty toward others into alignment with a personal one toward herself. For things to be in their proper order, one part of the self must inform the other what it is doing.

The unconscious mind wills wholeness and fosters integrity despite the superficial vagaries of the conscious mind. By means of the creative image it brought subconscious feelings into a conscious field of awareness, helping the lady have access to resources available to her in one area of her life but not in another. Once she could achieve the same autonomy in her role as a spouse that she enjoyed in her role as a professional, things would ease. It wasn't just numbers that were ticking off in the dream; the whole thing added up to years in a life.

Having reviewed her situation from the perspective the dream provided, the woman faced a choice: she could either continue to deny her own needs and suffer the consequences, or she could risk asserting her independence. She had to stop secretly "nursing" her anger against her husband, and ventilate it instead. Take those rose-colored glasses off, the dream urged, and see things the way they are—not as you wish them to be—so that you can really do something about it. For her blood pressure to level off the client had to begin to level with herself. Greater integrity of choice would result in a better integrity of mental and physical health. Once her self-esteem began to rise, her blood pressure would begin to fall.

THE FLASHLIGHT

By thinking and feeling associatively we perceived a cause-and-effect relationship in the dream sequences that was not evident at first glance. It was a relationship based on affinities, or *likenesses,* rather than on self-evident connections and *exactnesses.* For this reason it is important not to take a dream at its face value. Who knows what it all means? We're always only guessing and learning. Despite the fascinating dimension dreams might add to experience, they're never a substitute for it.

On the other hand, I am acquainted with someone whose life was saved by a flash of insight she had while dreaming. Unable to recover from the effects of the tragic death of a close relative, she was contemplating suicide; an inspiring dream filled her with a sense of spiritual illumination. When she awoke, she felt deeply refreshed. Not only had her mood changed; she had experienced a fundamental change in outlook that altered her life from then on for the better. And I've heard of other people who have had similar experiences. Thus, I believe it is a good idea to respect and trust the integrity of dream logic. Besides, seeking to interpret these creative images excites imaginative capacities that need airing. There is not just a wise man lodged inside us, there is an artist in there, too.

FEELING ASSOCIATIVELY: TIMING

Just as the unconscious mind has its own logic, it possesses its own sense of timing also. The eye of the unconscious mind rotates as if on a 360-degree axis, looking backward toward the past and forward into the future, and sometimes in all directions at once. Thus, in that nonlinear realm we can even occasionally catch glimpses of what might happen up ahead.

By means of the image the unconscious mind can familiarize us with a feeling in advance of an event. The prompting we've received is stored in a memory bank of feeling; it is deposited in a kind of living photograph album in the brain composed of remembered dream and other psychic images. By a process of association, we can make a decisive connection when the time is right for it in physical reality. Being sensitive to a remembered feeling can help us act or make a choice in a situation that might otherwise throw us off guard.

A friend asked for help in interpreting a distressing image that flashed before her mind's eye when she was resting one day, half asleep. She saw herself driving in the direction of her therapist's office when suddenly her car went out of control and she crashed. She wanted to forget the image but decided to think about it and play around with it a little. She had just had her car repaired, so even if the imagery didn't make literal sense she assumed it contained some meaning.

We discussed several possibilities. She was under intense pressure at work. In addition to her usual responsibilities as a business executive, she had started up a free-lance enterprise on the side, which she eventually hoped would become the jumping-off point for a new career. Perhaps she was pushing too hard, had gone into "overdrive" and was in danger of some kind of "breakdown." Or maybe she was afraid of continuing to see the therapist and was losing her "drive" to go there. Although these interpretations made some sense they just didn't click. We decided to let the matter drop, neither of us forgetting the image.

A long time passed. My friend began complaining that the people from whom she was to rent space for her new enterprise were behaving erratically. Their unpredictable attitude was alarming. She was apprehensive about whether they would stick to their agreement. We both remembered the image. What if these associates didn't come through and left her high and dry at the last minute? She'd feel immobilized, her hopes would be dashed, her drive to carry out the new venture damaged.

Then she had an insight. The imaginary crash had happened on her way to the therapist, or, metaphorically speaking, on her way to getting at the truth. The real fact was that if she wanted to increase the likelihood of her success, she'd start looking out for her own interests and wouldn't wait to see what her potential landlords decided to do. She would line up an alternative site, something she'd been too busy to do earlier. The feeling that she didn't have the "time" was preempted by the awareness that she ought to do it while there still was plenty of "time." By a process of association the memory of the feeling the car image had evoked helped her foresee—or forestall—an unwelcome outcome up ahead.

Sometimes the unconscious mind produces a shocking or frightening image. Nevertheless, its purpose is to provide us with gentle guidance. For although we may feel prompted to undertake action, we are not impelled to do it. The conscious self is responsible for deciding on the desired outcome. Whatever the specific meaning of an image, its ultimate purpose is to help bring about a higher degree of alignment between the conscious and the unconscious selves so that a person can act with integrity and make the most intelligent choice.

In the example of the woman married to the alcoholic, two aspects of the personality were brought into conscious alignment by a process of thinking and feeling associatively. In the case of the woman who imagined the car accident, two aspects of time were brought into alignment. Stored in the brain, a bad feeling the woman had about herself in the past coincided at the right moment with a bad feeling she might have about herself in the future if she didn't begin looking out for where she was going.

In this manner the unconscious mind, ever alert to possibilities, assisted the woman in making a choice in her best interest. It did not compel her toward a specific line of action; rather through the power of suggestion it provoked a greater state of self-awareness.

Like a skillful teacher, the unconscious mind sets creative examples before us in the form of puzzling and exciting images, stimulating us to figure out the answers to the questions raised. It takes our intelligence for granted, willing our complete autonomy and integrity. It wants to preserve and further the spiritual order in our lives without issuing a command.

THE INDIRECT MESSAGE

I prefer that when people speak to me about what's on their mind they be direct. But I realize I don't always speak my mind either. Sometimes I mean what I say, sometimes I don't. The clearer a person's intent is, the more direct the message. Things get garbled when his intent is unclear or he deliberately wants to cover it up. The best example is the classic one of the child who spills the glass of milk right in front of his mother and says he didn't do it.

Of course he did. He knows it, his mother knows it. What he's really saying is that he didn't mean to do it and doesn't want to be punished for an unintentional blunder. Why doesn't he say that straight out? A lot of growing up has to do with practicing how to communicate directly.

It is interesting that words can be misused in this manner. Their real function is to help us to be clear about things, to negotiate effectively for what we want.

It is different with images, though, because their function is to help us spell out those things that often defy definition. Whenever we deal with an image, or with the logic of the unconscious mind, we're dealing with an *implied,* not explicitly defined, set of relationships. Unlike the verbal message, which can either be direct or indirect, with an image we are always dealing with an indirect message. However, in this context the term does not refer to an act of duplicity, or to the desire to hide an intent; it refers to an act of suggestion and the desire to reveal a hidden intent.

We can use words to conceal feelings from ourselves. They can be employed to help us separate what we think from what we feel and throw us and those around us into a state of confusion.

Like a skillful chiropractor, the unconscious mind manipulates the self into proper alignment in order to help a person gradually attain a state of balance. It does so with willful intent but by indirect means, using the fine art of implication to apprise the conscious mind of a set of relationships it might otherwise repudiate.

When attempting to make something clear to a student, a teacher often gets a difficult idea across by using a concrete analogy. The unconscious mind is a guide; it, too, employs metaphor to drive the point home. It wants us to better perceive the connections between our thinking and feeling capacities. Just as a wise teacher seeks to promote an intelligent outlook in the student but will not make him adopt it involuntarily, the unconscious mind—through the power of suggestion—seeks to promote but not enforce a healthy relationship between the inner and outer self.

By this means the unconscious mind helps to create order without giving orders. Whereas the indirect verbal message hides the real point, the purpose of the imaginal one is simply to veil it. Like a sculptor who throws a cloth over a piece in process in order to protect it, the unconscious mind covers its work very much as part of a creative process, too.

PART THREE

The Universal Language

12

~~~~~~

Hidden Congruence, Juxtaposition and Superimposition

PASSING BY A FLASH

I'd like to relate an incident that will help you understand why I place so much emphasis on the use of the intuition. I've said that words in general help us to define things exactly and that images describe things more ambiguously. In practice, however, everyone knows that words can be used ambiguously, also.

Poets especially have been known to attribute new meanings to words. I remember taking the Latin exam in graduate school. How I sweated in vain to translate those texts! Armed to the teeth with rules of grammar, exceptions to the rules and lists of obscure conjugations, I just couldn't seem to make sense of anything until I had a flash of insight.

It was despair that drove me to it. The clock was ticking. I had to come up with a bright idea. I kept staring at the words in front of me. I knew how to translate them literally but that wasn't helping much; the meaning of the whole thing was beyond me. Then, I thought, Cicero, you wise guy, you're not thinking literally, you're thinking poetically. Suddenly between the lines of verse I saw the meaning he had implied. And I passed the test.

It is an important principle to grasp. Even when dealing with words, we need to learn to stretch the imagination. During the Latin exam what helped me was the realization that ultimately I could only sense the meaning of the text through feeling. Whatever technical know-how I possessed only represented part of the picture.

WHAT ARE THE ABC'S?

Now we are ready to investigate the nature of psychic imagery from a more technical perspective, examining what the basic components of the language consist of.

Just as there are three basic kinds of sentences, i.e., a declarative statement, a question and a command, there are three basic ways in which images tend to align with one another to form a psychic "sentence." They occur either near one another in consecutive sequence and veiling a hidden congruence, juxtaposed against one another, or they mingle, becoming superimposed over one another.

I am going to use a simplified example to convey these three concepts at their most basic level:

On Plate 5 in the color insert, the two colors, red and yellow, remain separate from one another; they are divided by space. On Plate 6 in the color insert, the two fields of color are in contact, yet their separate natures remain distinct from and in contrast to one another because they do not mingle; their boundaries are clearly defined. We might say that the colors red and yellow, although maintaining a dynamic connection, exist within a mutually exclusive relationship. As long as they do so, they both retain their unique characteristics. Should their boundaries blur, the two elements, red and yellow, combine to create a third new entity, the color orange, pictured on Plate 7 in the color insert.

Using the example of colors, we can see how combining two or more elements creates something new, by a process of transformative blending; this new something, seen as an entity in and of itself, is actually composed of the *now unseen* two original components, the red and the yellow.

To remind you of the separate parts of which the orange is made up, I've left traces of the red and yellow at the

outermost edges of the field of orange. If I had neglected to
do this, you would have to imagine the existence of the red
and yellow within the orange. Should you have encountered
the field of orange on a separate page and out of the sequence
of illustrations in which it is presented, you might forget to
do so. This is an important point, i.e., the need to imagine
the separate layers out of which the whole superimposed
composition is made up, and I shall return to it later.

The three basic kinds of psychic "sentences" we are
speaking of, whether occurring in dreams or artwork, also
have three components: they are either formless fields of
color; they are differentiated abstract shapes or forms; or they
are concrete objects or people (or any combination of these).
In the following illustrations we can perceive how two or
more objects might align with each other according to these
three patterns:

On Plate 8 in the color insert, the two elements, the
separate red and yellow strings, remain distant, divided by
space. However, they do share two characteristics in common, their size and the S-shaped curve. I will return to this
point later when discussing the concept of hidden congruence.

On Plate 9 in the color insert, the two strings are placed
next to each other, now comprising one thick string. Although joined, they could quite easily be pulled apart; their
respective outlines as two thinner pieces of string remain
quite distinct.

On Plate 10 in the color insert, the relationship between
the two strings has become more complex; they now comprise
a third entity, or cord. To perceive just how intricate the
relationship is between the separate parts on Plate 10, we
would have to imagine that the pieces of red and yellow
string consisted of translucent material. Therefore, when
intertwined, the cord they create together would most ac-
curately be depicted as shown in Color Plate 11.

If I were to attempt to disentangle the two pieces of
string, the orange cord they comprise together would be
eliminated. The red and yellow coexist as orange only when
they thoroughly mingle. On the other hand, were I to pull
apart the two strings on Plate 9 in the color insert, nothing
comparable is lost; they have no "orange" to lose. This is an
important distinction to note, because the concepts of juxtaposition and superimposition are closely related, and some-

times the difference between the two is difficult to ascertain. In the next example, we see how this ambiguity can arise:

FIGURE 24
Woman and Tree, Juxtaposed.

FIGURE 25
Woman and Tree, Superimposed.

In both pictures, the figure of a woman and the shape of a tree are joined. In Figure 24 these elements are juxtaposed; in Figure 25 they are superimposed. Whereas the outline of the woman's body and the outline of the shape of the tree are separate and distinct from one another in Figure 24, in Figure 25 they have merged. The one thing has so completely become part of the other that they cannot be distinguished from each other; they share an identity.

Were we to try to separate the two objects, we would be left with perhaps half a woman and a section of tree. The case would be similar were we to unwind the orange cord on Plate 11 in the color insert. We'd be left with two pieces of red and yellow string, i.e., remnants of "orange" *in dissolved form.* In contrast, when the woman and tree in Figure 24 are separated, no such shared and special mutual identity is lost.

There is another example that illustrates the point. Supposing these two objects, a snake and a pair of glasses,

FIGURE 26

were juxtaposed in the following manner:

FIGURE 27

or the ideas were superimposed like this:

FIGURE 28

In Figure 27, once the two objects are juxtaposed, a so-called third entity (like the thicker piece of string on Plate 9 in the color insert) is created, and we have either a serpentine scholar or scholarly serpent on our hands. Yet once the objects are separated, we have only lost the concept "scholarly" and still have a separate and distinct snake and a pair of glasses.

In Figure 28, however, were we to unwind the snake, we'd lose the concept "eyeglasses," because neither the snake nor the glasses could attain its separate identity any longer without the existence of the other. They depend for their existence on the continuing superimposition.

The autonomy of the field of orange on Plate 7 in the color insert is dependent upon the joining of the colors red and yellow. It is the continued merging of the separate elements within their superimposition that lends the thing its special identity, whereas within a juxtaposition, it is the ongoing autonomy of the individual parts that defines the unique characteristics.

Within each of these imagistic statements there is a coexisting of elements; in juxtaposition there is a linkage between them; in superimposition there is a fusion.

Here is another example illustrating the distinction among the three different ways of ordering elements:

FIGURE 29

| *Consecutive Sequence* | *Juxtaposition* | *Superimposition* |
| Attraction, | Cohesion, | Fusion |

The symbols depict the differing quality of relationship that exists among separate parts of the three kinds of imagistic statements. Recognizing these differences accustoms us to the creative terrain. Once you can differentiate among the three kinds of statements, you realize that no image, however plain or primitive, is as simple as it might appear. And no image, no matter how intricate, is too complex to be broken down into the simpler components of which it is composed.

In distinguishing among the three main ways in which images tend to arrange themselves, we've begun to acquaint ourselves with the creative language of imagery.

It is important to perceive the differences among the three types of imagistic statements, but it is equally important to see what they share in common. In each, there is a dynamic interaction about to take place or already taking place among the various components of the statement. This interaction reflects an invisible yet even more powerful interaction happening beyond them, because when observing a psychic image, we are seeing reflected in its parts the dynamic interaction of *parts of the psyche itself*. Parts of the self, of the personality as we know it, are coming together, cohering, fusing; what we are actually seeing in imagistic form is an integrative process at work. Images not only reflect this process, they are an intrinsic, vital extension of it.

HIDDEN CONGRUENCE: AN EXAMPLE

Images arranged in consecutive sequence sometimes do not appear to entertain a direct relationship to one another. Hidden congruence refers to the connection that exists between them not apparent at first glance. Identifying the hidden congruence helps bring the meaning of the statement into clearer focus. Here is a simple example:

FIGURE 30
Original drawing by author, rendered here by illustrator.

Looking closely at the drawing, we can identify a recurring shape:

FIGURE 31

The cloud, the sail, the girl's hair, the boat, the fish and the wave all share a common element—the belly-shaped curve. The premise is that whether the artist consciously intended to do so or not, everything in the drawing has a meaningful function within the piece and does not appear there randomly. The things do not seem to be directly connected—other than being depicted as part of the same landscape. Yet, as soon as we note the fact that they share a common aspect, the oval shape, their relationship acquires added significance. We can assume—by implication—that they are more closely related to each other than they would be if they did not share this common element, that they come together therefore *for a reason* at this particular moment in time.

It's the hidden congruence among them that brings the reason to light. Focusing on the curving shape helps us become more aware of forward, harmonious movement of all the elements in the piece; everything is acting in rhythmic concert. The fish leaps *out* of the water, the woman sails the wide, *open* sea in an *open* boat. Despite the clouds, the sky is *clear*. The emphasis, then, is on openness, *an opening,* on being in the clear, free of impediment. The hidden congruence among the images in this simple beginner's piece suggests a new pattern emerging in the psyche. It's a feeling of opening up that is liberating, exciting; it represents a desire to move forward despite or with the resistance. For example, the fish must resist the water to jump, the girl must steer with the wind—and sometimes against it—to progress.

But just at the point at which we become sensitive to the elements that share characteristics, we notice another significant occurrence. It becomes evident precisely to the degree that we are cognizant of the hidden congruence; there is an element that stands out in contrast to the others. We perceive the sharp rectilinear angle of the tiller in the girl's hand, comparing it to the repetitive and more curving shapes that surround it. In comparison to them, the tiller is the incongruous, or disparate, element in the drawing. The disparate element often provides an important clue to deciphering the message that the images as a whole contain, for it is out of the interplay among the congruous and incongruous elements that we begin to discern meaning.

The girl controls the movement of the boat by guiding the tiller. Thus, the drawing suggests that the forward movement within the psyche is contingent on conscious cooperation; it is not involuntary.

Viewed from the perspective of what the imagery might be saying about the opening of a client's creative drive— rather than from an aesthetic critique—the message indicates that the person is gaining rapport with the unconscious mind and is moving in sync with it. This is the first step in what portends to be a spontaneous and liberating experience, representing at the same time a stage of growth that is dependent for its further development on the cooperation of the conscious personality. Simple in both outline and content, the drawing proclaims significant movement in the direction of greater self-expression. I'd expect the client's next piece to reflect further positive change both artistically and psychologically.

Hidden congruence is a key to recognizing the relationship among objects arranged in consecutive sequence in dreams as well as in artwork. The "objects" can consist of a series of repeated similar shapes, or colors or other qualities that several unrelated objects might share in common. For example, someone might dream of a closed room in which a closed chest is standing, against which someone leans, arms folded across the chest, fingers clutching a lock. Clearly, the congruence among these elements is the idea of being closed or locked in.

Similarly, the hidden congruence can consist of a common missing element. Someone might dream of standing in a room, unable to close the door because the knob is missing, then trying unsuccessfully to button a shirt off of which the buttons have fallen, desperately reaching for another in the dresser drawer, only finding to his dismay that all the handles are missing, etc. In this instance the missing element, the frustrating experience of literally being unable to get "a handle" on things, depicts a person's inability to "keep things together," his fear that everything is "falling apart."

If in the first example the dreamer should suddenly spy a key lying on the floor, the disparate element, he might suppose he was approaching a solution to his dilemma at least on an unconscious level of awareness. And, if in the second case the person was relieved to unexpectedly see a carpenter standing in the corner of the space, he might likewise suppose a solution was at hand, again appearing on an unconscious level of awareness first.

The concept of hidden congruence, that is, the recurring component that connects several apparently disconnected elements, is but one tool to help you better understand the language of imagery. Like any grammatical element in a sentence, it only represents part of the whole message. Together with an understanding of the principles of juxtaposition and superimposition, hidden congruence builds a facility for interpreting images in a way that enhances their creative impact on our thinking.

JUXTAPOSITION: AN EXAMPLE

To the degree that we become aware of the shared element among several components of an imagistic statement, we also become aware of the disparate element.

Sometimes it is a sudden perception of the disparate element that helps us see the hidden congruence; sometimes it is our sensitivity to the hidden congruence that comes first, aiding us then to pinpoint the disparate element. Whichever comes first, it is out of the interplay among the components that the message begins to emerge.

Yet, the various elements of any imagistic statement are not always as simple as the drawing of the girl in the boat would indicate. Often one or more elements are compound in composition. For example, in English we have various compound nouns, that is, words made up of two or more nouns to form another word, like "guesswork" or "state-house." Likewise, in an imagistic statement any one element can be made up of several components. It is the combining of incongruous elements—the wedding of two or more disparate things to make a surprising connection—that I refer to when using the term "juxtaposition." The following picture illustrates this idea:

FIGURE 32

Here the artist creates interesting juxtapositions by making a collage out of a series of images.

Right where we'd expect to see the face or workings of a timepiece, we see a halved and open piece of ripe fruit instead. Two incongruous elements are wedded, and the unexpected connection brings insight. Perhaps, among other things, the image says the time is "ripe" for some special kind of action, or the outlook is brighter than apparent. Even if the time is difficult, it's not "the pits."

There is also a disparate element contained in the piece. The collage is composed of several concrete objects—e.g., the chair, watch, harp, piece of fruit (the hidden congruence)—and of the numeral 5 (the disparate element). It stands out in contrast to the other elements, although along with them it does share the shape of the curve. Thus, this particular collage shows both hidden congruence and juxtaposition at work.

Within the creative context of any kind of psychic imagery, the term "juxtaposition" refers to the joining together of two or more otherwise quite unrelated or incongruous elements to make another strange or surprising "thing," like this heart attached to an electric cord:

FIGURE 33
In this piece the artist spontaneously paints a haunting juxtaposition.

Juxtaposition also refers to the creation of an unexpected, provocative connection like this:

FIGURE 34

The same artist who made Fig. 32 creates yet another startling combination of images.

To acquaint a client with this principle, I sometimes ask him to do a simple exercise—to gather up a few objects that he might find lying around the house and to place them together in such a way that an unexpected or humorous connection is made among them. It's a fascinating task, and I suggest you practice it just for fun.

Once a woman brought in two pieces of burned toast joined together by a screw. Tightly sandwiched between the bread was a blue ribbon that said FIRST PRIZE. We speculated about the meaning of the image, deciding that although this person felt she deserved a prize for being a first-class nurturer of other people, she ended up feeling "screwed" when it came to thinking of creative ways in which she might better look out for her own interests. She was "burned out" and hoping to learn how to nourish herself by participating in the group experience.

Assembling unrelated objects in this manner or spontaneously pasting together images in a collage helps a person break through the barriers of the conscious mind and reach toward the dimension of the unconscious mind.

Experienced artists also make interesting discoveries when they experiment with their technique from this perspective, using it as a kind of jumping-off point. The aim is to deliberately gain more access to one's image-making process. Utilizing such materials frees a person from having to think about the technical aspects of drawing, and from being self-conscious about his abilities or from being afraid of how to fill a blank page. It exercises little-used muscles of the imagination, fostering a creative condition in the mind. The spontaneous connections provoke psychological insight and stimulate creative risk-taking abilities.

Juxtaposition is a powerful tool for helping a person develop his creative abilities while also furthering self-awareness. It sensitizes him to the workings of the unconscious mind. To combine images in fascinating ways and then to ask what the connections might mean encourages a person to expand his faculty for thinking associatively and intuitively. He gradually becomes accustomed to looking beyond the outer appearance of the image; like a carpenter learning how to read a blueprint, he tunes into the basic structure of the thing, striving to envision the creative whole while implementing the "plan" step by step.

13

~~~~~~

Superimposition

THE BRAID

The principle of superimposition is one of the most fascinating ways in which images tend to align.

Once joined by means of superimposition, the boundaries of the images merge and do not remain mutually exclusive. Fused in this manner, the individual components of the image remain inseparable. Superimposition represents a kind of psychic laminating process.

Thus, this is the most complex of the three principles: it reflects as much a philosophical concept as a technical idea. As we proceed, you will begin to perceive how the principle tends to operate on more than one level of meaning at once.

There are two kinds of superimposition: one is *explicit,* the other is *implicit.*

The word "explicit" in this context refers to the concrete representation of an image rather than to an abstract or suggested one. For example, here is a picture of a snake rendered in *explicit form:*

FIGURE 35

And here is the same image rendered in *implicit form:*

FIGURE 36

In its implied form, that is, when it is depicted in a suggested or abstract manner, the image of the snake is, of course, less literal. By association the wavy line could represent any of several things, e.g., it could symbolize a flame, moving water, hair, a current of energy, etc. And, occurring in a dream or work of art, it might stand for any or all of these things, depending on the context.

In implicit form, the significance of the snake image itself is less apparent, for through the power of implication a series of relationships is suggested, of which the snake is but a part.

For now, it is important to see that it its implied form, metaphorical connections are being suggested by the image rather than being explicitly defined. In written form, the difference might look like this: the poet states *directly*, "That woman looks like a rose." Or, he suggests *indirectly* that the woman is like a flower: "Lying before me, open, delicate, sweet, I breathe in her essence." Again, in its suggested or *implied* form, the flower image (like that of the wavy line) might represent several other things, such as a piece of fruit, the vagina, etc.

In its implied form, the image is more abstract; its shape becomes more ambiguous, less easily defined. Imagine a salt and pepper shaker. Sprinkled on a piece of waxed paper, the grains of salt and pepper are easy to distinguish from one another. Once they are added to a pot of stew, however, they are less so; as a result of the cooking process, the salt itself dissolves. To the extent that the condiments add flavor to the stew, their shape becomes less discernible, perceived no longer by one's sense of vision but predominantly by that of taste.

Similarly, with implicit superimposition the invisible elements inform the image with their presence, lending it unique character. But what they actually consist of must be intuited.

When speaking of superimposition we are actually describing a kind of alchemical process, akin to what happens when ingredients are cooked and change from one form to another before our eyes. However, in this instance the transformation is not just a physical one, it is spiritual.

Overall then, superimposition in terms of psychic imagery represents the creative means by which something is *changed from one form into another*. The change can be recorded in explicit terms, as in the phrase "I feel like a bird spreading its wings," or implicitly, as in the phrase "I feel ready to take off."

These pictures further illustrate the point:

FIGURE 37
Hair without a braid

FIGURE 38
Braided hair

FIGURE 39
Unbraided hair

Figure 37 depicts a head of hair in its natural, as yet untransformed state. In Figure 38, the hair has been combed into a braid. The head of hair and the idea of "braid" have combined; it's an example of explicit superimposition. In Figure 39, the hair, released from the braid, has been transformed as a result of the superimposition; it's an implicit image of hair that has been braided.

Let's imagine that the idea of braid is to the head as the salt and pepper was to the stew. In Figure 37, we have plain hair as we once had a simple stew without any salt and pepper in it. In Figure 38, we clearly have two things combined, just as we could clearly see salt and pepper granules sprinkled on the surface of the stew before they dissolved. In Figure 39, however, the hair has the residue or aftertaste of braid, just as the stew had a different flavor once the salt and pepper had been blended in. The idea of braid, like the presence of the salt and pepper, is more difficult to discern once it *has changed and been changed* by the thing it was added to.

If I were to encounter the image of the unbraided hair in either a dream or in artwork, I might suppose the wavy lines implied something serpentine as well as braid-like. Or, I might suppose they implied the presence of water and snakes, and not that of braid.

Just an inventive chef must discern the right balance of flavors when experimenting with a recipe, likewise, when interpreting images, a sense of balance, timing and "taste" are required. We need to scrutinize the whole picture, thinking and feeling associatively about the "ingredients" until we literally start "cooking" with ideas about it.

Superimposition, especially in implied form, poses a high challenge to the imagination. In reasoning about the layers of meaning of an image, we must exercise flexibility and discrimination. If we wander too far afield in our speculations, our interpretation can become farfetched. On the other hand, if we never dare to take a leap of the imagination, we will not catch sight of marvelous implications.

THE SEED

Keeping in mind the meaning to which a single image or group of images can aspire as a result of the process of superimposition, let us examine the seascape from a fresh perspective:

FIGURE 40

I've explained that the tiller stands out as a disparate element because of its angularity. It could represent the person's ability to think with the left side of the brain, to reason cognitively in a "linear" fashion. The image reminds the viewer that the girl needs to exert a conscious effort to keep sailing in the right direction. Like the fish leaping from the water and the boat riding with the wind, she must move *against and with the resistance to progress forward*. She realizes resistance is *a natural force*.

In this regard the drawing itself represents the client's first creative step in the right direction. It is taking place in the presence of some natural resistance to it, e.g., the fear of performing, the fear of change, the fear of expressing the child side.

Let us review the imagery to see if there are any superimpositions that can shed further light on the subject. Indeed, the shape of the girl's hair is similar to that of a seed; it is reiterated in the shape of the fish's body and in the oval outline that describes the boat. The idea of a seed suggests that the drawing represents a beginning, a creative sprouting. The image of a seed superimposed over that of the boat suggests that this beginning has momentum and force, is a propelling of energy outward and forward. Thus, the seed/boat image simultaneously prognosticates both growth *and* a change of position. To the extent that the imagery portends all this, the meaning of the fish acquires added significance. To be in touch with her subconscious creative resources, to see a "seed" of talent opening before her in this way, represents quite a "catch" to this budding artist.

There is another possible meaning that could be attributed to the image of the hair. It is flying free, and the shape is reminiscent of the tip of a paintbrush as well as the outline of a bird. Although of plain and childlike design, the drawing reflects the release of a natural inclination to paint. Letting go of her creative inhibitions is having a liberating effect on the woman and changing her self-image. Perhaps a new identity as an artistic person is taking shape. Even if it is at its nascent or "seed" stage, a metamorphosis of far-reaching consequences in both inner and outer terms is taking place. But, the woman will need a bird's-eye view of the situation to get past the rough spots (despite the balmy day, there are clouds), for without a creative vision of what she can hope to achieve, she might feel discouraged by her first attempts, decide to turn around and not continue the exciting trip.

If that's the case, then taken as a whole, the superimposition would imply this innocent piece represents a decisive and sensitive turning point. To be open means to be exposed and vulnerable as well as to be growing and developing. This little drawing represents a creative seed at the sprouting stage, one that will need care and protection. If nurtured, there will be a spontaneous flow to events, a creative advancement in both personal and artistic terms that follows its own natural course.

By means of superimposition, we see how the imagery can transmit a multifaceted message more complex in design than would appear on the surface. It provides a review of the situation on several levels of meaning while at the same time giving a forecast of its possible outcome.

THE BUTTERFLY

In searching for and analyzing the implied superimpositions, it's as if a person were a juggler who has to keep all the possibilities circulating in his mind without letting any drop. Eventually, a rhythm is established, a pattern to the pursuit emerges. It's easier to make assumptions when the super-imposition is explicit. In the picture of the braided hair or of the woman and the tree (Figure 25), we can see the separate layers that are laminated together. When the superimpositions are implicit, we need to use the imagination. The physical shape of the image that we can see becomes a jumping-off point for intuiting the presence of other layers invisibly melded with it.

To assess the accuracy of our assumption about the meaning of the imagery and the presence of the implied superimpositions in the piece just discussed, we'd have to wait and see how the client's work evolved. Like a cook who uses experimentation to modify the recipe he's testing, we'd then make the necessary adjustments in our interpretation.

In the following example, a series of three drawings derived from a case study of an artist, we can observe an image evolve and see such a superimposition taking shape. We have a context against which to test the accuracy of our assumption about this invisible layering process.

In the first picture we encounter the images of a woman and several butterflies in juxtaposition:

FIGURE 41
This exciting piece, drawn in charcoal, is filled with symbols.

The client brought this drawing to group shortly after beginning to work with me. She was an artist in her late thirties who had felt blocked for a long and frustrating period of time in which she'd been unable to produce anything to her satisfaction. She was quite pleased with this piece, and on closer inspection we can see why. It depicts a dramatic turn of events; the butterflies appear to be leaving her stomach—maybe she's overcoming her stage fright. The group support is helping to alleviate her performance anxiety. She's not so afraid to show who she is and what she can do. Perhaps she's also feeling closer to her instincts, is not so hesitant to express her "gut" feelings when she paints.

On the other hand, we might well suppose the opposite: the butterflies are entering the woman's stomach. Neither interpretation is exclusive of the other. In this case, the image might indicate the person was getting in touch with new, creative feelings about herself and her potential to be an artist, feelings that are transformative and liberating. To combine both suppositions: to the degree that the artist is able to let go of her fear and release her inhibitions, she makes room for an exciting sensation of positive change to enter.

In the next piece, produced approximately at the same time, a figure flies amidst the clouds:

FIGURE 42

The second drawing of a mysterious winged figure is also rendered in black and white.

Perhaps it's the same woman; if that's the case, her breast is hidden by her arm. Whatever her identity, there seem to be wings sprouting. Is it an angel? A goddess? All of these?

There might be an implied superimposition; we could

suppose the presence of a butterfly. This assumption casts important light upon the significance of the piece in terms of the woman's development both personally and artistically. Up to this point in her life—despite having graduated from art school—she felt stymied because she'd experienced difficulty projecting an image of herself as a professional artist. The block was depressing, representing not only an obstacle to her creative self-expression but also affecting her overall sense of well-being.

Communicating about the dilemma to others in group had eased her anxiety. The encouragement she was receiving to more freely express her child side was having a positive effect; her self-esteem was rising. The painting reflects the change, indicating her sense of identity is undergoing a transformation. It is sprouting wings. The feeling of liberation, of greater mobility expressed by this image and represented in the first drawing in the shape of the butterflies, is being carried over into this piece.

The idea of metamorphosis is becoming more fully incorporated into the woman's consciousness. Her self-image is changing; she has begun to acknowledge and respect her identity as an artist, and the awareness is having a powerful, healing influence on her. For one thing, it's helping to lift her depression. Maybe she's literally and figuratively "getting over" the block in this drawing.

Was our assumption about the invisible presence of the butterfly image in Figure 42 correct? Within the context of the progression of the three drawings, we can ascertain that it was.

In Figure 43 we can see the figures of a woman and butterfly superimposed explicitly. There's been a remarkable change in the imagery. It is vibrant, colorful, more daring

FIGURE 43

In contrast to the preceding pieces, this one is painted in pastel. The colors are bright and scintillating.

and expressive. A metamorphosis has transpired, and a beautiful figure—half woman, half butterfly—has emerged as if from a cocoon. We can more clearly perceive the message brought about by the fusing of the two images. A new sense of herself has been released, a feeling that through the power of her art, the woman has the ability *to change herself.* The internal emphasis is no longer on how others view the work but on what she herself sees and appreciates in it. She has been captivated by the magic of her own imagery and is no longer as inhibited by the critical voices inside her head that held her back in the past. Her art has become a desirous object; it has magnetic force and a transformative effect. She is attracted to it and attractive because of it.

The painting marked a turning point. From then on, this client identified herself as a professional artist; she worked much more energetically and with a higher degree of concentration and purpose. Above all, she began to associate painting with having fun. She had unlocked the doors to her creative imagination and experienced making art as a journey of discovery to delight in and enjoy.

THE INVISIBLE WAVE

Within the context of the series of three drawings, the implicit superimposition of the butterfly in Figure 42 was easier to discern than it might have been out of context. We see the hunch was correct because of the direction in which we perceived the imagery evolving in Figure 43. Often we don't have such immediate access to an overview. We have to rely on an intuitive feel for the meaning of the image and the direction in which it's headed.

Images have psychic force. They are composed of waves of energy manifested as form in time and space. Getting a sense of their invisible layers is equivalent to getting a feel for riding a wave; in this instance it's a wave of creative energy that's taking us where we want to go. We gain creative momentum by tuning in to the direction and intent of an image just as surely as we gain physical momentum by riding with the crest of the wave. With regard to the case just discussed, learning to appreciate the presence of superimpositions in her imagery helped the artist draw closer to her material and feel empowered by it. She thereby overcame a long-standing block and gained greater momentum for furthering her career.

THE CHANGING HOUSE

The principle of superimposition, whether implicit or explicit in form, is the means by which psychic imagery condenses, codifies and integrates information pertaining to many levels of the personality. The transformation that an image undergoes reflects a process of inner psychological transformation as well. According to this view, *form follows function*.

When the content of an image changes, then the form that housed it does, too. But the content carries a memory of the form it once held. Therefore, the new form that the content continually aspires to and assumes is a composite shape bearing the stamp of the forms that preceded it. The memory of a form and the experience it housed are always retained in consciousness.

14

Dreams and
Superimposition

THE EDIBLE PLAYING CARDS

I'd like to apply the principle of superimposition to a deepening of our understanding about the nature of dream imagery. All psychic images, whether occurring in artwork or dreams, are shaped by and reflect the selfsame aesthetic and psychological ordering principles

As we increase our ability to understand the complex nature of imagery, we will incline to be fascinated by our dream life. The greater access we have to it, the greater the momentum that builds in the creative wave we are riding. Understanding how superimposition works in relation to dreams is an invaluable aid in helping us to perceive the interconnection between *all* our images, exciting us to extend the boundaries of our imagination so that we see how the images we create, both on the inside and outside, spring from and are nurtured by the same source. It is a principle that helps us appreciate the all-inclusive nature of the image-making process.

The ideas of hidden congruence and juxtaposition can be seen manifested in dream images. Superimposition can be also. I'd like to demonstrate how these principles might operate in purely visual terms within the context of a dream.

A client, a divorced artist in her early fifties, found herself at the end of a long dream sequence at a table eating dinner with members of her family. On the table was a salad consisting of old lettuce leaves and a deck of playing cards. If the image occurred in a hidden congruence, it might look like this:

According to the client's rendition, however, it occurred in juxtaposition and actually looked like this:

If the two elements were to be superimposed explicitly,
the image might appear like this:

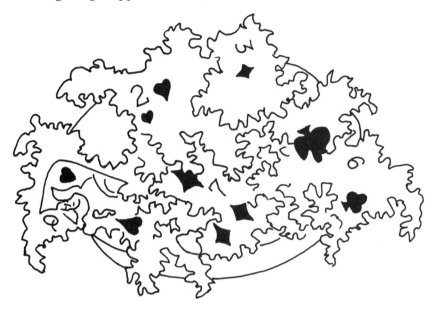

Were the salad bowl to disappear, the image would look
like this and the idea of "salad" would be implied:

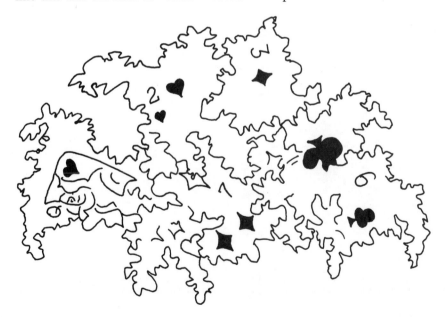

Familiarity with the concepts of hidden congruence, juxtaposition and superimposition helps us navigate and orient ourselves within the realm of images in visual terms. In that regard the ideas pertain to a structuring principle at work on this level. At the same time, they pertain to one operating on a psychological plane as well.

Whether encountered within the dimension of dreams or within the realm of art, all images are composed of highly flexible components. However, dream images, whose dimensions are psychic both in terms of content and outline, are pliable; artistic images rendered into permanent physical form are not. They are necessarily less mobile and ephemeral.

Freed from the normal restrictions that waking reality imposes, we more readily perceive the essential plasticity of images when dreaming. Things move about and change their shape even as we begin to focus on them. Everything within an image hangs momentarily together, as if the parts were all movable, revolving around an invisible axis.

The manner in which the particular components of an image are attached to each other, their temporary constellation (as illustrated in the various arrangements of the lettuce leaves and playing cards above), is secondary in importance to the fact that *they are joined* together for a time and that we remember making the connection upon awaking.

If we can fathom the invisible axis around which the parts are revolving psychologically, that is, determine what the *associative link* between them consists of, the reason for their coming together becomes apparent. We realize then that however the components of a particular image might be placed momentarily, that arrangement constitutes but differing visual variations on a theme, just as in a declarative German sentence one can vary the word order without changing the gist of the message. Establishing the associative link is the key that leads to understanding and appreciating the nature of the entire imagistic composition.

I'd like to put this idea into practice, since in and of itself it's a difficult one to grasp. The client just cited dreamt of the salad made of lettuce leaves and playing cards on a table at which she dined with her family. We might first conjecture within the context of the *dream* that the juxtaposed images generally reflected her growing awareness of the games her family played around the issue of nurturing. Thinking associatively, we might further surmise that this person had often felt herself to be a loser or victim in such games in the past. In fact, within her immediate family the burden of caring for an aged, cantankerous and widowed mother fell mostly on her. And, when she was married the responsibility for caring for the children had also fallen mainly on her shoulders, not those of her inveterately alcoholic and unsympathetic husband.

The associative link that exists between her current feeling of being the victim and the old familiar one of being deprived is the invisible axis around which the components of the dream image revolve. This person is *fed up* with her victim role and all the lines she's heard and recited to herself in relation to it. Thus, the salad is composed of old, unappealing leaves and tasteless paper. She doesn't want to eat it. A salad is made of raw food; perhaps she feels she's been dealt a bad hand, gotten *a raw deal* in life. To the extent she gains a conscious understanding of her own voluntary participation in the game, and makes a new choice based on the insight she's *won,* the raw deal becomes food for thought.

The numbers on the playing cards are exposed; her number—and those of the people who've been playing the game with her—is up. She's getting ready to turn over a new *leaf,* dis-*card* the old way of thinking and acting that have become unappetizing and no longer tempt her.

The same associative link sensitizes us to an implicit superimposition, one we might not have otherwise perceived. While working with this client, I had acquainted her with the theories of Transactional Analysis and the concept of the "script," a term referring to habitual patterns of emotional response we acquired as children, that have an unconscious influence upon our behavior when we become adults. It's the life drama or game we find ourselves embroiled in over and over again: things appear to happen to us that seem beyond our control, or whatever control we do exert is useless and has little or no influence on the situation.

This woman was tired of a script that dictated she would always have to take care of others, never be appreciated for it and be lonely to boot. Above all, she was drained and never had enough time for doing what she enjoyed most—her artwork.

I see the idea of a script superimposed over the image of a card, that is, of a piece of paper on which the elements of a tragic drama/game are revealed, like cues, for all to see. The elements of the script, or the playing cards, are moving into the woman's conscious awareness. The drama might continue as far as the other participants are concerned, but for her, the one whose eyes are opening, it's only a temporary state of affairs holding little threat to her well-being. Everyone's now holding an open hand. The consequences of such a game are not as deadly; there are no covert moves possible. Everything's aboveboard, the cards are on the table. The client can therefore avoid a surprising setback, immobilizing entanglement or unexpected entrapment in a situation that has become distasteful to her.

THE COMPOSITE COMPOSITION

In analyzing the content of the woman's dream, we see that the image is actually a composite shape in terms of its form, and it also embodies a composite experience in terms of the content it holds. Superimposition in the broadest sense refers to this idea. It stands on the one hand for a visual concept—i.e., it shows how two or more actual things can be superimposed to create an image—and on the other for the process whereby two or more intangible, invisible things can be superimposed and included as part of the image we perceive.

These two or more invisible "things" can consist of suggested and similar images, such as the idea of a paper script superimposed over the image of paper playing cards. Or, they can consist of two or more experiences that are similar and can be linked to the image associatively, as they were when we connected the distasteful feeling the client had about herself as a loser in the past, the unappetizing one she had about herself as a victim in the present and her response to the bowl of wilted leaves and bitter cards.

Sometimes, as in the dream just discussed, we can fairly easily establish an associative link between the events in the dream and events in the person's life. Making this connection immediately helps to make sense of the imagery. Then, as a result of the association we begin to perceive the intangible presence of superimposed images that bring the point closer to home. In the case of the script and the playing cards, it was not too difficult to observe this process at work. But not every dream yields so readily to imaginative investigation. We can establish the associative link and yet something within the dream remains elusive. It often takes a leap of fantasy, a positively intuitive hunch to perceive the superimposed form within the image. It is only our imagination—and the heart— that can bridge the gap between the seen and unseen elements of the composition, bringing their hidden presence and relationships to light.

AN UNLIKELY COMBINATION

It is essential to remember that the techniques for interpretation that I am describing are not just intellectual in nature but are also designed to encourage and foster the expression of the intuition. To illustrate how important it is to cultivate an imaginative attitude when dealing with any imagistic experience, I'd like to analyze another dream.

A female client, a medical doctor in her mid-thirties who had grown up and studied medicine abroad, dreamt of returning to the university where she'd acquired her degree. It was night and she found herself running from one room to another, up and down corridors. She was in an agitated state of mind and felt as if she were looking for something, she wasn't sure what, nor did she even know why she was there. Suddenly she arrived at the main entrance gate. To her dismay, she discovered it was locked and she couldn't get out. Breathless and disheartened, she felt frustrated, stuck.

When relating the dream in group, the woman recalled her experience in medical school. She remembered how little free time she had had to enjoy outside activities. Although she had performed well then and subsequently enjoyed her career, she now found herself in the same claustrophobic predicament.

She ran a holistic health clinic in a large city; this commitment was consuming, leaving her little time to enjoy leisure pursuits. We could see the connection that existed between the old feeling of being compelled to perform as a student and the current feeling of being compelled to work as a professional. Yet, the feeling of frantic movement, of running about without getting anywhere, of almost *being lost,* aroused another emotion in the woman, one she couldn't readily pinpoint. All at once, with the aid of intuitive insight, we perceived the presence of an invisible superimposition.

There is a feeling of congested activity in the dream. The direction in which the woman finds herself moving seems dictated less by reason than by the structural flow of the building itself. Her movements seem involuntary. The endless corridors, the shift from room to room, her breathless urge to get out, the sense of mounting pressure that finds no outlet for release—all this suggests blood coursing through the veins, even the heart itself, ventricles engorged, pushing and pumping under pressure. The locked gate at the end of the dream from which the woman cannot emerge could symbolize a closed heart, or her inability to give voice to an important emotional urge or desire.

The connection between a school building composed of inorganic material and a heart made up of muscle and blood seems unlikely, yet it isn't an impossibility. We might conjecture the emotional pressure the woman is under has been *building* a long time and potentially could have a deleterious effect on her physical well-being.

What is it that the woman seeks? What is it she wants to let out? They are one and the same thing, and the associative connection between the image of the heart and the university complex brings it to light. The woman wants to release something she has always carried within her but paradoxically also once left behind; it is her lost childhood, the freedom to express her creative, playful side that she prematurely gave up to pursue and meet the demands of an arduous career.

She has spent so long proving to herself and the world that she can act like a grown-up that she has almost forgotten what it's like to be a child. The pressure and pain she feels is caused by the child locked inside, screaming and pushing to get out.

At this point in the discussion, an interesting fact we were unacquainted with before came to light. The woman admitted she felt "heartsick" about the situation, that try as she might she could not make room for pursuing creative activities. Despite her outward success she longed to cultivate some of her untapped inner resources, but she needed advice about how to do so. As she thought about this she mentioned that her interest in holistic medicine had grown out of a physical condition she'd suffered from as a young intern—high blood pressure. Medication and proper nutrition had done much to improve the condition. But the dream experience indicated that the source of the difficulty might also be psychosomatic. To try to lower her blood pressure, she needed to establish a balanced and healthy relationship to the child inside.

We think of the heart as the seat of emotional pleasure and pain. The woman perceived how much pain it caused her to repress her creativity and sensed her need to release it. Just as she consciously and conscientiously nurtured a loving attitude toward her husband and her patients, she decided to cultivate a consistently loving attitude toward her child side.

As she began making space in her life for her artwork and creative play, another kind of space opened in her heart, one she thought there would never be enough room for. She decided to become pregnant, something she had long secretly wanted to do. She now viewed finding the time in which she could enjoy the rewards of motherhood, along with those of being a wife and a career person, as a challenge—not an obstacle—to expressing her creative imagination.

Her outlook became brighter and more lighthearted. Patients and clients attending her seminars on health care commented on her relaxed and playful manner. As her values shifted, even her appearance changed; she began to look and act like a person who was getting more pleasure out of life.

We can now perceive the reason for the unusual superimposition of images. A university is an important place of learning and transition, a decisive turning point in the life of a person preparing for adulthood. The heart is the center where we learn about our feelings. Often it is an important emotional experience that becomes a turning point in our lives, a key in helping us to see what we value the most. This woman's insight into the superimposition in her dream— her appreciation of the significance of a most unlikely combination—unlocked a critical emotional experience for her, one she'd never had, that of learning to value the child in her as much as the responsible adult. As such, it represented another decisive moment of transition leading her toward maturity and a fulfilled old age.

THE EYE OF THE HEART

Superimposition is a term referring to a rather complex process. On the one hand, it reflects a way in which images are visually arranged. On the other, it refers to the special means by which the psyche shapes, orders, organizes and integrates conscious with unconscious experience. It is the record keeper of the psyche, writing the history of a person's life in images, not words. It connects a series of experiences, layering them together through the power of association. To the extent that we come to appreciate the integrative process that superimposition represents, we more fully understand how watching our images grow and change is a special way of looking at ourselves growing and changing. Reading a life printed in psychic pictures is like looking into a kaleidoscope; the patterns are vibrant, changing, infinite. Yet, because the kaleidoscope possesses a magical characteristic, is like a mirror as well as a prism, we see that the pieces of which it is fashioned are parts of ourselves; we are looking at the moving mosaic of our evolving selves.

To arrive at an accurate understanding of the image in the doctor's dream, great flexibility and imaginativeness were required, not just an intellectual awareness of the three principles described. In approaching any image, we have to open our hearts as well as our minds if we wish to grasp its message. For it is by getting in touch with what we feel about the image that we become aware of its unseen implications; out of this sensitivity, illuminating insight arises. Like a secret written in invisible ink, the words the image speaks can only be read with the eye of the heart.

It's as if you had a fishing rod in your grasp. You have to wait for the fish to bite no matter how eager you might be to make a catch. When dealing with unconscious realities, it is the power of the intuition as well as that of logical reasoning that pulls the pieces into place. By utilizing the right tools, you are in the same fortuitous position as the smart fisherman. Standing ready, patient and attentive, you know the insight will come along as surely as fish will appear in the stream. But, you can't force it to happen any more than you can force the fish to bite. The best you can do to ensure your success is to be alert and to prepare yourself appropriately.

Sometimes my cello teacher, Vaska, a wizened and wise old man, would interrupt me when I was playing for him. His blue eyes twinkling, he'd turn around in his seat at the piano to face me and draw the shape of a heart in the air. I got the message.

I'd like to pass the same one on to you. While I've gone to some length to provide you with a technical understanding of how your imagery works, I've done so with the conviction that we develop the imagination best by exercising it. Thus, I've provided intellectual tools that, properly applied, will excite your imagination, prompting you to think with feeling. In this manner, an invisible net is fashioned out of the workings of the conscious mind, a net that cast upon the sea of that which is not yet conscious will bring forth a remarkable yield.

Part of our fascination with imagery is its abiding

mystery. Like sexuality, there is a *je ne sais quois* to it all. While it is true that we can become more adept at understanding what our images are telling us, there will always be something about them we just can't figure out. I like it that way, it's part of the magic.

Furthermore, as much as they are magnetizing and mystifying, there is also something irascible and unpredictable to their character; I respect that. Therefore, in closing, I'd like to advise you that it is always a good idea to approach any image in a friendly manner, inviting a hospitable response from it rather than egotistically demanding one in the spirit of provocation.

"I get it," as one fellow brightly said, "it's like leaving milk out for the leprechauns!" Right.

15

Warming up: Julia

A RITE OF MAGIC

By way of a warm-up to the discussion of the source image, I'd like to apply the principles of interpretation to the detailed analysis of a single collage. I hope to demonstrate the kind of insight you can derive by utilizing these tools.

In Part One, when pointing out the difference between the personal and the cosmic source images, I mentioned that the latter category pertains to a series of archetypal symbols occurring with regularity throughout my clients' work. To this group belong those of special mythological animals like the snake or dragon, the bull and the horse; winged creatures like the bird; landscape imagery such as certain bodies of water (especially the well and the river), the forest, the tree, the mountains; and planets and stars. There are special shapes like the egg, the spiral and triangle, and sacred objects like the chalice (or cup or other shallow, round containers). These images can be depicted in either explicit or implicit form; in this context I'd like to remind you, for example, of the two different ways in which the snake image was rendered in Figures 35 and 36.

While my investigation of cosmic images has not been as systematic as that of the personal source images, there are a few ideas about them I would like to share to orient you regarding their function.

First, although they do not necessarily appear in any given order, once you begin to unblock your creativity, they emerge with regularity in either your dreams, writing, artwork or fantasies. It's as if our creativity had been stifled or crippled by early repressive influences in the environment around us. But, no matter how long it has languished inside, no matter how atrophied the instinct seems, it can still wake up as if from a long sleep. Its awakening is signaled to us by means of these special cosmic images.

Another interesting aspect of the source images I've designated as comic (or generic) is their affiliation with the ancient creation myths of primitive cultures in which God was often worshipped as a female entity. Perhaps buried deep in the psyche of us all are distant memories of a time when we enjoyed a more primal connection to the Great Earth Mother and celebrated our connection to Her as something divine.

Whether that is true or not, in practice I've observed that exploring the nature of our originality inevitably means we will make unexpected discoveries about our origins. Tapping the source brings its own reward. The more creative a person becomes, the more creative his outlook on life in general. Things about him take on new meaning and he feels spiritually uplifted. The discovery of certain universal symbols in the unfolding of a person's creative instincts signifies an order in the universe in a larger sense.

For ages people have instinctively recognized the power and importance of ritual. Novitiates of ancient religions were initiated into secret rites of worship via ritualistic services. Within differing cultures, rites of passage have long been observed with elaborate ceremonies. In analyzing the function of the ageless, universal and ancient source images, we might conclude that nature herself, to celebrate the infinite power of her creativity, has devised a ritual to initiate all of her children into her mysteries. For me the cosmic source images are part of a mysterious psychic ritual—invisible rites of passage that mark an individual's entrance into a secret realm.

For a long time I wondered about the meaning of the images of the well and the chalice and wanted to understand their special significance. Gradually, as I became sensitive to the fact that the spiritual changes transpiring in my clients' personalities always seemed to coincide with the creative ones taking place in their work, I realized what they might be about.

I think of the chalice (or bowl or cup) as a symbolic dipper, and of the well as the unconscious mind. Our images are more than just vehicles we can use in unfolding our creative abilities. Because they spring from and lead back to a universal source, they are also transmitters of metaphysical knowledge. Each of us can find refreshment at the well within us; but each of us is also responsible for fashioning the dipper used to reach down inside. The creative images we produce form a container, the vessel we need for lifting water from the well.

THERE ARE NO EQUATIONS

I have said that it is foolish to try to write a dictionary of symbols which would attribute specific, definitive and lasting meanings to images. This is true to a large extent. On the other hand, I have just defined what I think the symbols of the chalice and well mean. Ahead, you will find that when I am interpreting creative pieces, I will frequently point out the meaning of certain symbols in this more universal and general sense.

The emphasis here is on *general*. Whereas we can often attribute a certain universal significance to an image, e.g., to dream of going shopping has to do with making a choice, we cannot specify what meaning the image will take on once it has undergone transmutation in the mind of the individual. Although we ascertain the shopping dream has to do with making a choice, we can't know a priori what the specific choice consists of.

Another analogy will further illustrate this point. We know that the function of a car is to provide transportation. But how a person feels about the car, what it means to him, what he uses it for, which one he decides to buy, how much he's willing to pay for it and above all, where he decides to go in it is highly subjective. We can make general statements about what a car is and what it is meant for, but we can't determine what a person's unique car history will consist of.

Whenever I risk explaining the universal function of a specific image, I do so with the awareness that *images do not have equations*. Each manifestation of an image is unique. Just as all the pictures of the tree, the seed and the star shared something in common, they were also individual and special manifestations. Their universal component represented but one aspect of them.

Thus, even while you keep one eye on the map I'm providing, I'd like you to keep the other on a question mark. Since being creative is the capacity to view the old thing from a new perspective, your own perception about the meaning of an image is going to be as—if not more—important than any I might attach to it.

Interpreting imagery is a bit like playing hide-and-seek. For every meaning attributed to an image, I've found a new one peeking around the corner.

THE STARFISH AND THE PHONE

I'd now like to turn to interpreting a piece I mentioned earlier. It was produced by a woman in her early forties, married with two children, who worked as a free-lance editor. She felt blocked and wanted to use Source Imagery to help open her creativity. Stifled and unfulfilled in her marriage, frustrated with her career, she felt there were valuable artistic resources inside her that she wanted to release through writing and painting.

But there were obstacles in her path. An only child, she'd grown up in postwar England and had shown pronounced talent as a dancer. Her family endured great hardship during the war and afterward had to struggle to make ends meet. There had been little time or money for furthering Julia's creative bent. The main reason they supported her taking dance classes was that a doctor had advised them as exercise to strengthen her weak ankles.

As a youngster of about twelve, she tried out for the Royal Academy of Ballet and had almost been accepted as a student. The family, in the midst of a move, was caught up with other concerns and did not push Julia to continue taking lessons. Not long after that, Julia became more interested in dating than dancing, so the matter was dropped and the whole thing forgotten.

Julia ended up blocked by default. Her parents by no means had discouraged her interest in the arts, but neither had they attributed particular significance to it. They did not perceive how important it was for her to find an outlet for her creativity. Thus, Julia had not inherited an internal model of support for furthering her artistic expression, and she needed to find one. Moreover, since that early experience Julia had not only felt discouraged about her creative abilities, she'd begun to doubt she even possessed them.

When she decided to enter the group, she at first had great difficulty enjoying the visual exercises we did together. Upon completing a project she'd be momentarily excited, then she would become dissatisfied and critical. Gradually, with support and encouragement, Julia began to overcome the critical voices inside that were preventing her from enjoying herself. A few months after joining the workshop, she brought in a collage she'd spontaneously produced that she was pleased with and proud of.

The piece represented an important step, reflecting an inner change that would help her overcome her block. It is well-composed and striking, revealing a turning point in Julia's artistic and personal development.

Analyzing this piece will help you put into practice what you have been learning about the principles of hidden congruence, juxtaposition and superimposition. Identifying how the images are ordered helps you make sense out of them, prompting you to arrive at the meaning that lies below the surface. The insight you derive from combining your logical with your intuitive faculties will show you how the piece is at once itself and more than itself. It is a special vehicle for transforming consciousness, precipitating spiritual awareness and furthering artistic growth.

Like a hologram, in which the whole picture can be reconstructed out of any of its parts, so too can the whole meaning within any type of artwork (or dream) be derived from one of its parts. Therefore, a person can begin working with the images in any piece by pinpointing the one that

strikes him first or *the most*. In Fig. 48, the heart with the
phone cord and receiver extending from it particularly catches
the eye. The heart is placed where we would expect to find
an ear. The artist has created an ear/heart image by means
of explicit superimposition. The heart is also juxtaposed with
the image of a phone. The receiver dangles down and almost
touches a starfish. Thus, the idea of a telephone exchange is
juxtaposed with a voiceless creature from the deep.

FIGURE 48
*The client created this fascinating collage by pasting together images
for magazines.*

It's as if the phone cord and receiver were acting like a fishing rod and hook. We can then assume the presence of an implicit superimposition between the ideas of a casting line and a phone line. We note a hidden congruence between the ripples on the water, the ripples in the sand, the curling hair on the head of the woman seated on the rocks to the right and the coiling phone cord. There is another hidden congruence between the fingers as extensions of the hand, rays as extensions of the body of the starfish, keys as extensions of the piano and tendrils as extensions of the peacock feather. We might assume the presence of an implicit superimposition in the image of the peacock feather itself; it could represent the writer's pen or even the painter's brush.

Any single creative act reflects the frame of mind of the person who enacted it. It sheds light on the larger frame of that person's life. Just as two people living together can influence each other, a person's creativity can have a major impact on his life. When attempting to interpret images, it's always helpful, therefore, to examine the larger context in which they arose. Let's apprise ourselves again of Julia's situation to better grasp the meaning of her imagery and ascertain its special message.

When she entered the group, Julia had voiced excitement about exploring her untapped creative abilities. Over the years she'd tended to focus on more practical concerns, like those her parents valued. Once a dutiful daughter, now she'd become a dutiful wife and mother; it was difficult for her to put her own needs before or even on a par with those of anyone else. Although her material need for security was satisfied, she felt deprived on other levels of her being.

Her marriage especially presented a block to self-fulfill-ment. For many years she and her husband had interacted predominantly as friends; the romance seemed to have drained from the relationship. Although they liked each other, they were incompatible in many ways. Julia felt a conflict of interests. She longed for independence yet feared it at the same time. She felt she should keep the marriage alive for the sake of the children. She had decided to renounce her own needs to further the interests of the family. As a result, she felt stifled both emotionally and creatively. She saw no other solution than the one of squelching herself. After all, since childhood she'd been suppressing her need for self-expression.

Her resistance to making a change was now so strong that she announced a strict hands-off policy regarding her relationship with her husband. She would not discuss it. Fiercely protective of her children, her elegant home, her idealized view of herself as a model wife, mother and daughter, she was unwilling to put anything in her present life at risk. She was hoping to achieve her aims without having to change anything.

Julia's attitude was blocking her. She, who so much desired to tap into what lay below the surface, was especially reluctant to look there; like many people, she was afraid of what she might encounter. But what lay there was buried treasure, the key to her creativity and its transformative power. What Julia was resisting was not change but rather her own capacity to effect it.

When Julia presented her piece to the group, she had set clear limits as to the level of self-disclosure she would allow. But she had diligently been doing the drawing and writing exercises; in this manner she'd begun to align herself with her unconscious mind in such a way that, despite her resistance, she was producing images that truly fascinated and inspired her. Also, the practice she'd received in giving and getting positive strokes was having its effect. No longer was she subject to the debilitating critical voices inside her head; she'd begun to nurture her creative child, regularly setting aside time for herself at home in which to paint, write or think about her dreams. Gradually, without realizing it, Julia was discovering that the way past her resistance was to go around it. Her creativity was arousing such strong feelings of attraction that she could neither deny nor suppress them any longer. Like a parent who entices a child by reading him an interesting story, the unconscious mind was beginning to bewitch her with its charms. She was finding that, for the moment, the only shock that awaited her on her quest was the one of self-discovery, not of loss.

A SHIFT IN ALLEGIANCE

Julia's collage is exciting because it depicts her newfound willingness to cushion herself *with* the truth instead of insulating herself *against* it. All at once the imagery brings into sharp focus her growing capacity to have confidence in her creative powers. She instinctively is harkening to an inner voice, losing some interest perhaps in her efforts to keep up a nice outer appearance for the benefit of others.

The face of the woman in the center of the piece is in shadows, her eyes are closed, her expression rapt. Her attention is turned inward; what she sees or hears lies within. An insight is dawning. It is not an outside force that will change her; it is the power of a force inside. This dawning awareness is depicted symbolically in the light illumining the heart cupped against her ear, shining around and beneath it. The source of this light is hidden, mysterious. It emanates from an inner sense, is generated by the power of spiritual perception.

What is the nature of the insight slowly dawning in Julia's mind? The imagery in the collage reflects a process of psychic transformation at work as much as it does the unfolding of Julia's artistic abilities. We're witnessing a shift in allegiance; Julia is about to change her mind. No longer will she heed the voices of the past that influenced her and held her back. Rather, she is gaining an increased capacity to be sensitive to her feelings. Precisely where we would expect to see an ear a heart is placed. The emphasis here is on Julia's decision to listen to what her heart is saying.

Her experience in group has been having its effect. It is not so much what she has heard, as how she has been taught to listen. During our exchanges about the meaning of images, she's been getting in touch with the feelings they evoke; she's practiced voicing what she senses, not just what she intellectually thinks about the images. She has learned to trust her intuitive responses.

As she has listened sensitively to others, so have they listened to her. This experience is now being internalized; Julia's growing understanding that the heart makes connections the mind cannot is transmitted by means of the superimposition between the heart and the ear. The heart really is an inner ear; Julia has begun to grasp that to understand what her images are telling her, she must listen with feeling.

This increased sensitivity to and appreciation of her creativity is necessarily about to affect other areas of her life. The superimposition prognosticates a general tendency for her to become more sensitive to her feelings. On the surface, Julia has appeared a model "woman." She did this at the expense of asserting her own power. She is about to discover that being a woman and being powerful is no more a contradiction than for a man to be both assertive and caring. Expressing her creativity is helping Julia break the old rules. Whoever heard of someone placing a call to a starfish? And, whoever heard of a woman who could be as in touch with her own needs as she was with those of others? Julia is reprioritizing, placing a higher value on the desires of her heart.

Opening up to her feelings is opening her up to the forces of nature itself, awakening within her a new trust in their power. The unconscious mind gives each of us direct access to nature's energies. The infinitely beautiful design of the unconscious mind is symbolized for Julia in the image of the sea. The large, powerful moving body of water with its myriad life forms is like the inner realm of the psyche—powerful, fluid, vast and full of intelligent life.

An awareness of the rich resources within her is reaching Julia's conscious mind. It is not an intellectual supposition but a nonverbal perception, an instinctive knowing that is rising to the surface. The idea that these resources are within reach is expressed by the juxtaposition between two incongruous elements: the phone cord with the receiver and the starfish. A person who goes deep-sea fishing uses a line and rod. Here we have a heart with a phone cord attached as a rod, and, in place of a hook, a receiver. The idea of fishing is superimposed with that of the feeling capacity of the heart. To make the creative "catch" her own, Julia needs to practice being receptive to her unconscious mind and the impressions it transmits by means of feelings and intuition.

Julia is discovering how appropriate it is to be in sync with her instincts. There can be a harmonious exchange between the conscious and unconscious levels of her being. But for this synchronizing to occur, a finely tuned sense of timing is important. Both the nature imagery in the piece and the hand moving across the keyboard imply the importance of timing. Water and music flow in rhythmic sequence. When we suppress our instincts and feelings, our timing tends to be off.

As a child, Julia was cut off from spontaneously enjoying her artistic nature. One characteristic of a starfish is its ability to regenerate a severed limb. The juxtaposition between the phone and the sea creature suggests two things. First, Julia is reconnecting with a part of herself she felt cut off from in the past; she is experiencing her psychic capacity to regenerate an atrophied instinct. It's not too late to begin again and recapture the passionate, spontaneous relationship to her creativity she enjoyed as a child. Second, the phone image suggests that this connection is the result of willful intent, representing no more an accidental occurrence than picking up the phone to dial a friend. The juxtaposition implies that making a connection with the unconscious mind is the result of a conscious choice. Starfish don't speak, at least not in a tongue we humans understand. The two-way communication between the conscious and unconscious minds is not a verbal one. Rather it consists of a flow of feelings and images that may then be cast into words or some other externalized shape. Linking with our creativity opens an intelligible exchange between the physical and the spiritual senses.

The starfish is a pivotal image in the piece. Like the hands cupping the heart, it is composed of five "fingers." As I mentioned, there is a hidden congruence between the fingers on the hands, the rays of the starfish, the keys on the piano and the delicate branches of the peacock feather. Understanding what the connection among the images says provides us with important clues about what the collage prognosticates in terms of Julia's creative growth and spiritual development. A piano implies the need for practice, and a starfish, for regeneration. The image of hands often connotes both the fulfilling of promise and the need for solitude, and the peacock feather connotes artistry, love of beauty and pride in one's creativity. Perhaps what is being regenerated in Julia is her lost capacity to write, a need she repressed (along with her love of dance) when she was younger. An innate pride in her creative ability and her desire to fulfill her promise as an artist are quickening.

In order to survive in the environment in which she

grew up, Julia had to block off a part of herself. She put important desires to sleep; they became unconscious. These once-dormant desires are now stirring, waiting to be integrated into the conscious mind. The peacock feather, which could stand for a writer's pen and/or painter's brush, extends from the head of the woman, who appears to be sleeping or in a deep trance. An important part of Julia has been asleep for a long time. She will have to wake this part of herself up. As her creative potential surfaces, this side of her personality awakens. It is a kind of rebirthing process that requires Julia's conscious cooperation. The hidden congruence might suggest that the way she can best serve this integrative movement is by regularly expressing her feelings in writing and painting. To do so would constitute in and of itself creative productivity, whose value lies predominantly in its subjective worth for Julia rather than its objective value as a work of art.

Julia must take what exists merely as a possibility and make it a reality on a conscious level. By casting her feelings spontaneously into images and writing, she gains access to her unconscious creative potential. As she reviews her work, sharing it in the group and thinking about it on her own, she ingests on a conscious level that which was unconscious. Gradually she learns to nourish herself with the fruits of her own creativity. Artistic talents unfold, rooting of their own accord. By learning to place a high value on what she produces, be it sophisticated or primitive, she strengthens its chance to survive and thrive.

Hidden congruence reveals a further insight into Julia's personal situation and her reluctance to undergo change. A starfish can alter its direction without shifting its position. Julia fears and wants to avoid shocking or unwanted change. She is, for example, unwilling to even consider the possibility of divorce. She prefers to wait for her husband to make the first move, or until some indefinite time in the future when she might feel free to take the step. In this regard the message the imagery transmits is reassuring, and she can take solace in it. The starfish image implies that by focusing her attention on herself and her creativity, she can begin to effect significant inner change without having to make a dramatic shift in her physical situation. This is welcome news for the hesitant pilgrim. Rather than needing to adjust her position in relation to someone else, she need only concentrate—for the time being—on making adjustments in relation to herself. Once there is an alignment between the conscious and unconscious selves, there will be a corresponding realignment between the self and the outer world. The collage therefore predicts a spiritual change, one that will ultimately alter the course of events in Julia's life just as surely as nature alters the seasons. Once she learns to trust herself, she will trust her ability to make the right changes.

THE MAGICAL STEPPING STONES

As I mentioned, when I was a young music student, my cello teacher would often encourage me despite my mistakes, telling me it was as important to play with heart as it was to perfect technique. By expressing her creativity—and this merely for the unadulterated pleasure it gives her—Julia is going to begin playing her life with heart. All of her relationships will eventually reflect the same integrity she enjoys in the one she cultivates with herself.

We speak of movement in a musical composition and the movement of a body of water. In Source Imagery the sea suggests a powerful movement of the psyche. Julia's piece proclaims new movement in her life, movement precipitated by feeling as much as by the power of reason.

Julia has connected with a transformative source of energy and is harnessing it to her own advantage. However, as much as her piece predicts a positive outcome, it also points to an immediate hindrance. To the right, a woman sits on a rock, staring out to sea. She represents that part of Julia which sits on top of her blocked energy. The block is hard to move, is cold and unyielding. It will take time to wear it away. Any creative block is a complex entity, breaking apart and dissolving one piece at a time.

Julia's collage predicts change but does not ensure it. Her tendency to squelch her creative instincts and silence the voice of her heart is a powerful regressive habit. Just as it was she who heard the message about her creative potential, it is she who can tune it out. In this special exchange the receiver and sender are one. There is no one who can heed the message better than Julia herself. She alone is responsible for what happens to her from now on. Forces in the past that held her back are no longer of concern. She is the one with the power now to release her creativity.

Opening to one's creativity stimulates an integrative process in the brain. Something has budged in Julia; part of the block has been removed, revealing something valuable. That mysterious light emanating from around the heart says that Julia is turning on to herself, is turning herself on. The feelings she's experiencing are attractive, irresistible. The excitement she feels about her creativity will inspire the expression of sexual and spiritual desires that have long been denied or discounted. Instinctively, Julia will realize that these urges spring from the selfsame source as her creativity, reflecting a beauty, power and validity of their own. As she turns on to her creative abilities, Julia warms to other parts of herself, aspects she will claim one by one.

The collage configures a creative awakening on several levels of the psyche simultaneously. It represents a step forward for Julia in terms of her ability to express herself artistically. At the same time, it depicts how she is evolving as an individual. It is like a page out of a magic journal recording a person's individuation process. It is the multifaceted nature of the creative experience itself that will help this woman forge a new sense of identity. By acknowledging her power to be creative, Julia simultaneously gains awareness of her unique vision of reality.

The innate capacity of each person to be creative and to grasp his unique artistic vision is exemplified in the occurrence of an important cosmic source image, that of the serpent. In Julia's piece there is a hidden congruence between the undulating S-like shape of the ripples in the sand, the waves in the water, the coiling phone cord and the wavy hair on the woman to the right. These sinewy shapes suggest the presence of a snake in abstract or implicit form. The appearance of the snakelike image indicates that on an unconscious level Julia is gaining confidence in her *power to be original*. Primal energy is stirring; a natural creative impulse is taking shape and making its existence known.

Because a new sense of who she is and can be is emerging, Julia will be establishing new and clearer boundaries in her relationships with others, setting healthier limits on the demands they make. There will be a better balance in her need to be responsible toward herself as well as others. But the process of clarification will take time. Like the gradual steps of a renovation, the changeover will occur in stages. After completing this collage, Julia began to dream that her house and yard were under construction. The first stage in reconstructing her sense of who she is consists of her efforts to align her conscious with her unconscious side. Artwork, like a magical mirror, provides her with glimpses into hitherto unknown or disowned parts of herself. The life she is building will bear the unmistakable imprint of this encounter, containing elements of her special creative vision.

Now Julia will actively be forging her own destiny rather than merely responding to the expectations of others. In the collage the concepts of up and down, inside and outside, are superimposed in a subtle manner. The woman's head, partially in shadow, is tilted back and pointing upward. But she does not stare at the sky. She peers downward and inward toward the ocean of the unconscious mind, with its living star. The star symbolizes one's sense of destiny. Perhaps what illumines the heart above the starfish is a ray of insight about Julia's destiny, transmitted from the depths of the unconscious. Into her brain there might be filtering an inkling of knowledge small as a grain of sand, precious as the diamond sparkling on the hand holding the heart, symbolizing the possible commitment Julia is making to herself.

We often speak of the unconscious as if it existed somewhere in us "down below." Does it? And is it "in" us or "outside" us, "up" or "down"—or all of these? In this piece what is below shines up above, and what is above shines within the watery heavens beneath. An inner realm is perceived as an outer one and vice versa. This complex superimposition implies that as Julia gains in her ability to express her creativity, her outer world will mirror the integrity of her inner one.

The man's hand moves across the keyboard; the image represents the idea that positive strokes have the power to evoke a harmonious response. Julia's ability to stroke herself for taking a creative risk has struck a resonant chord in her heart. It is as if her creative imagery carried sound; in it she hears the refrain of a melody from the distant past. Just as her feet once moved in rhythm to the music she danced to as a child, her fingers have the ability to dance with color when she paints.

The shape of the woman's head is almost egg-like. Like an egg cracking open so that new life might emerge, the imagery depicts the cracking open of new awareness, signaling the breakthrough of new life and an important impulse for change. But, this emerging awareness is fragile and needs careful handling. The heart is most carefully cupped in a pair of hands. Julia realizes it is not how she was handled in the past but how she handles herself from now on that counts.

Although the collage documents a subjective stage of growth in one person's life, it reveals the creative potential we all have to take hold of our destiny. The imagistic building blocks with which Julia is working are composed of magical stepping stones lying within the depths of her psyche but within the reach of us all. Each person has the ability to use his creativity to dip into the universal well of the unconscious mind. Everyone has a vision to claim; the unconscious mind times, with mystical precision, our awakening to spiritual insight.

PART FOUR

The Source Image

16

≈≈≈≈≈≈≈≈≈≈≈≈≈≈≈≈≈≈≈≈≈≈≈≈≈≈≈≈≈≈≈≈≈

Niki: A Case Study

THE WAVE

When she entered group, Niki was in her early forties and divorced, with three children in their early and late teens. Although she had little formal training as an artist, she had pronounced drawing ability and aspired to one day support herself as a free-lance book illustrator. She also wanted to open up her ability to paint, a goal she rightly saw as related to but quite distinct from the first. She participated in the group experience for a little over two years. Just before leaving she discovered she had breast cancer. In Niki's case we will see how the skills she'd gained to help open her creativity aided her in this crisis. She faced the disease and its treatment with inner hope and fortitude, bringing her art supplies right into the hospital. She attributed her rapid recuperation in great part to the inspiration and strength she derived from consciously tapping into the creative devices Source Imagery had made available.

Niki was a shy, somewhat self-effacing individual with little confidence in her creative abilities. At first she felt intimidated by other people in the group and tended to compare her own work unfavorably with theirs. She did not like to compete for attention and seemed uncomfortable when the spotlight fell on her. It was as if the critical voices in her head had told her she was stupid to think she was talented. These critical voices were so powerful that they held her creativity in check, preventing her from freely expressing and enjoying herself.

Before entering the group, Niki had worked occasionally as an illustrator. She wanted to expand and improve her capabilities, but something held her back. She had difficulty thinking of herself as an artist. Although she had made space for a studio in the basement of her house, she spent little time there. Despite her desire to take risks with her painting, she felt constricted and inhibited. A deep-seated fear of taking center stage and an almost insurmountable sense of inferiority were blocking her creative expression. She felt stymied.

While Niki participated in the group experience, her work changed and evolved. She began taking risks, experimenting with new techniques and materials, and she gained confidence in her abilities both as an illustrator and artist. The drawings, paintings and collages she produced during this period are fascinating. You can easily observe in them the emergence of a source image and learn to appreciate its function and complexity. Out of the hundred or more pieces that Niki made while working in the group setting, I have selected ten to discuss. (See Color Plates 12 through 21.) The series shows clearly how a source image evolves, reflecting and precipitating positive changes in the life and work of the artist as it itself changes shape and develops.

Niki's first piece (Color Plate 12) shows her drawing abilities. It looks like an illustration for a children's fairy tale and reveals how imaginative and talented she is.

Like Julia, Niki soon began to respond to the support she received in group; as she learned how to give and receive positive strokes, the child side in her opened. She began taking new risks with her work, daring to be bold, endeavoring to please herself when she painted.

The next piece (Color Plate 13) contrasts quite sharply with the first both in style and design. Drawn in pastel, a new medium for Niki, the scene is depicted in vivid colors. Niki is less focused on being technically exact. The piece has an exuberant, passionate quality.

The encouragement she received to express herself has evoked a powerful response. It's as if the encounter with the group acted like a flint stone igniting a fire; her gift, symbolized in the passion flower, has burst forth with blazing intensity out of the rock-hard block of resistance. Waves splash and dance against the stone island. And, upon closer inspection, we can see the soft, undulating contours of an almost female-like form taking shape on the surface of the rock in the foreground.

Despite her resistance, there has been a startling spurt of growth. Niki's hypercritical attitude is softening. Those voices are becoming less harsh. As with Julia, the ocean imagery suggests new movement transpiring in the psyche; a process of transformation has begun. The single flower, standing triumphantly, seems to symbolize not so much a sense of isolation but that Niki is taking pride in standing on her own and having others notice her.

From this point on, Niki continued to draw using brighter and more intense colors. In the next piece (Color Plate 14) we see the image of a wave appear again. Its color, shape and function have changed, however. Here it is juxtaposed against the image of a large, piercing eye.

Earlier I explained how images function as organizing principles. Like words, they help us explore and define our experience. But we may express far more complex responses to reality through the use of images than by the use of words alone. The drawing of the eye is exciting because in it we see how the image of the wave is beginning to take on special significance for Niki. A personal source image is evolving right in front of her eyes. A complex response to her interaction with the group and the Source Imagery material is having its effect. The image of the wave expresses a change that is taking place, translating this change into a form that can approximate its multidimensional nature.

The wave, stylized in shape, is not watery in character. Bright red-orange in color, its fiery tones are reminiscent of the passion flower. When something burns, it changes from one form into another; consequently, fire tends to connote a *shift in values*. Formerly, Niki placed great emphasis on how other people perceived the quality of her work. Yet no matter how much it measured up to outside standards of excellence, she derived little personal satisfaction from it. She couldn't acknowledge any compliments received because she viewed her work with a relentlessly critical, disbelieving eye. Like a player at bat who hits a home run without trying, every time she produced a picture she was baffled, considering it a quirk of fate and not a matter of skill. Any positive recognition she received fell on deaf ears.

But Niki has been affected by what she has learned about the need for positive strokes. A new feeling has been building and is making its presence known. When it first occurred, the wave was depicted as an extension of the ocean; in that shape it represented an important transformational movement taking place in the psyche. Now we can perceive a complicated process of superimposition influencing the form of the image. The idea of the ocean has been combined with that of the passion flower and even of fire itself. But, the red-orange wave flowing up and over the eye also suggests the flow of blood to the head. And the tips of the wave are rounded, looking almost like the curving fingers of a large hand.

An important feeling is beginning to grow in Niki; like the life-giving flow of blood throughout the body, self-confidence is bringing vitality into her artwork. Blood is a living substance. Like Julia, Niki is learning to respond to her images with sensitivity. She recognizes that they are not sterile, technical constructs but represent instead living entities. The wave now symbolizes a renewal of faith in the process of life and art.

The wave could be ebbing and drawing back like a curtain. We are witnessing, then, an opening; it is the opening of Niki's ability to see her work more honestly. The eye peers forward with unswerving intent. Perhaps Niki is learning how to assess her work from a more realistic viewpoint and with an eye for its true value.

Niki's new feeling about herself, exemplified in the fiery wave of blood, has to do with being loving. We think of passion as something that is fiery-hot and that stirs the blood. Niki's heart has grown cold and hard from a lack of self-love and self-esteem. Now she is warming to herself, learning that for her art to grow, she must nurture it with love as much as cultivate it with technical know-how. If she keeps an open mind, her imagery can teach her something valuable about herself.

The wave is like a hand. In group Niki mastered a special kind of eye-hand coordination, one that has nothing to do with physical skill. Niki learned to coordinate her feeling responses with her mental faculties. From now on her artwork would become a vehicle for expressing her feelings, and not just a sophisticated exercise in manual dexterity.

The wave is coming to represent something of special import to Niki. It exemplifies the idea that who she is as a person and what she creates as an artist are intimately connected. The wave celebrates the connection. It symbolizes the power of a life-changing insight and says art, heart, mind and body can no longer be held separate from each other. In this regard the wave represents the gathering together of many forces within Niki; it is a symbol for *unified momentum*.

Niki will no longer be at such odds with herself when she is being creative. Instead of battling her desire to be an artist, she will ally herself with it. That eye peering from behind the wave almost looks like a fish swimming forward. Within the context of Source Imagery the fish symbolizes an important *moment of inception*. Both the source image itself and Niki's newfound capacity to appreciate its impact on her work reach a significant point of development in this piece.

In the next drawing (Color Plate 15) the wave image has undergone yet another transmutation. Again it appears in abstract form, but here the image of an ear is superimposed with that of the wave. The idea of a sound wave is combined with the notion of a wave of color.

The wave has grown in size, almost dominating the piece. It intersects with a large triangle and in the lower left corner curls around the minute figure of a unicorn. In its new incarnation the image has acquired yet another layer of meaning, reflecting an important psychic change. When Niki brought this drawing to class, she was less self-conscious about showing her work than before and seemed pleased with the piece. Moreover, after I had finished commenting on it and was about to turn my attention to someone else's drawing, Niki interrupted to say that she hadn't finished talking and wanted to speak further. The group was startled; generally quite withdrawn, Niki was beginning to open up and communicate with more ease. A member of the group complimented her on taking the initiative, saying, "I understand why your wave is getting bigger. You're beginning to have the courage to make waves!"

Indeed, what had first appeared as merely a splash, then as a ripple, had gained sizably in proportion, now resembling a breaker. Up until this point, Niki had been in the habit of keeping her needs to herself. Having grown up in an alcoholic household, she was accustomed to either being ignored or criticized; she had decided it was safer not to be noticed. When she announced she had something to say, Niki was really deciding that people should sit up and take notice of her. She was acknowledging her own importance.

But where did this newfound sense of self-esteem come from? To the extent that Niki had been learning to trust her instincts and paint with more feeling, she had also been learning to trust her ability to communicate on other levels as well. Unconsciously, she was beginning to realize that being heard might be just as much fun as being seen. In this instance the source image itself helped to precipitate personal growth in Niki's consciousness, prompting her to take a risk in relationship to others. Just as she had begun to experience the beneficial effect of unified movement within, she was beginning to accept the notion that the group unity outside her could represent a positive influence. Niki grinned when the person told her she was starting to make waves. She liked the idea; she was tired of feeling isolated and cut off from others, and wanted to interact more spontaneously with them.

Niki's wave represented a breakthrough for her both personally and artistically, helping to generate within her a sense of belonging and connectedness. On the one hand, the wave has come to represent the feeling of energy that freely expressing creativity gives her; on the other, it has come to signify the sense of release she experiences by letting go and associating with others in trust. As the wave has grown in power, Niki's resistance and distrust have diminished.

Over a year had transpired since Niki began working in group and using Source Imagery. In general she had become more relaxed in her manner and positive in her outlook on life. Her artwork had also loosened up and changed. Occasionally she put her thoughts into writing and would share them with the group. Still subject to bouts of depression, she was nevertheless gaining confidence in her artistic talents and abilities to communicate. I mentioned the presence of the unicorn image in this last drawing. Its occurrence can connote the awakening of a poetic gift. The wave of energy that is emerging in Niki's artwork contains seeds of yet another potential talent.

The wave curls into spiral-like shapes at either end. The spiral, like the snake in Julia's piece, is an important cosmic source image. It is highly charged with meaning and spiritual implications. A spiral moves simultaneously in and down and out and up; in creative terms it stands for a point in consciousness where inner and outer reality are becoming more fully integrated. Once a person starts to unblock his creativity, he begins to realize that his images are vehicles for perceiving the world differently. An ordinary object or event like Niki's wave can be translated into its imagistic equivalent and suddenly gain new meaning and import. The object transformed no longer merely replicates something of material worth and dimension; alchemized by poetic vision, it has gained great psychic significance.

In general, the presence of the spiral indicates a person is beginning to perceive his life from a less materialistic standpoint; by means of his creativity he is learning that it is not what he experiences but what he makes out of his experience that counts. His inner response to an event helps to shape it. The altered vision of reality generates a new and positive attitude. Being creative operates as a healing force in the psyche, helping to make a burning ground of the mistakes and misfortunes of the past, which in turn, transforms it into a canvas that holds the promise of a brighter future. This continuous process of transformation and renewal is as essential to the psyche as it is to nature. The back and forth movement in which physical reality impresses consciousness, and consciousness impresses reality, is symbolized in the spiral. Niki's wave has become far more than an expression of her freed creative energy; it expresses our innate spiritual ability to transform life's experience through the power of spiritual vision. The spiral indicates that *a vital psychic feedback system* has kicked into operation, invisible in nature, far-reaching in consequence.

The triangle intersecting the wave is also an important cosmic source image. When it appears in the work of clients it indicates a vital shift in aesthetic terms. The capacity to translate feeling into form is generating of its own momentum the ability to find more sophisticated modes of creative expression, be it a new medium, method or outlet. The person not only feels he is original (which the snake symbolizes), but he is also beginning to bring an original body of work into being (which is symbolized by the triangle). Whereas this progressive step forward is prognosticated, it is more a promising announcement than it is the announcing of a promise. Like any creative forecast, it is subject to change—depending on which course of action the artist decides to take.

From this point on, Niki still tended to disparage her work; yet it was beginning to afford her an increased sense of purpose and pleasure in life. Like Julia she was beginning to heed the guidance of an inner voice as much as listen to the discordant directives of the critical ones.

The source image, like a carpenter's tool, has many functions; it helps us fashion a better world in which to live from both a creative and psychological angle. Each time it reoccurs, it appears in transmuted form, documenting a progression of psychic change. The image has changed because the content that it houses has altered, but the content carries a memory of its previous forms. Thus, the source image records in sequence a history of evolving consciousness.

THE SWAN

A personal source image is composed of many layers, superimposition upon superimposition. In the last drawing, for example, we saw the shape of an ear superimposed over that of the wave. The wave is colored in both red-and-orange tones, and blue-and-white ones, entertaining a significant similarity with the wave images of earlier drawings (e.g., Plates 13 and 14 in the color insert). This new manifestation of the image contains, by implication, characteristics of the old; it is not one but three or more waves. That explains its unique form. It crests and turns back upon itself both at the top and again at the bottom, where it branches simultaneously into several coils. This wave is quite special, flowing back in time and space as much as it thrusts forward, containing vital information about the creative unfolding of the artist.

Each time the source image appears in new form it has a higher charge of energy, because it contains within itself not only the characteristics of all those forms that have preceded it but new characteristics as well. Like a perfume to which many fragrances may be added, there is nevertheless a continual distillation process at work. The effect may be beautiful; certainly it is always powerful. Even in minute quantity, the source image stirs the consciousness of the viewer, effecting transformation. Ultimately, the size and shape of the source image are secondary to its impact.

Chapters in a book, or scenes in a drama, represent important turning points in the developing plot. Similarly, there are visual pieces that have the same function. In Niki's next drawing (Color Plate 16) we see the wave once again; here it is transformed into a giant, swan-like shape that almost appears to be suspended in air. The image is pivotal both for her artwork and career, illustrating the essential role the source image can play in the unfolding of a life story.

By now you will recognize familiar components in the evolving wave: the blue-and-white curling crest of the previous waves forms the main outline of the swan's body; the red-orange wings are shaped like teardrops, yet are reminiscent of the bird-of-paradise flower petals in Plate 13 of the color insert and the rounded tips of the fiery wave in Plate 14 of the color insert. They also resemble flames. Moreover, they are beginning to look like the points of paintbrushes. In this most recent manifestation, then, the ideas of a swan, wings, tears and of painting itself have been added to, or superimposed over those of the flower, fire and wave. Note two other important elements in the piece: the strong blue line bordering the drops of fire and forming part of the swan's body, and the red-and-black background against which the bird is moving. They also represent important additional components of the drawing.

Gradually, Niki has been changing. In the past she had been subject to bouts of depression that left her feeling despondent. Like many of us, Niki sometimes felt shackled by her sense of inferiority. Depressing thoughts like dark clouds temporarily blacked out any prospects she had for feeling optimistic. Niki sometimes sank into despair and lost sight of the goals she had already begun to achieve. In this state she tended to revert to feeling isolated and unable to lift herself above the clouds.

Although opening her creativity has helped to provide Niki with special tools and new insights, it represents but a healing device; it is not a panacea for the unexpected—and continual—ups and downs of experience. Despite resistance Niki is committed to her creative process. But, every change brings upheaval, leaving a temporary sense of disorder. To withstand such a period of psychic stress, a person needs to have an overview. Much as an architect's blueprint helps orient someone involved in a building project, spiritual signposts help orient a person toward psychic change, giving him an invaluable perspective of the whole.

I mentioned the strong blue outline around the tear-shaped wings of the bird. The drawing, like a magical blueprint, contains insight that will help Niki weather not only her current disorientation but also unexpected storms ahead. The presence of the bird, a cosmic source image, indicates that through her creativity Niki is gaining access to *spiritual foresight*. It is this invisible capacity, a strength of spirit, that gives an individual the courage to face change and upset, and to rise above temporary difficulties.

When discussing the concept of the meta-image, I explained that the unconscious mind posits images in consciousness that are part of a larger emerging design. In a sense each image we create has futurity. It points us toward the direction in which it wants us to evolve, helping us realize our destiny. The wings of Niki's bird are formed of wave, fire, tear and paintbrush, all symbolizing her capacity to rise above her fears, to stay in touch with her artistic promise. No matter what surprises she may encounter—whether of an inner or outer nature—a determination to keep her spirits elevated is growing. Despite moments of anxiety, she will stick to her commitment to change.

The value she has begun to place on her painting and her communication with others is having its effect; her sense of identity is changing. Like the duckling who outgrows its awkward shape, Niki is leaving behind an outworn image of herself. Clouds of dust seem to be dispersing above the swan's body; it is as if Niki has decided to brush off her limitations in order to more easily move forward. Beneath those clouds of dust and depression, something graceful and golden is emerging. Creativity has helped Niki swim free of the past, empowering her to see herself in a new light. The symbol of the swan helps connect us with the transformative power of letting the past go; its occurrence signifies making such a choice.

Sometimes Niki has felt angry and frustrated by her inability to express herself and give vent to her passionate nature. She has often turned the anger inward. This debilitating tendency, along with those critical voices, undermined her self-confidence. The swan floats above a sea of red-and-black. This color combination has special significance, indicating a radical change in an unconscious self-destructive pattern of behavior. Precisely what is changing for Niki?

When she first entered the group, Niki had been overly concerned with her drawing techniques and felt inhibited by a sense of inadequacy despite the technical training she had received. To her, being artistic meant being specially gifted. She identified being creative with putting on an excellent show, not with something that had to do with spontaneity. Like many of us who have survived deprivation in childhood, she imagined it was her lot to be unhappy in life. She did not suspect that anything of great beauty or value lay within her. If anything, she thought that what was in her needed to be expunged.

But now, like a gold miner prospecting for nuggets, Niki has made an invaluable discovery: she is realizing that beneath that dreary outer crust of anxiety and depression lies a wealth of bright resources. Instead of burying her feelings and letting them weigh her down, she's going to bring them to the surface, cast them into fanciful form, experience the wondrous release of unfettering her imagination. The piece prognosticates that from this point on, Niki will be less concerned with matters of performance and technique, and more concerned with the sense of personal gratification her work provides.

As happened with Julia, Niki is warming up. She is entertaining a more passionate relationship to her imagery. The drawing of the swan, like the drawing of her tree, has a fairytale quality. Yet, if we compare the two, we see that this one has greater intensity and power. With hindsight, we can look at that original drawing and see the source image present in nascent form in the wavy outlines demarcating the bark on the tree. But like a cell suspended in a chemical buffer solution, it had been lying in a dormant condition.

The experience of bonding with the group—receiving positive strokes that helped loosen her creativity—and learning to trust her feelings has changed the psychic environment. It is as if Niki had taken the image and transposed it from its seed state into a special growth medium.

The transposition has induced acceleration of an organic process. Within a relatively short time the image has changed, developed and undergone rapid maturation. At first it appeared in less well-defined form, seminal in outline but totipotent in essence. Now having attained a more differentiated expression, its complex functions emerge.

Niki has not just been mixing paints to get a creative effect; she's been blending unconscious insight with conscious perception. It is the aligning and merging of these two states that has precipitated the desired results, literally causing a fertilizing effect on her imagination. In the human reproductive cycle, the sperm itself must grow from a nascent to more mature state before it is ready to be released and "capacitated," that is, has the potential to fertilize an egg. Further growth of the mature sperm is retarded while it remains suspended in semen in the male body.

Whereas Niki's source image has gained in dimension and grown in complexity, it has not yet attained maturity. Rather, much like the sperm, it has reached a potent state of activity in an ongoing chain of developmental stages; it is currently ready to be released and become a link in a chain of even more vital, complex reproductive events. I mentioned earlier that this drawing represented a turning point. Unless Niki continues to take risks and make a concentrated effort to break out of old restrictions, both on a personal and creative level, her source image, like the sperm suspended in the male body, will (without losing its potency) become dormant. Although more fully developed than before, it will rest at a seminal point of evolution.

In reviewing the piece once more, you can perceive the peculiar shape of the wings of the bird. Three of the flaming teardrops are attached to the body and are formed like this:

FIGURE 49

The feminine, petal-like shape is reminiscent of the paisley design, a Middle Eastern symbol originally representing a flowering plant. A fourth drop, positioned slightly above the other three, appears in the shape of a seed-spark:

FIGURE 50

It is difficult to pinpoint whether the seed-spark is flying into and merging with the bird, or out of and away from it. In either instance we are witnessing a release of energy in potent manifestation. In all likelihood the seed-spark—whether flying upward and outward, or downward and inward—carries new life; in its most recent incarnation the source image reveals that Niki's image of herself as a woman and her emerging identity as an artist are at a critical point. This opening, like Julia's awakening, intersects with a moment of spiritual enlightenment; in Christian iconography the descending dove symbolizes the presence of the Holy Spirit and is associated with the celebration of Pentecost. Through her creativity Niki has gained direct access to an illuminating force within her that is as divine and regenerating as it is magical and whimsical.

After completing this piece Niki continued to draw mythical animals, beings and landscapes in pastels. Gradually, however, she began to experiment with new media, producing a series of collages and paintings in watercolors and acrylics. As her creative style changed, so too did her social life and job. She began working more frequently as a free-lance illustrator. No longer as inhibited about speaking in public, she began teaching a class on the writing and illus-trating of children's stories. Eager to make new acquaintances, she also became active in the antinuclear movement. Perhaps most important, she began working in her studio more often, enjoying herself and feeling at ease there.

Almost another year passed. Although still somewhat shy and insecure about her abilities, Niki was pleased with the progress she was making. Though she sometimes felt depressed and discouraged, her outlook on life was improv-ing. The image of the wave transformed into a swan with wings of fire and gold had prognosticated not only these changes but another important one as well; it signified Niki's growing desire to test her own wings, to wind down her association with the group and establish her independence. With the support and encouragement of the group, she readied herself over time for this step.

During this phase Niki brought an interesting collage to one of the meetings. Again we encounter a dramatic change in the wave image.

It is as if the woman in the center of the piece (Color Plate 17) had just emerged from the water. Droplets of moisture spray from her hair and about her body; she stands facing the light, head thrown back exuberantly, looking refreshed and renewed. Several pictures of Einstein surround her. Male and female, the vigor of youth and the wisdom of old age appear in sharp and complementary contrast.

The woman's hair, free and unfettered, flies back, swing-ing upward in the air, forming a large curve like that of the wave. Light shines through it, setting it aglow. The tips especially are translucent and look similar to spindrift blowing in the wind. Here, then, the images of hair, wave, wind and fire are superimposed. Like Aphrodite emerging from the ocean's foam, the woman seems reborn. Now the idea of creative movement within has merged with the idea of Niki's outer self. Getting in touch with the power of her instincts and intuition has altered her self-concept, releasing the im-aginative, playful child within her. The artist is revealed as

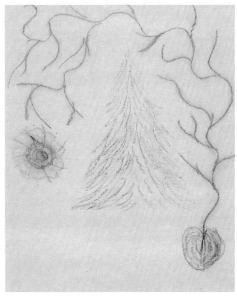

PLATE 1   *This drawing was made by a lawyer in his midthirties.*

PLATE 2   *A physical therapist, a woman in her early forties, drew this response to the exercise.*

PLATE 3   *One of a series of first attempts by the author.*

PLATE 4   *This vivid drawing was made by a woman, an engineer in her twenties.*

PLATE 5 *In consecutive sequence (hidden congruence)*

PLATE 6 *Juxtaposed*

PLATE 7 *Superimposed*

PLATE 8   *In consecutive sequence*

PLATE 9   *Juxtaposition*

PLATE 10   *Superimposition*

PLATE 11   *Superimposition*

PLATE 12 *(left) In this first piece, the wave appears in seminal outline as markings on the bark of the tree.*

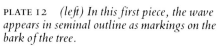

PLATE 13 *(right) The image of the wave begins to emerge with more clarity. Notice the water splashing against the rock.*

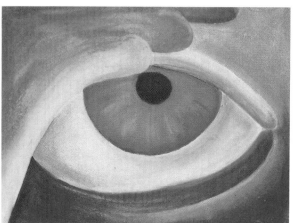

PLATE 14 *(left) The wave emerges more fully as a brilliant red-orange form to the left of the painting.*

PLATE 15   (right) Now the wave assumes
even more dramatic form, its shape
dominating the entire piece.

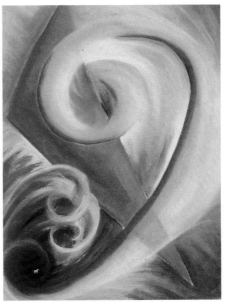

PLATE 16   (left) In this painting the wave
undergoes an important change. It takes on
the shape of a large floating swan.

PLATE 17   (right) Again
the wave undergoes a
metamorphosis. Its form
and its presence are
suggested in the sweep of
the woman's hair flying in
the wind.

PLATE 18 *(left) Every time the image changes shape it gains a new layer of meaning. In this underwater scene perhaps we are seeing the wave from a new perspective.*

PLATE 19 *(right) We may imply the presence and power of the wave even in this peaceful seashore scene.*

PLATE 20 *(left) Like many other clients Niki is discovering that creativity is an important means for expressing her feelings.*

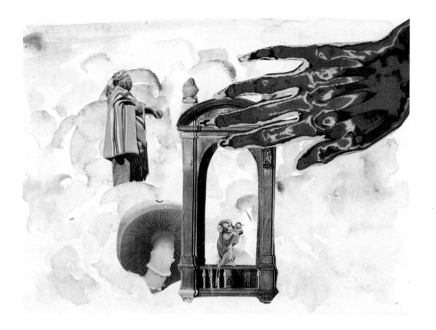

PLATE 21 *Learning to appreciate her creativity has also opened a new level of spiritual awareness in Niki. There is a mystical feeling to the imagery in this piece.*

PLATE 22 *The artist has created a special hand to act as a bookmark. Like the fingers of a magician, those of the artist also mystify, causing us to see amazing things.*

PLATE 23   *These are pages from one of the magic books of the author, who finds much refreshment in contemplating the images within its pages.*

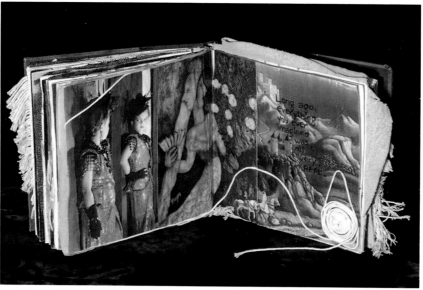

PLATE 24   *The words on the right-hand side of the book read, "Long ago, everything you ever imagined was all very real." The poet García Lorca writes, "I will go very far to ask…the Lord to give me back my ancient soul of a child."*

woman, the woman is revealed as artist. Inner feeling and outer expression are one.

If Niki once had a self-destructive tendency, she now shows a healthy instinct for self-preservation; the female figure, rejuvenated and full of vitality, stands forth in praise of life. Creativity is helping Niki to feel in better balance with the world around her; she senses her rapport with the natural elements, and it uplifts her. Just as Einstein symbolizes a genius for grasping the natural laws of the universe, so Niki is beginning to trust a natural order within her, one that reflects a universal predilection toward evolution.

The wave has come to symbolize creative movement for Niki. At first she hoped to experience greater movement in her artwork. Now she realizes that taking risks with her creativity has precipitated greater movement in her life as well. Prior to her encounter with the group, Niki had lacked inspiring adult role models in her life. Her father, a remote, somewhat passive figure, had not been very supportive either as a parent or spouse, although he enjoyed outstanding success in his career. Niki's mother, who had a poor self-image and a drinking problem, was depressed and resented her role as wife and mother. Consequently, Niki grew up thinking that men were smarter and more effective than women. Afraid to express her emotions, she shared a prejudice common to many, believing that being sensitive necessarily implied being irrational, that being in touch with her emotions meant being out of control. To be smart and rational she had to hold her feelings in check.

Niki had learned to distrust her feminine instincts. Now she is beginning to appreciate the beauty, power and intelligence of her emotions. She's letting go of the old negative head trip and coming to recognize the genius of woman. The upper right-hand corner of the picture of the woman (in the center of the piece) overlaps with one of the pictures of Einstein, intersecting exactly with one of his eyes. Niki will no longer view herself from a self-diminishing viewpoint; rather, she will prize both her mental faculties and her feelings, seeing them as but differing aspects of one intelligence.

THE MAGICAL FLIGHT

Having accomplished many of her initial goals, Niki was preparing to leave the group when she learned she had breast cancer. Just at a point when she was beginning to feel on top of things perhaps for the first time, life seemed to have dealt her an unfair blow. She decided to stay on longer because she felt she needed support to weather the crisis. Instead of fighting the anger and depression the news occasioned, she made a choice to put her feelings to work for her and to vent them in a creative way, using her imagination to help her maintain as optimistic an attitude as possible. Her courage and new values were being put to an acid test.

The next piece (Color Plate 18) is part of a series of collages and paintings she produced while dealing with her anxiety and undergoing treatment for the disease. It depicts Niki's struggle to maintain a positive outlook on her situation despite her despair over the setback.

Here we encounter a wave not of light but of darkness. We are dealing with the appearance of things below the surface, for this is an underwater scene. If before Niki felt she was riding the crest of a wave, now she seems submerged beneath one. A strand of air bubbles traced in silver reminds us of the presence of the vibrant woman surrounded by droplets of water in the previous piece. A cooked fish and boiled lobster claw dominate the foreground. A lamppost rises from just behind the claw, piercing the layer of darkness in the upper right-hand corner of the picture.

There is an interesting use of boundaries and edges: the fin of the large fish dangles off the collage, the lamppost also rises over the edge of the watercolor portion, connecting it with the black paper which has been torn and pasted onto the painting. It is almost as if Niki had deliberately produced a less than perfect piece—wanting to overstep, even break, some rules. There's a touch of defiance in this work. Instead of succumbing to a sense of defeat, becoming passive in the face of adversity, Niki is pushing her limits, struggling to keep her art alive. Just as images in the picture spill off one field and merge with another, so are differing directions in her life mingling and mixing with each other. Is she moving forward or back, will she live or die? Is there hope in the face of affliction? The lamppost burns in the deep; the creatures swimming underwater are cooked; does anything make sense after all?

Like someone swimming in the ocean who has been caught and pulled under by a wave, Niki feels disoriented. There is a hidden congruence between the fin of the fish (demarcated by a straight silver line), the silver antennae of the lobster, and the lamppost (outlined in silver on one side). Each of these elongated shapes represents a different kind of conduit for energy: the fin helps guide and propel the fish through space; the antennae transmit sensation; the pole carries electrical current. Niki is frightened. She's stabbing about in the dark, attempting to guide herself through and beyond her feeling of panic. In confronting the fear of death, she's not at all sure whether the disease will overpower her. Is it worth the fight, or is her "goose" already cooked?

Using the Source Imagery tools, Niki is accessing an unconscious reservoir of humor and irony. In order to regain her balance she will have to lighten up her attitude. Those circles might represent bubbles of laughter that are welling up over the absurd tragedy, or tears that are spilling over at the tragic absurdity. The silver lines represent special conduits; they symbolize the magical power of brush strokes. During her first stage of development Niki learned how to let go creatively, to let images spontaneously well up in her and to express them freely. Now—even while staying in touch with that spontaneity—she is deliberately playing with images to evoke a specific effect. She is wielding her paintbrush more consciously than ever before, yet less self-consciously than when she was inhibited by her performance anxiety. There is a paradoxical correlation between her willingness to take her creativity more seriously and her efforts to lighten up her approach.

Now she is going to deal with herself and her scary situation with the same light touch. A paintbrush may be implied in the presence of the lamppost. The ability to paint about her experience acts as a beacon; her brush is a magical conduit that helps her reach down into her depths to find the guidance and strength she needs while dispelling the shadows of uncertainty. Because she has learned to play fearlessly and intelligently with her images, Niki has earned the right to take her art more seriously.

Thus, the dark wave may not represent a threatening

force; it might stand for the realm of the unconscious. Niki has gained a respect for the power of the unconscious mind as a source of inspiration. Can she utilize her newfound trust in its mysterious energy to guide her in ways she might not have thought possible?

The lamppost, inasmuch as it symbolizes Niki's faith in the creative process and the unconscious mind, stands for more than a paintbrush; it's like an electrical antenna with the capacity to receive as well as transmit. In the past, Niki tended to get caught in the clutches of depression. She kept her anger and fear inside. This time her rage almost reached the boiling point. Yet, because now she had an outlet for her feelings, an outlet that could help her understand them, she was not held prisoner in the old trap. Instead of immobilizing her, the anger has energized her. The red tip of the lobster's claw seems to touch the end of the pole; the contact signifies that her anger is empowering Niki toward constructive action.

At about the same time Niki produced this piece, she decided to participate in a workshop conducted by Dr. Bernard Siegel, who employs visualization techniques to help people deal with life-threatening diseases. Niki was determined to put her faith in the healing power of the unconscious mind to work. As I mentioned earlier, she brought her painting materials into the hospital with her. She knew that as long as she kept her spirits up, her chances of achieving positive results were improved. During her stays in the hospital she maintained a healthy attitude by using her imagery and her painting to vent her frustration and to keep herself on track.

Niki came to see her fate as a challenge, not a cross. The cancer that threatened to eat her body became food for thought; she did not permit it to feed a depression. Just prior to the crisis Niki had begun to feel on top of things. The threat to her physical well-being shook her self-confidence. But mobilizing her inner and outer resources in such a single-minded manner has had a galvanizing effect; now Niki feels *in charge*. She has learned not only how to survive being tossed about by life's largest breakers; she's mastering the art of riding them.

One other important theme occurs in this last piece. Just as human beings have an instinctive urge to parent biologically, so do they want to propagate in a more spiritual sense.

We could view our images as spiritual offspring, a special offering to the universe. Images are like seeds containing the imprint of our personalities as surely as our children carry our genes. This idea may be expressed in a person's artwork by means of a small reiterated form, like the silver circles ascending in a line toward the top of Niki's piece. The little air bubbles could be like eggs hatched from the body of the fish before it died; to this extent they might symbolize Niki's unconscious awareness that through her creativity she can transcend the limits of mortality no matter how brief her life.

In my work I have come to recognize sharply delineated vertical (or horizontal) stripes and lines as symbolic representations of psychological limits and/or of a person's desire to push through limits to a new plateau of self-realization. In this piece we notice that the fish is headed in the direction of the vertical post. Niki is pushing through the barrier to self-expression that the threat of death has posed, to reach serenity on the other side.

Niki's world view has changed. The waves she has dreamt about, the waves she has painted and the figurative one she has ridden have brought her to a new place in life. Over several months she successfully completed her treatment at the hospital and began working full-time as a free-lance illustrator and book editor. She had realized her original ambition without returning to school for further professional training, but she had been willing to work hard on many other levels. Now her extended effort was bearing fruit. Once again she prepared to leave the group.

The next piece (Color Plate 19) was brought in during that period. Like Plate 13, it is a collage and watercolor painting. Its imagery reflects her new attitude:

The scene is peaceful. A woman, sitting beneath a flame-colored umbrella, rests on the beach with a male companion near the water's edge. A bird flies overhead. To the left, a large bird-of-paradise flower extends out into space from an empty picture frame, as if from a window. Slightly above it and to the right, several children peer out of an open window from beneath a half-drawn shade. A large urn appears in the lower left corner, and a giant strawberry lies in the foreground to the right. We see many old themes repeated—the water, the flower, the red-orange colors, the white bird—and some new ones—the strawberry, the urn and the frame. Why do familiar images keep recurring even as new ones appear?

On an extended trip, a person often takes a few familiar items provided they don't take up too much room. He might bring a favorite pillow, a picture or a candle holder. The objects vary from person to person and often have more sentimental than material worth; their value has grown over time and exists in the eye of the beholder. They provide a sense of comfort and continuity. Although such a collection might be small, it carries with it the atmosphere of home, reinforcing the idea that home consists as much of *a feeling environment* as it does a specific location.

The traveler will also cull new objects from the things he has acquired on a trip and add them to his growing collection. These carry with them not the connotation of home but the flavor of certain places and events he wants to remember. They are valuable because they represent feelings aroused when he traveled, perhaps to places he may never see again. Eventually the collection of things from home and souvenirs of travel join, becoming a large container that holds the memories of subjective experience within a series of objective forms.

Psychic images fulfill a similar function. My clients often describe their creative opening in terms of a journey or inner voyage of self-discovery. While the body is the vehicle by which we travel through life, it is a finite container for experience. The urge to find a lasting vessel in which to pack our experience of reality is innate. We, like the traveler, have images reminding us of "home" as we pass through time and space on our "trip" toward the unknown. In this sense home refers to important relationships, the emotional and physical environment we like to create around us, and major experiences we have had in the past. And along the way we collect new "images" that record important relationships and experiences we are now encountering.

No matter how economic in his use of space, a traveler needs something into which to pack the items reflecting his journey. Developing a creative outlet is the means whereby we fashion this container. It is a process that takes time. Even accomplished artists find they feel awkward when it comes to dealing with more and more complex images. But like the traveler who occasionally misses a connection, we must find the fortitude to keep on going even when we feel we might have missed the boat.

Once we have made a commitment to casting our images into form, we have embarked on a special voyage and begin a selection process. What images will we take, and what new ones will we add? Unlike the mere traveler, we don't have a permanent suitcase. We have to keep fabricating one to accommodate our changing needs. A major purpose that unblocking creativity served for Niki was to enable her to make a more suitable container for the important images in her growing collection. She wanted keepsakes of her inner voyage. An instinctive awareness of her art as a container for this experience is transmitted by means of the urn in the lower left corner of the picture.

Niki has discovered that being creative fills a critical need in the psyche. Surrounding ourselves with the images we have come to prize gives us a sense of continuity, helping us feel at home and at peace with ourselves. It is as important for us to devise a container to hold them as it is to have a place in which to live.

When Niki learned of her disease, it was as if she had received an eviction notice. The threat of death compelled her to make a move. Just as a person who is moving sorts through his belongings, Niki reviewed her life's history, sifting through her experience to determine exactly those things that she most wanted to keep. The overwhelming fear that she would lose all had swept over Niki like a dark wave. Yet in this tranquil scene, it is as if the storm had passed, as if the currents had borne her away to a safe place. Here there are no mighty breakers, only the gentle lapping of the tide against the shore. Once again the face of Niki's wave has changed; her vision of its underside has altered her perspective of reality. In the quiet light of day, Niki has a chance to see what treasure was stirred from the deep and swept ashore. Her picture has a contemplative quality, reflecting this need of hers to take stock and rest.

Because it forced her to turn her attention inward, the crisis has had a cleansing effect; more consciously than ever before, Niki used her creativity to get in touch with feelings and images that would help her maintain her emotional balance and find peace of mind. In this extremity she made an important discovery: her creativity represented more than a means of self-expression. The power of inner concentration that she had begun to cultivate by using her imagination came to her aid, offering a surprising avenue of escape; inside she came in contact with a timeless well of inspiration, which refreshed and restored her. For a moment, even within the midst of turmoil, things stood still. Being creative helped her find anchor and a spiritual resting place, precipitating a change in perspective that is reflected in the overall tone of the scene at the beach.

Creativity represents an innate capacity we each have to enter—at will—an altered state of consciousness similar to the one we might entertain on an ideal day at the ocean. The elements seem to conspire to relax and refresh us. Time stands still before the endless movement of waves on the shore, the flight of birds overhead; the rhythmic interplay of wind, water, sand and marine life seems to have gone on forever. And we know it will endure long after we die. For a moment within time, we are not disturbed by its flow but surrender to it in trust. In accord with the will of nature, we experience peace of mind. In that altered state which is so akin to creativity, time moves and stands still all at once. Like a bird airborne, we pause in magical flight beyond time's reach and glide suspended over the uneven terrain of life, uplifted by the coexistence of two realms of being, the physical and the transcendent.

As Niki began to rely on her creativity as a source of guidance and inspiration, new horizons opened to her; though a captive within the realm of time she felt free, no longer subject to its weight. Like a bird released from a cage, her spirits rose. Being creative linked her to a source of power and energy that helped her transcend the limits imposed on her by the thought of death. This spiritual experience is reflected in the wave turned into a calm tide. Whatever storm should pass upon the surface, Niki has found a harbor, one she has created for herself, in which she may take refuge and find peace.

I mentioned that the traveler needs a container for his collection of objects. On her voyage Niki has learned that her creativity offers a spiritual container for experience. Her artwork defines the boundaries of an inner home, is a measure of the feeling environment in which she best functions and grows. Just as a person needs the privacy of his physical space, so he needs the solitude that a creative space gives him. Within the invisible walls of this retreat he gains access to spiritual resources that help him reframe his perspective of reality in a positive light.

We admire the self-reliant traveler his economic mode of living; he carries everything he needs with him wherever he goes. Someone who has begun to frame a more spiritual outlook for himself by means of his creativity carries his home on his back, too; his sense of self is more complete than before. Equipped with special tools, he can build a private space whatever the outer circumstances.

To be self-contained in this way gives a person a feeling of independence. Through her work in the group, Niki has become more self-reliant. Like an architect, she has the knowledge to build spaces not only within physical dimensions but in spiritual ones as well.

Niki places a high value on her ability to feel self-contained. Several images in the piece convey this idea. Beneath the unlimited expanse of sky, the man and woman rest on a large white blanket; like an empty canvas, it delineates the self-contained space of the artist, who resting on nature's shore is inspired to new design. The two window frames suspended in air symbolize her capacity to reframe reality, giving shape to a creative vision she fashions with her own two hands.

The image of the umbrella is interesting; small, fragile, its color is a bright red-orange like that of the flower, which we know has come to symbolize Niki's love of painting. Despite the insignificance of its size, the umbrella is a valuable device offering the couple temporary shelter from the sun. It is easily carried from place to place. Likewise, Niki's small paintbrush is a powerful instrument, helping her define a space of her own. It is the primary means by which she expresses her creativity, and an ingenious device for transporting herself from one emotional clime to another, affording shelter and protection. Niki, who has come to more fully recognize the temporary nature of life, realizes how important this spiritual mobility is; she knows that any space she inhabits defines but a momentary resting place for the spirit.

A visit to an exotic new place whets the appetite of the avid traveler. A spiritual traveler, Niki's thirst for experience cannot be quenched. The images of the flower extending outward into space, its petals open like the eager fingers of a giant hand; of the large urn waiting to be filled; and of the children peering from the window eager to go outside transmit to the viewer the idea that although she feels self-contained, the artist is more open to life than before.

This paradoxical state of being open and closed raises another question. The children gaze out from under a half-drawn shade, the flower leans half out of the window, the woman sits half exposed, half covered by the umbrella; that is, what appears to be outside is partially inside, and that which is inside is likewise partially outside. What does this dual state of being mean?

Unblocking her creativity has helped to establish a better rapport between Niki's unconscious and conscious mind. There is a greater integration in her life. That which she produces bears the stamp of her imagination, and her imagination is continually stimulated anew by what she experiences in the world. The integrity of Niki's work lies in this harmonious blending of inner with outer reality. Like a traveler who has settled in a foreign land, Niki has created imagery that acts as a bridge to bring two worlds together, gradually fusing them; thus, her images exist simultaneously in a realm half inside and half outside herself.

The images reflect parts of Niki's being just as any one of nature's elements reflects nature's whole essence. As nature endlessly shapes substance into form, so does Niki incline toward giving form to her experience. The hand of the artist within is an extension of nature's, continually giving rise to life even as it disappears. Niki's wave reflects the power of nature's *infinite activity* and of the artist in rapport with it.

But where did this image originate? Like consciousness itself, the source is difficult to pinpoint. Just as the world has come into being through the dynamic interplay of natural forces in the cosmos, so did the wave come into being through such forces at work in the psyche.

During the voyage, more than one change of consequence has transpired; as a result, Niki's conscious will *to be creative* has become integrated with an unconscious will *to create*. Her new piece celebrates this wedding of purpose. The figures of the man and woman resting together on the sand represent the coupling of the male and female sides of the psyche. The marrying of their physical forms, in either explicit sexual terms or implicit romantic ones, often depicts such a dynamic point of integration. There is a hidden congruence between the V shape made by the man's arm (bent at the elbow) resting on the sand; one of the woman's legs (which is also raised and slightly bent); and two of the flower petals, which seem to be both grasping onto and reaching beyond the window frame. This shape in Source Imagery stands for the presence of *creative tension;* the image of the flower itself for our attraction to nature. There is a natural urge for the release of creative tension in the psyche just as much as there is an instinctive urge to satisfy the sexual drive. Niki's paintbrush, symbolizing her attraction to her creativity, is the implement she employs to attain that end. Like the act of union between male and female, it has *integrative force* in her life, bringing seed images to birth, new forms into being.

The integration that the wedding of male and female depicts here implies a further idea. There is another hidden congruence in the piece. The figures of the man and woman seem small in comparison to the expanse of the coast around them. Similarly, although the flower itself appears quite large in comparison to the frame, the glimpse of sky which the window circumscribes is small in comparison to the expanse of horizon surrounding it. The juxtaposition of the small against the large physical elements in the scene highlights a juxtaposition of a more abstract nature; it points to the contrast between those elements in Niki's artwork that are of a personal nature and limited in scope, and those that are universal. This signifies that Niki knows her imagery has a twofold function: its ability to link her dynamically with her own unconscious creative processes, and its power to connect her with creative processes at work in the world at large.

The source image represents a vital link between differing levels of awareness within the psyche. It acts as a bridge, connecting a person's subjective and objective reality. Even while it reveals the importance of his own creative vision, it helps him accept and understand his insignificance within a larger design. The flower bursting through the frame suggests the great pride Niki is beginning to take in her work; if before, the flower had the power to spring right out of a rock, now the sky's the limit. But this is a respectful exuberance, giving vent to the sheer joy of achieving a breakthrough; it's not a sign of hubris. For what shines through and around the flower is open sky and sunlight, a scene depicting nature's handiwork, not that of the artist. Niki knows her imagery is the fruit not just of her own endeavor, but reflects the influence of a creative force ever at work in the world. She is at once the formed and the forming, the created and the creative, a vital link in a never-ending chain.

To the extent that Niki has gained a vision of her destiny, her anger has dissipated. She accepts her condition; more than that, she accepts the limits of the human condition itself. There are still voices inside that might subdue her enthusiasm, stirring up feelings of self-doubt; but now, if she chooses, she can use her insight to overcome their influence.

A luscious strawberry, ripe and tempting, lies in the foreground of the picture. It looks like a big heart or even a beach ball. Could those children be longing for food? Would they like to get out and play? Through her exposure to Source Imagery and her interaction with the group, Niki has grown to love the child inside her. She is in touch with its healthy, powerful instincts and realizes that to continue growing she will have to treat it with sensitivity, viewing it with a loving, tolerant eye. She will coax her imagination out into the open instead of keeping it inside.

In the group, Niki learned to trust others with her images. There they flourished in a supportive environment. Like seeds, her images needed to be planted in the right medium to grow. The strawberry is a fruit that bears its seeds boldly on the surface. Niki will need courage to continue bearing—and baring—the seeds of her heart in her painting. But, she knows these images will thrive if she remains playful and loving in her attitude.

The freed child in Niki infuses her artistic side with a sense of wonder and innocence. Before leaving the group, Niki brought a poem to share; she had transcribed it as a beautiful abstract watercolor, painted in soft, delicate hues similar to those in the last ocean scene:

> Listen to the wind
> It is free.
> It rattles the leaves
> And swishes the grasses.

It makes waves,
Small and delicate ones
To caress the shore,
Large gigantic ones
That change the face of the earth.
Listen to the wind, free,
Guiltless.

Once again we encounter the image of the wave. Here
it appears in invisible shape. It is neither a wave of sound
nor color; it is formless, composed of moving air. In the
poem, Niki has regained the stance of the proud, free woman
depicted in Plate 17 of the color insert. She feels in rapport
with the forces of nature, especially that of the wind. Like
time—whose influence we feel but whose presence we cannot
see—the wind moves constantly over the face of the earth,
an unseen entity known only by its effect.

Upon the ocean's surface, stirred by the invisible force
of the wind, waves appear and disappear in rhythmic sequence, rising up and falling back into the depths. A poem
is created by the rhythmic interplay of waves of sound and
moments of silence. In Niki's mind, the whole earth is like
God's palette, an endless ocean of color and ever-changing
forms, rising up and returning to an unknown source of
being.

Niki, poised like a bird in flight, listens to the wind.
Her creative movement, directed by instinct, follows a natural
course. The strokes of her brush are unselfconscious and
rhythmic, reflecting the power of nature to render intelligent
design. In this innocence there is no resistance. There is but
cooperative intent, a spontaneous spirit of co-creativeness.

Niki's magical flight through the universe is reflected in
the images she leaves behind. Like a sculptor who fashions
a mold, whatever she creates makes a lasting impression.
Psychic images leave more than one kind of impression in
their wake; imprinted in consciousness, they become part of
an invaluable archive, recording the history of a soul as it
evolves in a procession of ever-changing forms.

17

≈≈≈≈≈≈≈≈≈≈≈≈≈≈≈≈≈≈≈

The Cosmic Chameleon

THE BRIDGE

Niki's case illustrates how a source image develops over time, stimulating and reflecting changes in a person's life. In an earlier chapter I explained how any one image is continually transformed through superimposition into a more comprehensive manifestation of itself; I called this more fully realized form the "meta-image." Just as Niki's wave was already present in the wavy lines demarcating the bark on the tree in the first drawing, so is a future wave contained in nascent form within the image of her last piece. The meta-image is always in a state of becoming; thus, as the source image evolves, it is as if a new facet were being cut on this larger entity of which it is a part. Although we may not perceive the meta-image as a construct in and of itself, its growing luster inspires us. Like a jeweler who works with but doesn't own his gems, we never possess the object we are so patiently fashioning. Yet, the greater the degree of energy we expend in working on it, the higher the value with which the object is endowed. The emergence of the source image happens within the framework of this all-embracing, ongoing dynamic process. It is an intrinsic part of a psychic feedback system the aim of which is to precipitate further creative growth.

It is difficult to pinpoint which factor was the primary

causative agent in the chain reaction of creative events I've described up to this point. Did the source image stimulate the growth of Niki's talent, or did the developing of her talent stimulate its occurrence? And did psychological change precipitate her creativity, or was it just the reverse?

The question is difficult to resolve. Ultimately, the origin of the source image is mysterious. Whether or not we choose to discover and access the energy they contain, these images represent essential keys that help us open and express our creativity. Their spontaneous occurrence in the work of my clients indicates to me that we each possess a repository of such fascinating images; it's like a psychic bank account we are born with that we can choose to draw upon whenever we like.

I believe their presence implies a universal predilection for creativity. Any individual who so desires can become more creative by actively tapping into his unconscious image-making resources. The supply of material there is unlimited. It is as instinctive an inclination to want to wake up and be creative as it is to fall asleep and dream.

In describing Niki's work I have tried to show how intimately connected her artistic development was to her growing understanding and appreciation of the images she was producing. The two processes could not be separated from one another. It is my contention that familiarity with our inner image-making process stimulates and advances creative self-expression more effectively than technical training.

The rearranging of priorities was essential for setting into motion the natural chain reaction of psychic events we observed in Niki's imagery. Her case illustrates that to the extent an individual can become more literate about the meaning and nature of his imagery, he can begin to give it more creative expression. Being able to read the messages the image contains increases the active vocabulary of the imagination, just as reading literature enriches the mind. The more we can see in what we produce, the more we produce to see.

When interpreting the imagery in Julia's piece, I mentioned how closely related the opening of our creativity is to stimulating our sexuality. In Niki's case we see that a creative opening may precipitate a quickening of spiritual awareness.

Our understanding of the nature of the source image will help us better grasp the connection between creative and spiritual self-realization.

A person can, of course, derive pleasure from creative activity without concerning himself with this dimension of meaning, just as he can participate in the sexual act without special concern for the emotional content of the relationship. Nevertheless, the opportunity for such an experience exists as a natural extension of the moment. The idea of a relationship helps describe what it is that exists between a person and his source image. Niki's image kept growing and stimulating creative and spiritual change because she maintained a commitment, an ongoing dialogue with it. The integrity of her intent to continue fostering that special relationship had a healing impact on her life.

How is it that the source image becomes a vehicle for a spiritual experience? Earlier I defined the concept of an organizing principle by using the example of a house, whose structure evolves in a certain orderly sequence. The source image evolves in a similar way. Although it is difficult to pinpoint exactly when, where and in what form it might occur, the source image generally appears at first in fragmentary shape as part of a drawing, dream or conscious visual fantasy. At each occurrence its intent and design becomes more clearly defined. Its evolution, prompted by mysterious forces in the psyche, reflects a coherent order and consistent logic.

In examining the evolution of Niki's wave, we saw how it changed shape at each occurrence, undergoing rapid, dramatic transmutations (as, for example, when it turned into a swan). With each transformation it gradually gained a new layer of meaning, attaining greater significance. As it did so, it became more highly charged. Even when it assumed an invisible shape as the wind in the poem, the wave evoked powerful memories of its previous incarnations. We no longer needed to see the wave in physical form to remember all the meaning it had accrued. Like a musical phrase that reminds us of an entire symphony, a few words evoked an entire procession of organized psychic events.

Niki's wave unfolded in a certain chronological order. We can date when each drawing or painting was made. You will recall that images keep a record of events in chronological sequence. Yet, if we pause for a moment and review Niki's images, we can perceive within any one drawing intimations of both past and future waves. Each single occurrence of the wave is inextricably wedded to the whole, the emerging meta-image. The wave no longer simply moves forward on a horizontal line from the past toward the future; it simultaneously oscillates on a vertical axis that is time-transcendent, containing aspects of the past, present and future.

Imagine, for a moment, someone who hears a familiar phrase from a favorite piece of music. He eagerly anticipates sounds he knows are to come. He recalls with pleasure the many times he's enjoyed listening to the piece. His past, present and future experience of the music intermingle. That phrase, which he might hear at three twenty-five on a Friday afternoon, is part of his larger experience of the piece, an experience that cannot be limited to its expression in the present.

The source image is analogous to the phrase, the meta-image to the entire piece of music; the former represents but a single point on an invisible continuum of change. In that the source image unfolds within an orderly sequence of timed events, it is part of an evolutionary process and is a time-oriented manifestation; inasmuch as it is part of a less visibly definable design, it is to an equal extent a time-transcendent phenomenon.

As we examined Niki's work we noticed that even as the image of the wave changed its structural components, the essential identifying characteristics—the colors blue and white, the idea of water, the theme of fire, or the large curve—kept recurring. No matter what form the wave temporarily assumed, these characteristics cropped up with the regularity of a recurring melodic phrase in a jazz improvisation. Whatever creative pattern Niki might weave, it is as if there were a psychic armature acting as a support. The image, constantly in a state of flux, always took shape or was flashed out around a few highly flexible elements. At each new incarnation it represented a subtle blending of the old with the new.

In this manner, that which is outworn is constantly shed but never discarded. As nature herself keeps reworking the substance of which she is composed, creativity helps us rework our own substance. Picture a cross section of the planet Earth. Its outermost crust keeps shifting and changing while multiple layers of compacted substrata reveal events transpiring below the surface over aeons. That which takes place on the uppermost level, or in the present, is but one component in a picture of change that is coming into view through evolution.

When discussing the living glyph, I explained that creative images integrate conscious with unconscious awareness. And, like the core sample, they contain a historical record, transmitting in a single moment intelligible messages in coded, compacted form. Their careful analysis can prognosticate the possibility for change in the future based on patterns of change that have occurred in the past.

Whereas any psychic image is a complex composite of material, the source image singles itself out in one important regard. Just as a person can examine a specific point on the earth, he can investigate, through the source image, a special place in consciousness. It is a cross section of psychic substrata, revealing the potential of his evolving creativity.

Through the special intelligence it contains, the source image can help each of us move in a creative direction uniquely suited to us. A person can be inspired by the works of great artists, but the only means for transporting himself to his own creativity lies buried deep in the psyche.

By developing our source image, we can be carried not only to a creative place in consciousness but to an awareness that is spiritually uplifting. Jung's concept of the archetype advanced the notion that certain symbols are common to the species, that they form a link between cultures and generations of man. Even as they undergo transmutations, they nevertheless contain timeless truths.

Just as we inherit a reservoir of collective archetypes, I believe we also have a repository of personal ones. Certain symbols in the individual's consciousness seem to act as timeless beacons in the mind, guiding him toward creative fulfillment while disclosing knowledge perhaps gleaned over lifetimes of experience.

Being creative is a birthing process whereby that which was of value in the past is cast into new form, bringing evidence of a continuity of individual consciousness. Within the meager, pliable boundaries of a symbolic framework, the source image condenses our impressions into a space as small as a microchip. There are endlessly fascinating bytes of information it can yield to the open mind.

It is as if there were a mysterious intelligence at work helping to filter out the nonessential while keeping what is of lasting value. Within the limited span of one lifetime we can perceive the condensing process at work; in Niki's case we saw an increasing amount of information being compressed into the image of the wave. From this point on, the simple word "wave" has the power to transmit to her the recollection of a critical period in her life. It will remind her of how she met the challenge of a life-threatening disease by utilizing the spiritual resources of her creativity.

Just where is the "wave" we are referring to here? In what realm does it exist? As an active figment of Niki's imagination, it is no less real for its invisibility. Quite a trick, this—the capacity to pack so much into so little. If there exists for Niki a wedge in space and time through which her hard-won knowledge might slip, this is just the size and kind of shape it must assume to do so. If psychic images are zodiacal suitcases, the source image is a cosmic chameleon. It may be difficult at times to see, but it is always there. And I suggest it has the ability to carry upon its powerful but slippery little back news that death does not erase.

The source image can span time and space in consciousness, helping a person actively integrate differing levels of awareness. One might speculate that Niki had precognitive awareness of how important the creative act was becoming for her. In the next piece (Color Plate 20), produced months before she learned she had cancer, she already seemed to sense that her source image had the power to help propel her from a dark place in consciousness to a lighter, more life-affirming one.

Within this context the source image represents a point where inner reality and outer experience combine to further spiritual growth; it is an individual procreative act transpiring below the threshold of awareness, as spontaneous and automatic as breathing. Whether or not a person is attuned to its presence, it makes its appearance felt with as irrepressible a regularity as the urge to mate. It may take on as unassuming a form as the decorative design selected for a placemat, or the imposing shape of a striking painting. The question is not so much how, but when and why the source image arrives.

The connection our source image sets up between an unconscious and conscious creative process acts as a bridge, joining these realms of experience in such a way that the individual is provoked to cross barriers inhibiting self-expression. By virtue of the pathway it clears, it precipitates an evolution in personal growth that is metaphysical in nature.

THE ARCH

While a source image spans differing realms of consciousness within a given lifetime, it has an even more far-reaching function. It has the capacity to carry great weight without bending beneath the strain. Like an archway whose strength derives as much from the manner as from the material of its construction, the source image, because of its unique design, disperses energy as it contains it. Its character enables it to act as a causeway, joining vastly disparate memories. Past, present and future coalesce within its symbolic shape, helping to make sense of what otherwise might appear to be a disconnected, meaningless series of events.

The source image is a mystical arch or threshold opening up a space in consciousness through which the self may pass on knowledge to the selves that have come before and will come after. It is a psychic loophole in time, providing an opportunity for a creative exchange.

In another collage, produced with subconscious perspicacity in the period before she left the group, Niki again indicated her intuitive grasp of the significance of the source image. (Color Plate 21.)

Like the skin and bones that support and define the boundaries of the artist's hand, the source image is an organizing principle that lends creative structure to human experience. Nature manifests her energy in a multitude of ever-evolving forms; we, as an extension of nature, also manifest our energy in a variety of evolving forms. To be creative means to jockey ourselves into conscious alignment with the creative principles at play in the universe. The same force that impels the colors of sunrise informs the bristles of the painter's brush, the fingers of the sculptor's hand.

We perceive the intelligence of nature in everything she creates, studying her phenomena under a microscope to better understand her workings. The heightened awareness of our relationship to the source image sheds light on the inner workings of the psyche and the metaphysics of existence. For Niki, defining the meaning of her source image from a spiritual as well as aesthetic perspective has helped to reshape her view of life.

Through the arch we can glimpse the outline of a statue. A sculptor creates contours through the power of conscious choice. Dealing with the source image has had a strong impact on Niki; if she lets the Inner Sculptor guide her, she also can make conscious choices that alter the contours of her experience. In the painting everything seems to be floating in a cloudlike aura similar to the nimbus drawn around the head of a saint. It is as if the hand of Niki's inner artist were raised to bestow a blessing on her work, helping her to give it the status it deserves.

Niki has begun to look through and beyond the physical outline of the image into its inner workings, perceiving its hidden spiritual significance. To the extent that she sees that creative expression is intimately connected to her spiritual growth, its stature is raised in her eyes. Artistic activity then assumes dimensions appropriate to the important role it plays in her life. She is empowered to re-establish priorities, not only *making* but *rearranging* things to accommodate the change.

Much as a child can quicken a deeper understanding of love in a parent's heart, so does the source image awaken spiritual awareness in the heart of its progenitor. Niki perceives in the progression of forms that have been evolving beneath her fingertips an intelligent consciousness at work, a consciousness that continually frees itself from that which contains it to uphold its integrity and maintain its independence. The looser her grip upon the finite form, the greater Niki's grasp of the enduring nature of its content. The artist who wields form by his will and the spiritual visionary who perceives a higher will within that form, together comprise an architect of destiny, one who builds his life by a divinely inspired design.

18

~~~~~~~~~~~~~~~~~~~~~~~~~~~~~~~~~~

The Magic Circle

ANGELA'S CIRCLE

As the biological child carries genetically coded information from the parent, so does the psychic child within each person carry special information concerning his creative destiny. Gaining access to this side of our personality is an essential part of freeing our artistic potential. The structural development of creativity along naturally ordained lines is dependent on the secret workings of this psychic coding system as much as the physical child's growth is dependent on genetics.

Within the work of the clients I have encountered—both professional artist and layperson alike—source images seem to manifest themselves frequently, if not always, unconsciously. Nonetheless, they have an important influence on the development of people's talents and personalities. Much like a plant that needs a supporting stick in order to blossom freely and mature, a person derives support from a source image in his life even if he, like the plant, does not have eyes to see it.

Moreover, even when made aware of its presence, a person often loses sight of it and is repeatedly surprised to find it reappearing as if of its own accord. Like the change within any growth process, that which the source image evokes arises imperceptibly but steadily. However, with hindsight we can perceive in clear sequence the stages of development it occasions. Just as we can observe the opening of a flower through the camera lens by means of time-lapse photography, we can perceive the dramatic unfolding of a source image by means of a visual overview.

In the next case, we can see how the artwork of a client named Angela evolves as the source image, a circle, undergoes a variety of transmutations.

FIGURE 51
Here the circle dominates the center of the painting.

FIGURE 52
The circle forms the eyes and mouth of a primitive mask.

FIGURE 53
In this playful piece the circle undergoes an interesting transmutation.

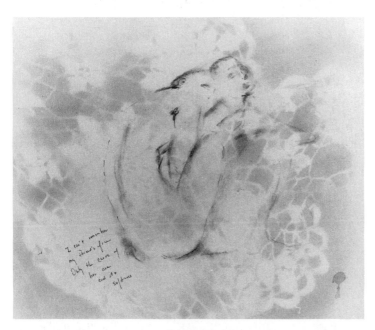

FIGURE 54
Here the figures of the two women are superimposed over the circle.

FIGURE 55

The superimposition becomes more complex.
Now the circle assumes the shape of the planets with their rings.

FIGURE 56

The client's paintings are becoming bolder.
The colors are exciting and dramatic.

FIGURE 57

To the right in this brilliant watercolor the circles appear again like eyes in the face of a totem.

FIGURE 58

In this black-and-white sketch the circle suddenly undergoes another dramatic change, turning into a chrysalis-like shape.

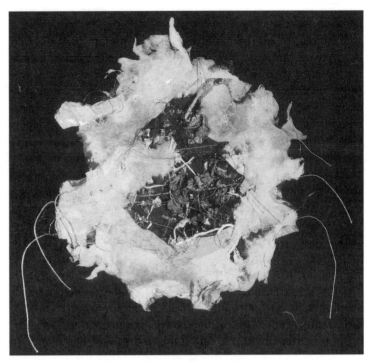

FIGURE 59

*From this point on, the client's work becomes increasingly original in design.
This beautiful circle was created in a paper-making workshop.*

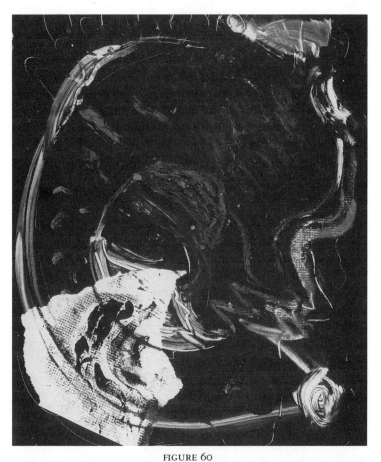

FIGURE 60

The client is experimenting with a wide variety of media. She especially likes making monoprints. A brilliant blue and bright red dominate in this piece.

Like Niki's wave, Angela's circle has clearly definable contours, but it is more abstract in nature. We know what a wave does. The word evokes an association with a specific physical phenomenon. Angela's circle doesn't "do" anything, nor does it evoke an association with one specific object; it is simply "there," a shape that keeps recurring in her artwork. Like the wave, it continually undergoes transmutations, ushering in with each mysterious turn of its psychic wheel a change in her consciousness as well as in her painting.

The examples of her work selected for illustrative purposes spanned just over four years. During that period Angela produced approximately two hundred sketches, paintings and collages. She and I often took note of how persistently the circular shape made its presence felt. At several points I suggested she paint a piece with this shape as the main focal point; it seemed we were acting in instinctive rapport with it. By periodically turning our attention toward it, we were adding a timely extension to the support stick of her creative growth.

A major goal Angela had set was to view herself as a professional artist. She felt handicapped because she lacked credentials. A single parent who worked as an editor to support herself and her teenage daughter, she found it impossible to enroll in school full-time. As Angela learned how to stroke her child side and gained inspiration from the exercises assigned, she grew more confident of her abilities; her artwork began to evolve in a manner similar to Niki's. Although Angela used the Source Imagery techniques to interpret her dreams and better understand the images in her artwork, she did not try to directly interpret the meaning of her source image. She simply acknowledged its presence, realizing it provided a special construction around which her talent might flesh itself out.

Just as Niki's image was examined, it would be possible, in retrospect, to analyze and interpret Angela's image, tracing the presence of the superimpositions and arriving at a deeper grasp of the changes occurring in her psyche. But in analyzing Niki's source image, I wanted to convey first and foremost the sources of such an image's high charge of energy. A person does not need to own his house to call it home; similarly, he doesn't need to "own" the meaning of a source image to recognize its function or to appreciate its value.

Angela wanted to see herself as a professional artist. By the time she had produced Figure 60 on page 237, Angela, like Niki, was at a dramatic turning point in her personal and creative growth. She was participating in various workshops, art and drawing classes, having finally decided that she didn't need to go to art school in order to qualify as an artist. Her productive intent and personal appreciation of her work were qualification enough. She is currently planning to enter her work in a competition.

It is interesting to note how the imagery in this piece reflects her significant change in outlook. The circle has evolved into a fetus-like shape. At the same time, it looks like a painter's palette. The source image has helped bring Angela's sense of herself as an artist to birth. Her personal growth and her creative development go hand in hand. Despite the personal nature of its content, the source image houses the objective unfolding of a talent with a validity and meaning of its own. A psychic building block, it has simultaneously effected change in Angela's consciousness as it has transformed her artwork.

When we view a source image, we are perceiving a place in consciousness as well as a space in reality. Through it we experience the fulfillment that integrating our inner and outer worlds can bring.

The case studies I've presented up to this point depict the emergence of such an image in a form easily recognized. I hope I have whetted your appetite and that you are ready to undertake the quest for your own source image. I wish I could encourage you by saying you could quickly pick it out. But it isn't all that easy; I've just supplied a few essential clues that will head you in the right direction.

Identifying a source image is part of a process in and of itself. Unless you are blessed with the intellect of Sherlock Holmes, the riddle can be irksome and resist quick resolution. In certain instances, it has taken years for me to perceive what the source image consists of in a client's work. That's why I want to emphasize the importance of creating an environment in which it can take root and grow. It will inevitably make its presence felt. But in the meantime, like me, you might have to stumble around the garden for a while in a state of blind faith until all at once the source image magically pops into view. It will stand there in your path with unabashed clarity, bright and unmistakable, like a lone yellow mushroom in a carpet of green moss. You won't miss it—for once you have solved the mystery, you will see that it casts a special light all its own.

VERA'S MOOSE

It is difficult to pinpoint a person's source image because often it is of a highly abstract nature, consisting of a constellation of shapes that, only when viewed in their entirety, form its contours. For example, in the following case I first felt convinced that the surprising and recurrent figure of the moose in Vera's work represented her source image.

FIGURE 61
The client drew this first piece in response to the tree, seed, and star exercise.

FIGURE 62

Her desire to integrate love of family ties with her creativity is reflected in this piece, her response to the bridge exercise.

FIGURE 63

She begins to open up, experimenting with a variety of media.

FIGURE 64

Once she loosens up, the client regains the love of drawing she had as a child.
The moose makes a startling entrance.

FIGURE 65

In this collage the head of the moose peers out at the viewer from behind branches.

FIGURE 66

The client's growing regard for her creativity and her desire for a spirit of community are reflected in this piece.

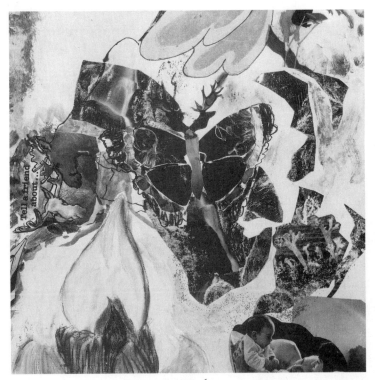

FIGURE 67

A butterfly with antlers instead of antennae dominates the center of this piece. The moose appears again to the left.

FIGURE 68

Nature imagery predominates in this collage. The figure of a leaping child symbolizes joy in natural expression.

FIGURE 69

The client experiences great release of feeling through her creativity.
Her style is becoming freer and dramatic.

FIGURE 70

The client produced this interesting collage in a workshop she helped to lead. She is combining her creativity with her counseling work. She appreciates the guiding force of images.

Then, with time and the perspective of an overview, I perceived that her source image consisted rather of a constellation of shapes that, when viewed as a whole, looked like this:

FIGURE 71

Looking back we can see the form already occurring in the first piece Vera presented, in which the shape of the entire drawing itself comprises the image (Figure 61).

Actually it was the shape of the antlers, not the animal itself, that more exactly coincided with the lines of Vera's source image. The antlers provided the clue that helped us perceive its presence. They represent one of the more crucial transmutations the source image underwent during an important phase of its evolution. Like a recurrent dream, the persistent moose had to knock on the door of our conscious mind several times before we recognized the purpose of its visit.

As we review the drawings and collages we see the image occurring in a variety of shapes and sizes: in the composite form of concrete and abstract shapes in the right-hand field in Figure 63, in the antlered butterfly with the abstract shapes surrounding it in Figure 67, in the shape of the leather pouch holding the mother's baby in Figure 68, in the combination of abstract forms at the bottom of Figure 69, in the cluster of feathers at the bottom of Figure 70, and elsewhere.

Always the image is a V-shaped form, whatever the thing or things that make up its content. There is a centripetal feeling to this source image, as if it had the capacity to draw its contents toward center, as opposed to Angela's image, which seemed to be building momentum away from center, expanding with centrifugal force.

We see the feeling of containment that the image exemplifies reflected in an early piece, Figure 62, Vera's response to the bridge exercise (described on page 281). In the lower left-hand corner of the piece there is a photograph taken of her and her younger son at his birth. Her hand and arm cradle the infant next to her breast. The edge of a coverlet, her hands and the naked body of the baby together make up the now-familiar V-shaped curve. Why didn't we recognize this image sooner?

Perhaps because the source image is a very personal thing. It fulfills a private as well as an aesthetic and suprapersonal function in our lives. Just as parenting serves the individual as well as the species, so does being creative serve a uniquely intimate as well as more impersonal role in development. That may be why it appears in veiled form at first, revealing itself to our eyes only when we are mature enough to handle it with sensitivity.

Vera, a pastoral counselor, is married and the mother of two boys. When she first entered the group, she voiced her desire not only to express her creativity but to somehow weave the many threads of her life together into an integrated whole. She sensed an integrity to the direction of her life, but somehow felt as if she were continually losing touch with it. Her various commitments appeared to conflict with one another; she felt disorganized, as if she couldn't make any headway even though she was always so busy. Despite her regular spiritual practice, her attention was repeatedly being pulled away from center.

As a natural extension of the creative exercises I gave her, Vera began to reorganize her activities, making and keeping agreements with herself to set her priorities straight. An active person with humanitarian interests, she gradually began cutting back on obligations that kept her from concentrating on what she valued most, her family relationships, her counseling work and developing her creativity and spirituality.

Gradually she felt a holistic theme entering her life. Those activities that nourished the growth of her inner self became the focus of attention. Her ability to discriminate between what was essential and nonessential grew. It was almost as if the time she spent sorting through the images in her artwork helped her to discriminate and organize things on other levels as well.

We can see this process reflected in the imagery and words of Figure 66, a picture Vera designed for a T-shirt midway through the group experience. One of the groups she was in planned to participate in a march around the Pentagon; she was commissioned by them to do this piece. It is striking how well her objective interest in a political cause and her subjective interest in her own creative development dovetail here.

The lower portion of the circle together with the figures of the older woman and the young girl form the outline of Vera's source image. The shape is repeated within the form of the yarn being held, in the curve of the elbows, in the V-shaped outline delineating the necklines of the tops both figures are wearing and in the shape of the child's ponytail; in short, it's everywhere.

The appearance of the young girl signifies the beginning of a major inner change. Vera had yearned to have another child, a daughter, but because she was in her forties the thought no longer seemed realistic. The idea had saddened her. Suddenly it became apparent that she wanted to nourish the creative child in her, turning as much attention toward it as she directed to others. In this regard, the picture represents a psychic milestone; Vera realizes that she has an obligation to protect and foster her own creativity. It renews her, empowering her to be more effective in her relationships with others.

Vera is concerned with pulling together rather than with separating and compartmentalizing the differing aspects of her life. As a result of her shift in focus and the ability to set priorities, she was able to attain the feeling of integration and wholeness she desired. Her most recent piece, Figure 70, which she conceived as a personal icon, was created at a workshop on spirituality that she participated in and helped to conduct.

Inspired by the techniques used in the Source Imagery workshop, she devised an exercise intended to help people expand their personal relationships, leading them to a deeper understanding of the feelings they had about God. She asked the participants to create a piece that expressed *in images* how the act of bonding among themselves reflected the nature of the bond they felt with God.

As a result of the creative exchange that ensued, the men and women in the group voiced the feeling that they had not only drawn closer to one another but also to an internal source of spiritual energy. The sense of internal integration that the source image had helped to precipitate in Vera expanded her ability as a counselor to quicken similar feelings in her clients.

I mentioned that certain images keep recurring in our dreams and artwork. By now you have ascertained that not all of these are source images. What's the difference?

Again, the image of a house is pertinent. Moving furniture around within one's dwelling is a strenuous task, but far easier and less involved than moving from one home to another. Favorite pieces of furniture and bric-a-brac create a familiar environment. Should we change dwellings, such possessions help us feel at home again. But the new setting exerts its influence upon the interior decor. There is a subtle interplay between the two, together creating the overall atmosphere of the place.

Each time we change the design of a house or shift the position of the furniture, there is a corresponding change in atmosphere. Imagine for a moment that the house could retain impressions of all the incarnations in design and decor it has undergone. This is what the source image has the capacity to do. It is the building that houses our creativity, and recurrent images are the pieces of furniture we place within it. Niki's bird and Vera's moose are recurrent images; the wave and the V shape are source images. Both types of images are intrinsic to creative expression. By nature, their functions fulfill differing needs of the psyche.

Just as walls provide a structural support, so does a source image provide a framework for our imagination. But suppose a person's house was blown away, leaving him with just a few possessions, or that as a result of theft he was left with the house but none of its contents? In the former case the belongings alone would carry on past memories, just as in the latter case the house would do so. Although each comprises an entity in its own right, neither could really be home without the other. In psychic terms each is part of a closed loop system, wherein one end of the feedback path regulates the other.

It is the source image that provides the unique setting for our creative experience. More than a container, it is a magical caldron, the recurrent images the ingredients lending it a special flavor.

Because it is much easier and less expensive to cart furniture about than it is to move a house, each of us inherits only a few source images. Bequeathed to us as part of an unconscious trust fund, their value accrues over time, part of our growing creative estate.

CLAUDIA AND THE MEANINGFUL TANGLE

In both Angela's and Vera's cases we saw how the source image provided a framework for their creative expansion on a number of levels. We also noted that whereas once identified, the shape of a source image can be clearly discerned, it most often takes time to perceive what form it might assume.

Another characteristic of the source image makes its recognition a challenging task. For example, in Niki's second piece the source image assumed a seed shape, i.e. splashing water. We could easily see the connection between the seed and its full-blown manifestation as a wave. But, what if the source image occurs in only partially realized forms as *a fragment and not* a seed? We could imagine that Angela's circle evolved even more mysteriously. Instead of arising from this shape,

it arose from this one,

or even this,

The next case shows this principle in operation. In Claudia's work we see the circuitous route the source image weaves as it evolves. Like Vera, Claudia was married. She had one small son when she first entered the group; a second was born later. Prior to getting married, Claudia had been a teacher, a school counselor and a communication skills trainer. When I first met her, the responsibilities of motherhood were her primary focus. She believed, however, that one day she would pursue a career again and wanted not only to develop her artistic talents but to gain insight into a new direction she might move in professionally. She wanted her work to be as creative an experience as that of motherhood.

As had Vera, Claudia wanted to integrate her roles as wife, mother and professional. Sensing that in a few years the intense amount of energy expended in child care would lessen, she intended to actively lay the groundwork for making a future change. She believed that by cultivating her creativity she could better learn to maintain a balance between caring for the needs of others and furthering her own ambitions. Moreover, she felt a strong desire to make an economic contribution to the family, and this was a motivating factor in her quest for self-discovery.

Claudia was very sensitive to the spiritual experience that opening her creativity represented. She did not attend church on a regular basis. She considered her concern with personal growth and expansion a kind of spiritual pursuit. But, something was missing. She enjoyed the companionship a dedicated group of feminist women offered her, yet she lacked that sense of special connection that belonging to a religious community can provide.

In this regard the act of expressing her creativity was to be a significant event for Claudia. During the process she had learned how to access a regenerative source of spiritual energy. Making this inner connection activated a feeling of wholeness in her, a sense of direct communion with a cosmic force or transcendent intelligence that could guide and inspire her. While she respected the religious beliefs of others, Claudia no longer felt the outsider because she chose not to belong to such an organized belief system. She felt validated in her ability to have a spiritual experience of consequence, knowing that her own heart offered her as sacred a sanctuary as any house of worship. Her creative quest and the quest for significance had gone hand in hand.

Because of the unique way in which Claudia's source image has unfolded—and is still unfolding—I found the recognition of it a challenging task. Each person's creativity opens up at its own pace. Although a supportive environment accelerates the developing of latent talents, a person's abilities, once freed, bloom of their own accord.

I remember the excitement with which I harvested the first vegetable from a little seashore garden. A city dweller, I couldn't believe the fruit had grown out of the seeds I'd planted. To me there was something magical about the process despite the role I'd played in helping it along. Overcome with delight, I ran to the phone to announce to a friend, "My garden's had a tomato!"

There is a cycle to the manifestation and evolution of every living organism. This includes the imagination as well. I can identify the major components of Claudia's source image up to this point, but I cannot yet fully grasp what it will look like in its entirety. Although she and I have worked together for a long time, and have witnessed creative changes in her life, the image is—to my way of thinking—still in a formative stage. But it is because the image is still emerging that it is interesting to discuss.

FIGURE 75

This is the first drawing the client made for me. It is her response to the tree, seed, and star exercise. Notice the carving shapes on the left hand side of the treetop and the line spiraling out of the round object to the lower left.

FIGURE 76

The curve has become much larger in this piece, and the spiraling line has evolved into a long, zigzagging shape.

FIGURE 77

This is the central panel of a triptych the client created in response to the bridge exercise. Several overlapping curves appear in sequence. Observe the large, zigzagging line at their base.

FIGURE 78

The opening to the box is framed by the curving branch of the tree. The leaves are made up of jagged intersecting lines.

FIGURE 79

A third theme emerges, that of the network. Notice the fibrous flesh of the fruit.

FIGURE 80

Here the idea of a network is reflected in the image of the woven baskets.

FIGURE 81

In this piece the images of the network and the curve combine.
They undergo an interesting change, coming together
in the shape of an intersecting highway.

FIGURE 82

The curve, the zigzagging lines, and the network occur together in this piece. The idea of the network is superimposed with the image of a bird's nest.

FIGURE 83

The client is not just breaking out of a shell, her block is cracking open. Her creativity has explosive force in this exciting collage.

The image seems to be composed of three major parts: a U-shaped curve, as in Figure 76; a curling line, like the one on the apple in Figure 75; and the weblike pattern made by a series of intersecting lines, as on the surface of the woven basket in Figure 80 or the bird's nest in Figure 82.

In Figure 75, the U first appears in barely recognizable form as a series of blue curves outlining the left-hand side of the treetop. It next appears in the cave-like opening to an inner landscape in Figure 76. It is repeated—in chainlike formation—in Figure 77, Claudia's response to the bridge exercise (see page 281). Whereas the U shape in Vera's work took on the function of a container, in Claudia's it appears to function predominantly as an entryway.

The idea that the source image delineates the entrance to a special place is evident in Figure 78, a three-dimensional structure Claudia built in response to a meditation concerning the inner child. In this piece the simple curling line, which spirals from the top of the apple-shaped object at the base of the tree in Figure 75 and evolves into a long, zigzagging loop in Figure 76, appears in more full-blown manifestation as the arching extension of the leafy branch of a tree. It is made up of a series of intersecting lines, a theme that begins to emerge with clarity from this point on.

In Figure 79, the two motifs appear side by side. Notice the U shape of the mailbox and the undulating pattern created by the red leaves at the bottom of the collage. In this piece the idea of webbing, or a network, is juxtaposed with that of the U shape and the attenuated, zigzagging line. Behind the head of the woman, a round piece of fruit rises like a sun. It is translucent, and we can perceive the fibrous pattern of the flesh.

The three ideas—that of the U shape, the long curving line and the interlacing network—are superimposed in Figure 81, where we see a highway forming huge interconnecting loops.

In what creative direction is Claudia's source image leading her? In Figure 83, the U appears in the shape of a giant pod-like image that has burst open and, as if scattering seed explosively in all directions, created a complex network of intersecting colors, shapes, images and lines. The piece is a veritable hodgepodge of passionate activity.

Thus the concept of the network, or of a complex series of interlacing lines, is superimposed upon the design of the entire composition. It is as if the U shape, the web and the curving line had led Claudia to a place where she might express herself without restraint. She seems less inhibited, no longer so self-conscious about the orderly placement of images on the page. She trusts that there is an organizing principle within her, helping her wield the brush *of its own accord*.

This is a process she may enjoy. When she was growing up, Claudia's parents placed a great emphasis on a neat appearance and proper manners, so much so that Claudia was actually uncomfortable when she tried to paint. She liked working in her magic book (a special diary described in Chapter 22) the best of all because, as she put it, she only made a "little mess," which was easy to clean up.

Being creative does mean being able to deal with a mess and feeling comfortable about it. One is bringing something into being; the first stages can be difficult, even painful. It is similar to the physical process of birth, which, though awesome and wondrous, is a bloody business.

When we consider the body's venous system, we realize it is composed of a vast, pulsating network of connections without whose presence we would die. Just as the heart pumps blood through our veins to keep the body alive, the psyche pumps imaginative energy through our consciousness. It is important to recognize the close link between biological and creative activity. In the unconscious mind there is a blood tie between sexual reproduction and the creative process; at their core, both are instinctive, ecstatic acts that celebrate nature's fertility and regenerative power.

The intimate, unconscious connection between sex, birth and creativity is depicted in the next painting by Claudia. Here the U-shaped curve has taken on the form of the vagina, and the leafy intersecting lines are like pubic hair around it:

FIGURE 84

The images of the curve and the intersecting lines continue to occur with regularity. Here their shape is reminiscent of a woman's vagina.

Less than a year after painting this piece and about midway through the group process, Claudia gave birth to her second child. She brought us photos that documented the experience of childbirth in explicit detail. She freely shared the intimacy of the moment and what it had meant to her, trusting us to acknowledge the primal, sacred moment that giving birth represents.

This self-revelation was an important turning point. Claudia had no compunctions about our witnessing her nakedness as she let go of the child within her. The painting of the abstract landscape that looks like a vagina signified that she was gaining access to the same kind of excitement about a natural creative process that she felt about having sex or giving birth. And just as she realizes her offspring is a part of her own body, so does she know herself to be inextricably part of nature's body in both a biological and psychic sense.

The blood tie that exists between the human being and nature is nothing to be embarrassed about. Nor can it be kept secret. But to acknowledge nature's power is to acknowledge our mortality and physical finiteness. Birth is but a brief part of a larger cycle in which we all participate. We may try to forget death, but we can never erase it. Being creative teaches us how to celebrate living in the face of dying. It is a spontaneous response to the touch of our cosmic parent.

The next piece illustrates Claudia's awareness that she is part of nature's cycle of birth, growth, decay and regeneration.

FIGURE 85

The use of mirrors in this collage is interesting. The client sees aspects of herself reflected in her work that have perhaps been held in check. The creative child is being released.

The young naked woman peers around the giant tree, staring at the older one. A self-portrait of Claudia gazes out at the viewer. And a small child innocently licks an ice-cream cone, blissfully unaware of the significance of it all, simply enjoying the state of being alive, unselfconsciously a part of the whole.

Releasing our creativity keeps the connection alive and healthy between the human spirit and its source. It nurtures our enjoyment of nature's bounty, helping us participate in the dance of life while at the same time preparing us for an inevitable departure. We are nature's reflection, part of a vast, pulsating network, cells of consciousness in a cosmic web she eternally weaves. Whereas Claudia's source image is still taking shape, her spiritual values have become more clearly articulated and grounded in her day-to-day experience.

Those scribbly lines in Figure 76 remind me of the markings I used to make on the page when I was young and learning how to wield a pencil.

Perhaps the concept of writing itself is superimposed over the squiggly lines in Claudia's early picture. If so, the image suggests that the act of writing will help her thinking— and her source image—to evolve, bringing important connections to light, helping to clear the way and indicating the path of her destiny.

There is a close, dynamic relationship between writing and the image-making process. Each of these creative activities reinforces the expression of the other. The two are inseparable psychic companions.

In my experience these two modes for communicating tend to intersect in a person's creative awakening. From then on, it's which road he prefers to travel that shapes the direction in which he moves. The idea that writing and imaging are closely interrelated is reflected in a recent piece of Claudia's that she did in her magic book.

FIGURE 86
*Notice the transmutation the three images, the curve, the intersecting lines,
and the network undergo in this piece.*
They are superimposed with the image of the enlarged branches of a tree.
The image suggests a roadmap or venous system.

We see the image of the U shape in the heartlike curve
of the flower in the upper left-hand corner of the page and
in the leaf at the lower right. The image of the network also
appears; here it is superimposed over the upside-down image
of a tree. The larger branches look like roadways on a map,
or even remind us of the arteries within the human body.
By means of implicit superimposition we can surmise that
in Claudia's mind the differing aspects of her life and her
creative direction are beginning to join; everything is organ-
ically connected to the living, growing body of the whole.
And the whole derives its lifeblood from the multifarious
connections of which it is composed.

A little book that looks like a mirror reflection of
Claudia's magic book lies suspended above the map. There
is writing on one page and a drawing on the other. A hidden
congruence exists between those intersecting pathways on
the map and the interfacing lines of words and color. Although
for now she might not know where she's headed, Claudia's
life is moving in a meaningful direction, because now there
exists an ineradicable congruence between her heart's plan

and her mind's intent. Her soul's treasure—the capacity to be creative, symbolized by the image of the book within a book—lies open before her. Whose story is written on that map? The seeming tangle of paths that Claudia treads as a mortal being and the one she follows as an immortal soul are not separate. To read the book one of them is writing is to understand the secret language of the other.

Learning to trust her creative instincts and take pleasure in them has opened up new avenues of self-expression for Claudia in relationships with her children, spouse and career; it has helped her perceive how all these activities fit into a larger spiritual scheme of things, and how they are a direct expression of it.

Claudia is working part-time while considering her next step. She has used her dreams and images to guide her to this point, though perhaps it is in writing, not in painting, that her artistic growth lies. In another recent piece in her magic book, Fig. 87, the curly line has evolved into what looks like, among other things, a giant C in reverse. Like the enlarged initial letter that stands out on the pages of a medieval manuscript, the prominent abstract shape might represent the first initial in a series of written thoughts that could inspire and guide her, as her images have done.

FIGURE 87

The more often these significant shapes appear the more intriguing and exciting the form they assume.

Just as it is impossible to say in which direction a source image will evolve, it is impossible to determine what face creativity will assume once released. This awareness is reflected in Claudia's painting in the image of the coin upon which several faces appear carved in relief. Writing may well represent an important step in Claudia's creative development. Perhaps the C stands less for Claudia than it stands for commitment, the commitment to more fully discover the shape of her creative nature.

Her source image has guided her to this point. It has become an entryway to an alternate reality. The following collage suggests the elusive nature of the source image. Never an end in itself, it represents a psychic passageway to a new state of consciousness.

FIGURE 88

Like the tales of A Thousand and One Nights, *the client's images make up a neverending story. It's as if she had rubbed a magic lantern. Creativity is helping make her dreams come true.*

As we look at this last piece we wonder about those objects the woman contemplates. Are they lying somewhere outside her and yet to be internalized? Or do they represent something beautiful and mysterious that, formerly inside her, now lie in the open for her to appreciate.

This riddle reminds us that the function of the source image is to raise as many questions as it reveals answers. It provides us with a better "now," even as it points in the direction of the "what next."

I noted earlier that Claudia's U shape predominantly symbolized an entryway rather than being a receptacle, as it was for Vera. Yet, when we perceive the shape of the basket in Figure 80, and the nest in Figure 82, we recognize that for Claudia this image can sometimes assume that function, too.

In Figure 82, it protectively houses young life. We see a small black egg-like shape behind the heads of the fledglings. The egg, a cosmic source image, represents the awakening or integrating of an unconscious part of the self into the conscious personality. And the bowl-like shape of the nest is symbolic of the cup or chalice, also a cosmic source image. Furthermore, the overall shape of the large blue curving lines (converging with the birds and egg) and the strokes of pink and orange adjacent to them forms a shape similar to the C in reverse in Figure 87.

Remember that each single art piece we make is connected and related to its predecessors and successors; each is but a fragmentary aspect of the meta-image continually coming into view. Like a blueprint, individual creative acts are a reminder of the ultimate intent and not the goal itself.

Viewed from this perspective, Claudia's U shape and the web have undergone an interesting transmutation when they occur in the shape of a nest. Each stroke she paints, every line she writes, like the interconnecting loops of the nest, are part of a tapestry she is weaving, one thread at a time. Together they house the spirit of the artist within her, a part that wants to become stronger and more independent.

As I discussed earlier, cup-like receptacles belong to the image complex of the chalice and represent the instinctive awareness we each have that creativity allows access to a cosmic reservoir of spiritual energy within us. It is as if we each had to fashion our own cup in order to refresh ourselves at this universal source. Like water springing from an underground well that is yet to be discovered, we suspect—even smell—its presence but have to dig about on our own to find it.

Our creativity is a dipper reaching into this eternal well. The pod-like U we encountered in the collage in Figure 83 originally formed the picture of a well, which Claudia then cut into pieces, unwittingly creating a superimposition that contained this idea.

We now have a better appreciation of that piece. The blue petal-like shapes in the middle of the collage, one of which extends over the middle of the open pod, look like wings. Above it the somewhat androgynous figure of a woman wearing a top hat peers forth with a determined gaze. It is as if the birds in the earlier piece had taken flight, leaving a symbolic remnant of their blue nest behind, indicating by their gesture that the artist in Claudia was ready to take flight.

In reviewing Figure 87, we can also see traces of the nest. Perhaps that dark shape that looks like an initial letter represents the black egg. It has grown, breaking its shell, spilling its valuable contents out. The circular ancient coin could represent the magical surface of the well revealed; in it, Claudia sees the faces of her differing selves reflected. Through the power of spiritual insight that creativity affords, she now perceives them as indivisible aspects of one being, and recognizes the One Being within its multitude of individual manifestations.

No one can escape his spiritual origin, whatever his religious leanings or philosophical inclinations. Its presence is as natural as the air he breathes. To discover and bring forth our creativity is to promote a healthy rapport with the environment. Is this "environment" inside or outside us?

Being creative means living in a world where there is no such division, a world rife with endless magical connections. Claudia's loop, Niki's wave, Vera's container, Angela's circle, all links in a chain of ongoing psychic events encircling us with their mystery.

Where does it end? It is not a finite cycle but an eternal spiral. To enter the magic circle you have but to take one step, cultivate one small change in consciousness at a time. Although you might not recognize your source image overnight, I suggest you doggedly keep looking around for it. The search is as exciting as the discovery.

The last section of this book is devoted to the hands-on experience of Source Imagery. It contains a series of special visual and writing exercises for you to explore and experiment with. By opening and stimulating both modes of communication, I hope you will more likely be able to find your way, to devise your own map to the creativity inside.

PART FIVE

The Magic Book

19

The Heart of the Child

WILDFLOWER SEEDS

A friend told me about spreading a can of a variety of wildflower seeds over a garden; she had to wait, of course, to see what she would get. Since they were all wildflowers, she couldn't miss; there were bound to be some happy surprises.

Similarly, once it has been stimulated, you cannot predict what direction your creativity will grow in, nor precisely what images will take root. However, there is much you can do to assure yourself that the creative seeds planted, whether in your artwork or magic book, will flower. I'd now like to introduce a variety of exercises intended to help you put into practice the ideas I've presented thus far. I will also provide a few hints about what you can do to support and reinforce this process.

First, there is a series of creative exercises aimed at unblocking visual image-making faculties. Second, there are exercises aimed at releasing the hidden writer, a part of us that yearns to get a word in edgewise. Finally, I will include some guidelines for creating a source or magic book, a very special and exciting creative journal to keep.

A new acquaintance once asked me, "What is it that makes you think you have something special to say about

273

creativity?" It was a challenging question to which I did not have an immediate answer; I gave it a minute of thought. "I suppose," I said at last, "that the writer in me is not in the closet anymore, and now that she's out, she just won't keep her mouth shut."

I think of one client in particular when considering this issue of finding one's writing voice. She wrote poetry but felt blocked; in addition, she had great difficulty reciting the poems in public. In fact, a fear of what others might think of her work so intimidated her that even when she was alone, their imagined presence had the power to strike her dumb.

I'm convinced that my new acquaintance believed she had something special to say, too, but that she also was stuck. Perhaps what she really wanted to say to me was "How did you find your voice? I'd like to find mine, too."

The client overcame her block, but achieving this goal was part of a process. One night in group when the time came for her to share her material, she flung her arms wide open in a gesture of self-confidence, boldly announcing she wanted to recite some of her poetry. Like Niki, who had decided to make waves, she was declaring her right to make creative noise. No one minded. Rather, we enjoyed and benefited from it.

I was not surprised, however, to learn of a setback that occurred soon after. She related a dream in which she found herself in a closet with a beautiful blond youth. She liked him very much, but quarters were cramped. To their relief they discovered the door was not locked, so they decided to go outside. Just as they were leaving, a policeman appeared and tried to force them back inside.

Although she had begun to open up, the client was still up in the process of learning to overcome the old taboo against uninhibited self-expression. Her subconscious anxiety about the repercussions of her change were reflected in the presence of the police officer. One must silence the voice of the critical parent and set aside self-invented taboos about giving vent to creative desires.

What's wrong with them, anyway? Does that mean we have pretensions of becoming a Michelangelo or Picasso? Are we secretly hoping that our creative genie is actually a creative genius who, like some kind of superman, can leap tall buildings in a single bound? I think most of us would be thrilled if the genie were to grant us a series of little wishes—we're not asking for the moon—and if but one came true, that in itself would represent a big change.

Many people have a blind spot when it comes to recognizing the extent and magnitude of their creative potential. The difference between the acquaintance who had not yet found her voice and the client who had found hers but feared losing it again is this: the former person could be stopped, while the latter was rapidly becoming *unstoppable*. Once a person begins to form a loving relationship with the unconscious mind, he can lean on it for support through the rough times. My client's dream did not represent a hindrance; it pointed to an open door for which she needed the strength to pass through. It encouraged her to overcome whatever remaining obstacles she'd placed in her own path.

Trusting the process is the sine qua non of succeeding with the Source Imagery material. I hope that reading this book has turned the ground of your mind, making it garden-ready and prepared to nourish the seeds of creativity so that they may thrive like the wildflowers, scattered on fertile territory.

THE IMAGE BASKET

I mentioned this particular client's temporary setback because, in my experience, no matter how excited someone gets about the results of working with the Source Imagery techniques, the voice of the critical parent (initially, at least), interferes with the connections he's making, just like static on the line. A person must keep reminding himself of how important it is to nurture and encourage himself by giving the child side consistent strokes and attention. There is an axiom in Transactional Analysis which states that the Adult can't function without the cooperation of the Child. We each have a responsibility to learn how to take care of our child-self properly if we want to get where the grown-up part of us wants to go.

No matter how strong the intent may be to implement a new course of action, the only way to actualize it is by consciously and assiduously *stroking the child*. When the child is content, the whole self sings. I'd like you to refer once again to the diagram of the Parent and Child (page 24) before proceeding. Give some thought to what it is *your child* wants to do next in terms of beginning a creative project.

Keeping in mind it's the child we're trying to hook, I'd like you to consider from the list of exercises in Chapter 20 which one or ones turn your child on the most? In terms of materials, which ones do you want to get first?

Children like to have choices. I remember a wizened old lady who ran the penny candy store in the neighborhood where I grew up. She didn't talk much. All day she'd stand there while we hung around in a state of interminable indecision trying to figure out what to buy with our limited cents. Dawdling and chewing over in our minds which candies to select was time-consuming, as there were varieties that sold for three—instead of one or two—pieces for a penny. Then there was the matter of color and taste. What a delicious dilemma!

I'd like you to regard the act of selecting your art supplies as a trip to the candy store. What colors do you like best? Which kind of medium do you want to try out? Magic Markers, pastels, fluorescent Crayolas? There are paints, too. I especially like acrylics, because they are easy to mix, water-soluble and fast-drying. They come in metallic colors like silver, bronze, gold and pewter, which are fun to mix with other shades, giving them an interesting tint.

To explore the possibilities can be intriguing and exciting to the child inside you. To him the array of choices is not intimidating but a treat.

There are also clay mixtures that are self-hardening. You might choose to respond to the exercises by making three-dimensional objects as well as by drawing.

It's important to have a place to put things, a big box or basket in which all these supplies can be kept handy. You can also collect memorabilia lying around the house, odds and ends, pieces of fabric, all kinds of flotsam and jetsam from the effluvia of life. Everything is grist for the mill. The critical parent will like that. He'll think the kid is about to clean his act up, not make a mess.

It's a good idea to have at least two baskets ready, especially one for collecting a variety of images: photos (which can be photocopied), cards, magazine pictures, etc. All these will be useful for your collages.

Here is a review of the few essentials you will need. Along with a collection of interesting images, some paper and coloring materials you should have on hand:

1. A jar of Elmer's Glue-All.
2. A jar of acrylic gloss medium.
3. A few paintbrushes.
4. A few pieces of mat board.
5. A variety of shiny materials—several shades of glitter, sequins, metallic confetti, metallic pens, pieces of gold and silver foil, etc.

I'd also like you to give some thought to what sort of notebook you would like to use should you decide to create one of the special diaries described in Chapter 22. You can invest in one or two different kinds depending on what type of journal you prefer to keep. If you are predominantly interested in writing, I suggest a loose-leaf variety. A convenient zip-up kind can sometimes be found at the five-and-dime. Another type is bound and contains acid-free paper that you can use for painting as well as writing. It comes in a variety of shapes and sizes and is sold at almost any art-supply store.

Like a child who has plenty of toys to play with, once you have gathered these materials you can start having fun trying the exercises ahead.

20

Opening the Artist's
Eye

In Part Two, I introduced you to your first creative exercise,
The Tree, The Seed, The Star. You may now experiment
with the next several exercises in any order you like, but I
strongly recommend that you do so only after having
completed this first one. I'd also like to recommend that you
save the last visual exercise in this section for some time after
you've begun practicing others and have gained confidence
and facility in wielding the new tools. I try to keep such
conditional requirements to a minimum, but there is a certain
optimal order to mixing the ingredients in this recipe.

When I was a teacher, I used to get a kick out of giving
my students an assignment that had the cryptic title "Machine
Consciousness." Inevitably hands would shoot into the air.
"What do you mean?" they'd say. "You want to know how
many pages it should be?" I'd ask. "No," another would say
in despair, "what do you *mean* when you say something like
machine consciousness?" "Oh," I'd respond, keeping a straight
face, "I simply mean 'machine consciousness.' " "Yeah,"
would say a student whose temper had run short, "what I
really want to know is, not what *it means* but what the heck
do *you want?*"

278

"Aha!" I'd exclaim gleefully. "I knew it! You're trying to figure out my expectations. But the point is not what I want you to say, it's what *you* want to say. *Your* response is what *I* want." I would go on to explain that they could interpret the topic any way they chose. They could draw, sing, compose, photograph, act or write out whatever they liked as long as the subject had to do with what the term meant to them.

The same thing goes here. You can produce *whatever you like* in response to these exercises. Although I give fairly precise guidelines as to what the focal point should be, whatever you want to make is what's supposed to be evoked. Every response is "right."

When they get an idea they like, many artists don't produce just one version of it but a whole series. They don't get attached to a piece of paper. They buy stacks of them, and if they don't like one attempt, they'll try another. The same thing may hold true even when they like one particular effort; they still go for another. It's like asking for a second piece of pie. Why not?

You should remember to take a few moments to relax, closing your eyes to meditate before starting any exercise, concentrating on the rhythm of your breathing. This essential step will allow you to get in touch with your child and to establish contact with your unconscious mind.

After you have meditated you need not rigidly stick to the directives outlined in the exercise. Let your imagination have free rein. Feel free to work with your own ideas at any point. You can draw, paint, collage (Exercise 1 contains a description of a simple collaging technique), sculpt or do a combination of any of these. Once you have begun experimenting, you'll figure out ways to mix and combine media on your own. And, as my clients have discovered, once stimulated you'll only need to refer to this list for an occasional boost.

Exercise 1: Future Hopes and Aspirations

This exercise can be done over a period of several days. To begin, I'd like you to visualize for a few moments some of the things you'd like to see happen in the future. What are some of the material things you'd like to have? What intangible things would you like to experience such as changes in your career or in relationships? Come out of this meditation when you are ready, and take some time to tear or cut pictures from magazines, old calendars, etc. that best approximate the kinds of experiences pictured in your mind's eye. These images do not by any means have to exactly duplicate what you saw. After you have outlined goals by means of the meditation, it's important to then let go of the conscious intent you've identified. Simply select those pictures that instinctively attract you the most.

If you like, you can set the pictures aside for a while, taking time to mull things over. Like starter dough, which is active even when heaped in a mound, your ideas will be brewing. Then you can begin again.

Gather the pictures and any other materials you'd like along with a piece of mat board (any size) and meditate again for a few moments. Once you're ready, start moving things on the board as if playing with the pieces of a puzzle. Look for surprising connections. Pretty soon you'll see an arrangement you like. Then go to work.

To begin, brush some acrylic gloss medium over an area of the board. Then position the images you want there, brushing more medium over them once they are in place. Although the glue is whitish and cloudy, it will dry clear. The Elmer's Glue-All is useful for attaching larger or bulkier objects to the collage.

Exercise 2: The Toy

Think back to a time in your early childhood. See yourself as a small child dressed in a favorite outfit, playing with a favorite toy. Can you see it? What was it? Did you actually own it or only wish for it? Picture it as clearly as you can. Imagine this toy with full intensity. See it in detail. Embellish it with your imagination. Then see yourself giving it to your inner child as a gift to be enjoyed always. Relax and come out of this meditation. When you're ready, draw a picture of it, adding whatever other elements you'd like to the piece.

Exercise 3: The Window

Imagine you could build a magnificent window in your house, one you'd sit in front of for hours, gazing out at the view. Visualize your window in detail. It can be any shape or size, made of any material you like. Once you have pictured it clearly, take a moment to relax and let the image go. Now conjure the window again. This window has special properties. It's like Merlin's window. Looking through it you can see a scene in your future; you have a view of something you'd love to experience. When you're ready, draw a picture of what you've seen. Embellish it with pictures from the image basket if you like.

Exercise 4: The Mirror

Before meditating and beginning this exercise, I'd like you to think about the idea "mirror" for a few days. What kind of thoughts does it conjure? Sometimes a person or relationship, or perhaps an experience, has acted as a mirror. Maybe you remember a particular mirror you have looked in and have strong associations with. What was its shape? Where was it? Why do you remember it? Or describe something else interesting you have seen yourself reflected in.

Once you've given the matter some thought, proceed as you have with the other exercises, meditating, then visualizing how you would like to respond. Perhaps you would like to include writing along with whatever else you create.

Exercise 5: The Bridge

Picture a bridge in your mind's eye. Like your window, it is very special. Where is it? What is its shape? What is it made of? Once you can see it, imagine yourself crossing it. To the left and to one side of the bridge is a scene from the past you are leaving behind. To your right and in front of you on the other side is a scene in the future you are moving toward. You notice that you are carrying something across the bridge; it is a symbol from the past you want to take with you into the future. What is it? When you finish meditating, create your bridge using whatever materials you'd like, such as string, pieces of wood, etc. Paint or collage the scenes from the past and future at either end of the bridge.

Exercise 6: The Key

Once you have meditated, imagine a key. It is special. What color is it? And what is its shape? Let the image go, and relax for a moment.

Now picture your key again. This time you notice that it is lying in a very unusual setting. Where? Make a drawing of the key showing where it is placed.

Exercise 7: The Magical Beast

Almost everyone has an animal he admires for its beauty and particular kind of power. Think about your favorite animal. Once you've identified it, take a few moments to meditate. Now picture this animal in your mind. As you imagine how it looks, you notice it is endowed with certain magical qualities. Fascinated, the child in you wants to touch and become friends with it. This animal is strong and awesome but approachable. He has some fanciful characteristics. He can be any size, shape or color. Once you have conjured him the way you like, draw a picture based on the image.

Exercise 8: The Magic Carpet

Imagine that you own a magic carpet, kept hidden in a secret place. At night it takes you wherever you want to go, and no one is the wiser. Take it out of its hiding place and examine it. What makes it so special? It's very beautiful. The fabric is embedded with unusual designs and magical objects.

Draw a picture of this carpet. Have fun pasting or collaging things onto it to make it come alive.

Exercise 9: Aspects of the Future Self

Take a few moments to relax. Now pick out three qualities you'd like to express more fully in the future. Keep your ideas simple and to the point. Once you've identified these qualities, jot them down on a piece of paper.

Now meditate again for a few moments, recalling each of the qualities one by one. See each word in your mind's eye. Then, *in place of the word,* imagine a symbol embodying that quality (e.g., in place of "love," an image of a heart). Once you have identified the three symbolic shapes or objects, picture them together in a drawing. As you look at the drawing, you notice a surprising element, something you didn't expect to find there. What is it? When you're ready, draw this picture.

Exercise 10: The Future Self

Imagine yourself as a child walking down a long country road. The day is bright and clear, and you feel content. The road extends far into the distance. To the left is an old stone wall and miles and miles of beautiful meadow. To the right is an endless row of tall and fragrant dark-green trees. As you walk, the sun filters through the leaves, making beautiful patterns on the ground.

Suddenly you notice a figure approaching from way up ahead, a speck against the horizon. As you see it coming toward you, you become very excited. You know now that you are on this road for a special reason. You look forward to the coming meeting with your whole heart.

As the figure gets closer, you realize why you are so thrilled. The approaching person is you—the you that you want to become in the future: stronger, more beautiful and powerful, with a healthy love and great respect.

You feel this love emanating from the presence as it draws near. Completely unafraid, you leap into one another's arms and embrace. You feel the strength of this presence entering you, and you are safe and secure.

Then the figure smiles and you know the two of you must part. Before the figure fades, take note of how it looks, especially what it is wearing. Form a clear, detailed impression in your mind.

Once again you are on the road, walking by yourself and headed home. But, just as you are turning to leave, you see before you on the ground a beautiful, magical object. It is a gift that the future self left with you as a token of the meeting you will always remember.

Create a picture of the future self and the object it bestowed on you with love.

SOME HINTS

Whenever you decide to do an exercise, you need not concern yourself with reproducing on paper exactly what appears in your mind's eye. Concentrate only on *having fun* and capturing the spirit of the thing. You can begin working with only a vague impression of what you've imagined. This is not a test but a trial run, a step in the right direction. And whereas it is satisfying to draw a whole picture and complete a piece at one sitting, it is also important to recognize that many exercises evoke thoughtful responses requiring time for their completion.

Occasionally you might find yourself beginning a piece, setting it aside and coming back to it over a period of a few days or even weeks. If so, there is nothing to prevent you from having more than one piece in progress at a time. In fact, such a situation is desirable and to be encouraged. No one likes having only one outfit to wear; an interesting variety of combinations keeps us from getting bored.

So it is with imagery. We need creative pieces that are an outlet both for the serious side of our nature and for the more carefree one. We can make playful, lighthearted or superficial pieces as well as deeper and more significant ones. To the extent that we become flexible, allowing ourselves time to complete some pieces slowly, we give the unconscious mind room for working its magic, in myriad ways unbeknownst to us.

THINKING ABOUT IMAGES

Once you've started having fun producing artwork and have compiled a few pieces, you might want to step back and think about what you see in them. What images, shapes, colors or themes recur? What aspects of a drawing attract you the most? In future pieces I'd like you to feel free, on your own, to explore drawing or developing those shapes and themes that appeal to you. By relying on your instincts, you will find new capacities for self-expression gradually opening up.

In the next chapter I deal with writing. However, there is a simple exercise I'd like to introduce now that will empower you to connect with the feeling elicited by your imagery.

Exercise 11: Writing a Verse

Pick a piece you have created that you especially like. Meditate on it for a few moments, recalling how you felt when you were getting ready to make it and then began working on it. Write down the thoughts and feelings you had in several sentences or phrases.

Then, looking at the picture again, recall the thoughts and feelings you had when you were well into working on it and ready to complete it. Write these impressions down.

Finally, review the picture again and recall the thoughts and feelings you had about the piece after you finished it and were looking it over. Write these ideas down, too.

When you've got your list, read it over from start to finish, underlining the phrases that impress you most. Now write a four-line, free-style verse, expressing your ideas in briefer, perhaps more evocative form.

I'd like you to make a practice of occasionally going back over the images you have produced, taking time to appreciate them and the feelings they arouse. Writing about them is an optional but valuable experience; it will greatly enhance the benefit you can derive from working with your images. If you feel blocked, you will find ways to overcome barriers to this form of creative self-expression in the pages ahead.

21

≈≈≈≈≈≈≈≈≈≈≈≈≈≈≈≈≈≈≈≈≈

Freeing the Writer's Hand

THE CLOSET

When I said the writer in me was out of the closet, the image was an apt metaphor. Most women I've met can identify with the experience of going to a closet filled with clothes one day and finding to their dismay that all at once they've "got nothing to wear."

What's happened? A closet is a selecting and storage space. We often keep items in it that are still in good condition but which we never use. Somehow when we put them on, they neither fit nor look quite right. Our image has changed. Yet we are afraid to discard them, thinking one day we might wear them again. So there they hang, year after year, taking up space and never being put to use.

There are other kinds of unworn items, perhaps something we bought on a lark. Something a little flashier or more daring than what we're used to. We bought it on an extravagant whim. It hangs there waiting for its day to come.

Then there are the good old regular clothes we wear day after day until they fall to shreds, practical things we live in. Along with these are elegant, sexy, perhaps even theatrical clothes for evenings out; professional-looking clothes for work; sportswear; and sloppy items for when we are feeling low or don't care how we look.

The state of a closet reflects a larger fact of life. We are all a composite of past, present and potential or future selves. And at any given point in time, that self is composed of differing aspects: the outrageous side; the conservative side; the introverted, shy side; the extroverted, assertive side; etc. Just as there are pieces of clothing we've outworn, there are parts of ourselves we are ready to let go of and new parts to discover and express.

Once in a while we decide to clean the closet. This act involves more than dusting and vacuuming. A genuine closet cleaning means going through all those things hanging there, discarding, recycling and giving away some, finding unexpected uses for others.

It is satisfying to get rid of the unnecessary junk. Until it's gone, there's no space for new things. And the selecting process is a sifting one; we are able to discern and make clearer choices about the new image we want to project.

The same applies to writing. Writing offers us invaluable assistance. Like the friend who stands beside us, helping to decide which items to keep and which to give away, the writer in us helps sift through our options and make choices clearer, enabling us to let go of aspects of ourselves that have long since outworn their usefulness and to identify new aspects that will empower us.

A FRESH SLATE

Why do we find it so hard to write? It need not be if you will take the time to experiment with the following exercises. Just as making images comes naturally to us, so does making sense out of words. To want to enjoy writing is the same as wanting to dance, sing or paint. It's a natural extension of the artist within us.

But early experiences have left their imprint and we often find ourselves inhibited when expressing our thoughts on paper. Like the client struck dumb by the voice of the critical parent whenever she wanted to write, we too remain silent where we would rather speak out.

It's as if we need a giant eraser to wipe away the

memories of all the red marks we've ever received so we can start with a clean slate. As in the previous exercise section, there is one exercise I would like you to do before proceeding with the others; it will initiate you into a new perception of writing, helping to erase attitudes that are holding you back.

NEW BEGINNINGS

Exercise 1: The Teacher

Take a few moments to relax. Then think about some teacher you've had in the past, someone you may or may not have liked but who stands out in your mind. Try to remember how the person looked physically, the kind of clothes he wore, his manner of speaking, characteristic gestures, and so forth. Once you have fixed the image clearly in your mind, write a paragraph describing the teacher as vividly as possible. The twist is this: write the paragraph in such a way that I would not only be able to picture him clearly but could also figure out whether you liked him without your having said so directly.

Doing this exercise will show you that it is easier to write when you have a clear image about what you want to say. In this instance it is the mental picture of the teacher. You don't necessarily need fancy words and a sophisticated grasp of grammatical rules in order to write clearly and effectively. Powerful writing is honest writing—writing that directly communicates your feelings. In writing a response to this exercise, you will continually look for words that best reflect and correspond to the feeling evoked by the mental image. When they match, you will feel satisfied, as if you are saying the "right" thing. The right thing when writing is to find the correct correspondence between word and feeling.

In the context of this discussion, to write means to make a "picture" in words that exactly reflects what you feel. Each of us has the capacity to form such mental pictures and communicate them intelligibly to others. The next exercises will help you develop and reinforce a new attitude about writing.

FORGOTTEN SENSE, FOUND ESSENCE

Having completed the initial writing exercise, you may proceed with the others in any order you prefer. Again, I'd like to remind you to begin each one by meditating for as long as you like. It's important to relax in this way; you'll feel less afraid and your ideas will flow more readily. The first connection to concentrate on is the one with the unconscious mind, not a piece of paper.

In some instances I will ask you to identify and write about a figure from the past within a very specific context. When this is the case, I would encourage you to pick a character you feel comfortable with. To benefit from the exercise, you need only select a real figure, not one of Dostoyevskian proportions.

I recall a workshop I once participated in which dealt with the importance of expressing one's emotions. One unfortunate fellow spent the better part of an hour thrashing around on the floor, sobbing his heart out in an effort to "release my bad feelings" while everyone else had moved on to a new exercise. It probably did him some good, but what I found interesting about the experience was his apparent belief that the extended expenditure of energy represented an end in itself. He evidently didn't understand that the idea was to bring it all to an end. I like to think of writing as a means to transcend suffering, for the release of joy. It is an effective way to create order out of confusion.

With that aim in mind, I encourage you to establish contact with your writing side; it is a part of you that gives special insight and a discriminating perspective. It helps make you feel and act more intelligently.

Once you have begun to enjoy the effects of these exercises, gaining some degree of ease in expressing yourself on paper, I hope you will begin writing your thoughts and dreams down in a source book, which I describe in the last chapter.

Exercise 2: The Daydream

Identify and describe a favorite daydream concerning some goal or aspiration in your life. Embellish it with any new details you'd like, and then write it down. Set it aside for a while.

Later, either the same day or over the next few days, pick it up again. As you read it, you'll notice how satisfying it feels to have put into words those thoughts you have concerning things you'd like to do. As fantastical as the daydream seems, does thinking about any part of it empower you to set a new, realistic goal? What is it? Jot it down.

Exercise 3: The Childhood Daydream

Some of us can recall a favorite daydream we had as a child or in our early adolescence. We imagined we had some special talent, that we could do something unique and magical. Meditate on this for a while. It takes time to remember some of the finer experiences of childhood.

Once you identify such a fantasy, write it down. Put it aside and come back to it later. Reading the daydream will help to remind you of a quality you had as a child, perhaps one that you liked but have forgotten you once possessed. What is it? Write about it. It is not too late to reclaim some beautiful or worthwhile aspect of yourself that might have been left behind. What is something in the present you can do to reactivate this childlike way of being? Write about it.

Exercise 4: The Authority Figure

This exercise is similar to the one about the teacher, but it consists of two parts. First, identify an authority figure from the past, a relative, acquaintance or employer who stands out clearly in your memory. Form a visual image, recall your feelings about him and write a paragraph describing him.

Then draw a line and proceed with the second part of the exercise.

Thinking about this person has perhaps stirred up some unresolved feelings. If you could say to him whatever you wanted, something you couldn't say then because you were too inexperienced, or intimidated, what would it be?

Write a dialogue, getting everything off your chest. You can be serious, but it's a good idea to use some humor, too. Write two distinct versions if you like, one serious and one in a lighthearted vein. Whatever you decide, remember you are the author and director in this script and now have the power to make the person respond exactly as you wish.

Exercise 5: Saying Good-bye

Think of a relationship you had which ended abruptly because of circumstances beyond your control. Perhaps the person moved away, unexpectedly broke up with you or even died. You never had a chance to say good-bye in a way that you would have liked. With hindsight this person's worth and the value of the relationship have become clear to you. Imagine having a conversation with him in which you say everything you wanted to.

When you finish thinking about this exchange, take a piece of paper and at the top outline briefly what in reality happened between the two of you, describing the separation itself. Then draw a line. When you are ready, write a fictitious dialogue based on the insight you gained while meditating on your imagined conversation. Speak clearly and honestly, voicing what you want. Have the other person respond to you in such a way that you know you are being heard. Allow him to say what he would like, too. The point of this dialogue is for you to reach a satisfactory and happy closure with each other.

Exercise 6: A Special Person

This exercise involves identifying the unsung hero in your life. Think back to some point when you met or interacted with a person, however briefly, who had a positive influence on your life. Who was it? What did he look like? Write about him and the experience, describing the nature of the valuable gift he had to share or the worthwhile lesson he had to teach.

Exercise 7: The Magical Space

Think about a place you have visited that, because of its unique design or layout, had a magical feeling to it. See it again in detail. Recall the sensations and feelings aroused in you when you were there. Write about it when you are ready.

Does it still exist, and can you go there again? Is there a place similar to it that you can visit now? Perhaps instead there is a change you can make in your own environment that would symbolize or help to evoke a similar feeling. Think about it and allow yourself to invent something creative.

Exercise 8: The Letter from the Future Self

Imagine yourself ten years from now. See yourself in marvelous circumstances, enjoying life to the hilt. What are you doing? Where do you live? Whom are you with? How much money are you making? Let your fantasy go wild, the sky's the limit.

Now imagine that this future self has decided to write to you, describing his life. What he has to say is entertaining and—even if somewhat absurd or ridiculous—highly encouraging. When you're ready, write this letter to yourself and see what surprising insight you come up with.

Put the letter aside and come back to it later. What as-yet-untapped aspect of yourself does it get you in touch with? What would you like to do about it? Write these thoughts down, too.

This next exercise combines visual and writing elements. You may need time to think about what you'd like to do, and when you implement your ideas, the project might progress in stages. You should enjoy this process and learn about getting creative results by knowing when to push and when to back off. With time you'll see how things can fall into place almost on their own. Being creative is part of a two-way relationship. It's as if you were entering into a dance with the unconscious mind. You need to cultivate a sense of when to take the lead and when to follow.

Exercise 9: The Fairy Tale

While meditating, think about two different sides of your personality that appear to be in conflict, such as the shy side and the more extroverted one, or the conventional versus the artistic side. Be sure to choose something you can comfortably handle on your own. Once you've identified these parts, imagine them personified as separate characters in a fairy tale. One is the hero or heroine, the other might be a mythological creature or some other magical animal or being. Write a story about them, endowing them with fanciful names and personalities. It is a tale of adventure, in which the conflict between the characters is *magically resolved*. Illustrate the fairy tale with pictures you either draw or collage. This is an experience for the child side of you.

THE SANDBOX

In experimenting with the preceding exercises, I hope you have come to the happy conclusion that it might be easier and more enjoyable to write than you ever thought possible. I hope you have made some other interesting discoveries as well. Writing about a past experience inevitably helps us to put things in a new light. We gain an appreciation for hidden meaning and purpose, which allows us to recast the event in our mind.

It's enlightening to get this kind of perspective. Details once missed may now stand out. Of course we inevitably alter the picture, sometimes even dramatically, fictionalizing certain aspects of an experience in order to make sense of it, or to turn the outcome around. Yet that new experience created by the mixing of elements from the past and present has its own integrity.

What is the experience we register as reality: the event that indeed once took place, or the event that we choose to create from it? What we write about an experience is an intrinsic part of the whole thing.

I like writing because, like a sandbox, it offers me an arena in which to play with time as much as I want, creating an endless variety of forms out of the stuff of my life. If I don't like one version, I can try out another.

It's not just an act of childlike whimsy. When we write, we are acting in accord with the creative force of psychic images. Like sculptors, we use words to fashion ever-changing, transcendent vessels for experience.

22

≈≈≈≈≈≈≈≈≈≈≈≈≈≈≈≈≈≈≈≈≈≈≈≈≈≈≈≈≈≈≈≈

The Magic Book

THE OWL AND THE PUSSYCAT

When I was a child, I used to like it when my mother sat by the bed and told me stories before I fell asleep. If she wasn't there, I'd make them up myself. Everyone knows it's important to feed the imagination of a child. Why do we ever stop?

We need to invent new ways to feed our imagination in the present. Keeping a source or magic book is an excellent way to do this, at once entertaining the fantasy of the child and fascinating the mind of the adult.

There are two kinds of creative journals to describe: one, the source book, centers on writing and includes pictures; the other, the magic book, focuses on artwork and includes writing. It's a question of emphasis and a matter of choice. Some of my clients keep more than one kind of journal. I suggest you might like to do so, too, for the child inside enjoys options.

The function of both of these books is to provide a private place in which you can experiment with and express your creativity, a place where the magical seeds that your images represent can incubate, free of outside interference. It is like a secret garden where they may grow undisturbed, in whatever direction they like. Much as you might visit this garden for the pleasure and pride taken in it, you'll also find comfort and peace of mind there.

Just as a garden makes a personal statement about its owner, your book will—and must—contain many personal statements about you. In my experience, source images arise most clearly and quickly in *a personal environment*.

A source or magic book provides just such an ideal environment. It's a place where you can create art, revealing your heart without fear. Like the owl and the pussycat who set out to sea with plenty of money and honey, this private book represents a safe passage to hidden places in the psyche. It sometimes seems that parts of our personality have been at odds for so long that we've forgotten they were ever meant to be friends. Yet, like the lucky if unlikely pals in the children's poem, if we invite them into a magical space where they can become reacquainted, they too might sail off in a beautiful pea-green boat and live happily ever after.

FLUID STRUCTURES: THE SOURCE BOOK

I'm one of those people who like things to be organized. Everything in my kitchen is labeled. I suppose in this way I try to create a little oasis of order in which to feel I am in charge. The labels seem to represent push buttons to an invisible machine called "Nothing Will Go Wrong Here."

In this regard I'm reminded of an experience I had as a fledgling college teacher. The students in my class seemed listless and disinterested, and consequently I felt I had lost touch with them. Discarding the syllabus, I suggested they tell me what they wanted to do. I did get their attention using this approach; their spirits perked up immediately. But, to my chagrin, we spent the better part of a semester figuring out what they wanted to do and not much else.

The experience taught me that it is always good to provide the child in people with some kind of structure, something solid to lean on when they are learning something new. As much as it is desirable to release our feelings, we should also maintain a sense of direction and purpose in the process.

The idea of the source book is to provide a fluid structure, one that is flexible enough to allow the child space for free expression while at the same time being tensile enough to provide a sense of safety and security.

To that end I've found it useful for a journal to be organized. Divide it into three sections, viewing them as separate but interconnected channels that are helping to cultivate one large, creative field. The first section, called "Dreams," is for recording and writing about them. The second, "Reflections," is space for creative writing. The third, called "Images," is meant for artwork. Of course, these are only suggestive guidelines; inevitably, such a project takes on its own shape and gains its own momentum.

The best book to use for this purpose is a medium-sized loose-leaf notebook. For the person who likes to keep his thoughts organized, this type of journal acts as a file; he can play around sorting and adding and deleting to his heart's content. A bound book does not offer this kind of flexibility. Of course it's nice to have such a book look special, so you may want to select a loose-leaf notebook (in a zip or snap variety) covered in leather or vinyl.

In "Dreams," you may record whatever dreams or parts of them you remember. In the beginning it's sufficient merely to write down what you happen to recall. However, it's a good idea to cultivate the habit of thinking intelligently about dream material. In order to derive insight and begin to explore what meaning a dream might contain, I've found a simple format that seems to work quite well.

Exercise 10: A Guide for Writing About Dreams

After recording the dream or dream fragment, draw a line and list the images that make a particularly strong impression when you reread the sequence. Then look this list over and jot down *why* they stand out. What makes any one of them especially unusual? Soon you will make a few associations with experiences and feelings the images bring to mind. If you keep writing about them, you'll gradually see sense beginning to emerge. More important than forming conclusions about what the dream means—for it can mean many quite different things—it is essential that you have a creative and playful interaction with the dream material.

In the section entitled "Reflections," I'd like you to record thoughts about your life. You can describe actual events and people, or you can dwell on describing the feelings you have experienced. There need not be an orderly sequence to these descriptions. Be less concerned with recording *dates* than with recording *episodes* that stand out for their particular significance and special characteristics. Practice responding to the writing exercises in Chapter 21, or write about and quote passages from books that have been inspirational and therefore represent creative "source" material. Experiment with poetry—anything. Like an electrical outlet, this section is a place where you can plug into your personal communication power plant.

The last section, "Images," is for pictures. Again, no particular plan or design is needed. It is a place for drawing and collaging that appeals to the artist in you. What images do you like and want to keep? What do they symbolize? This is a space for learning about what images attract you and why, a space that invites you to keep conscious track of important events and changes in your life by means of pictures rather than words. It is the voiceless part of the journal, the Technicolor version of the story, in which you step out as creative art director of the show.

THE MAGIC BOOK

If you can't tell a book by its cover, you definitely can't tell a source book by the guidelines. No two have ever looked alike. Each reflects the unique personalities of the people who have created them. It is similar with the magic book, whose design possibilities are as varied as the individuals concerned. To create one, you will need the sort of artist's sketchbook described earlier. I recommend you choose one with archival-quality paper. You'll also need a supply of palette paper or ordinary household waxed paper for placing between the pages of the book when they are drying.

There are few set guidelines for beginning a magic book. As with the source book, it offers a private space in which to take risks with creativity. Within its pages you are choosing to talk predominantly in images rather than words. If you want to write, do so either by printing something onto the page directly or by typing a passage onto a separate page that is then pasted into the book. The words themselves may then become an integral part of a picture (see Plates 23 and 24 in the color insert).

In the magic book there are no "sections" to be named. It is as if the separate channels irrigating a field had joined and begun to flow together. You can making paintings based on dream images. You can include your writing as part of the artwork itself. The whole collection becomes a colorful picture book, alive with your life's story in its many different aspects.

It is the magic book that especially thrills the child. Like entering the world of dreams, opening its pages ushers you into a time and space that is out of the ordinary. It's a place where you can reshape elements of the past and present or, as if on a magic carpet, project yourself into the future by means of the image alone.

You can use any of the visual exercises in Chapter Twenty to get the journal launched. My clients have used many different kinds of material for making their books: feathers, string, fabric, aluminum foil, costume jewels, watercolors, acrylics, pencils, etc. Some have cut shapes out of several pages so that one can look through them as if through a window, into other pages of the book (see Plate 22 in the color insert). One person is creating a colorful autobiography by photocopying old snapshots and collaging them into her journal, making an "image" album instead of a photo album.

Whatever you decide to do, the main point is that it represent not a sketchbook of artistic ideas but an art book of creative sketches. I hope that by viewing a few pages from the magic books shown in Color Plates 22, 23 and 24, you will be inspired and motivated to begin your own.

WHY CALL IT A MAGIC BOOK?

To me there is something positively magical about our capacity to create an infinite variety of forms. We're all using the same basic stuff, yet the possibilities are limitless. One person's safety pin is part of another person's bracelet.

But there is another reason for my using the word "magic." Images are an extension of a psychic force ever operative within and around us. They are not just arbitrary figments of the imagination, random creations of a wandering mind; rather, they are part of a mysterious, mystical arrangement, an expression of order that goes beyond the limits of the rational, conscious mind.

Why do images have such power? Perhaps, like the veins in the body, they are part of a vital, invisible psychic network not only connecting aspects of the self but linking each of us human beings to one another—joining us into one living, intelligent, creative entity.

"Reality's just a collective hunch," a gifted comedienne, Lily Tomlin, once said. I might add, what is it but *a group image,* one as subject to the magic of creative change and evolution as it is to the vagaries of chance.

HOW WILL I KNOW WHICH ARE MY SOURCE IMAGES?

As I've said, identifying a source image is like trying to solve a riddle. In one sense, all of our images are source images in that they are an expression of and a link to our unconscious mind. But I want to encourage you to use the power of your intuition to understand and discover which of them actually are source images.

In the final analysis, what does a source image represent but the invisible markings the self has inscribed in the mind, as if in evidence of the soul's existence. We may not fathom the depths, but only remark upon the wonder of this inscription.

I want to support you in continuing your quest to better understand the workings of the self by means of the insight creative images afford. And I do not invite you to attend to a boring, dreadful task. I'm asking you to a party. For it is only when you are having fun and thoroughly enjoying the trip that you are apt to stumble by surprise on a source image and the insights it affords, discovering they fall out of a grab bag you are holding in your own hands.

Above all, I hope that by now you recognize that your unconscious mind is an ever-present, built-in personal guide and benefactor, the single greatest creativity teacher you will ever have.

Epilogue

THE IMAGE WHEEL

I have sometimes dreamt of myself standing before a canvas, holding an invisible paintbrush. I am fascinated by the shapes taking form on the surface almost as if by themselves. Am I wielding the brush, or is it the handiwork of some force outside of me? As I peer at the emerging scene I notice the black-and-white outlines filling in, fleshing themselves out in color. Then—almost by magic—I am *in* the scene, transported to a living landscape I have created by my own but invisible dreamer's hand.

Within the context of such a dream it is easier for us to grasp that it is we who create that which we experience. In the real world we cannot easily make this connection because forces beyond our control wield their influence.

But, in reality, might there also be a creative *invisible* force at work like the one in the dream? To what extent do I *co-create* the scene I inhabit?

The Gaia hypothesis maintains that all living and non-living entities are invisibly connected, part of a self-regulating system that keeps its environment constant. According to this view, the earth alone does not create life; rather, it is we—operating collectively and in concert with inorganic things—who help to create the earth as we know it.

If I as a single biological entity affect my environment by virtue of a mere *breathing presence,* then how much more so do I as a psychodynamic entity have the ability to influence it by virtue of the power of my thoughts and feelings.

The artist who dreamed of the edible deck of cards is currently working on a series of paintings called "Art, Bread and Life." It is interesting to see the card image change. In one piece she plans to alternate slices of bread with postcards depicting the works of favorite artists. It's a powerful idea. That which she creates is a real slice of life and, conversely, whatever life throws across her path is food for creative expression.

I envision the pieces of bread and the single cards spread out like a fan before the viewer. Are they disconnected entities—flat, two-dimensional representations of the "real" thing—or are they connected, round, multidimensional entities radiating like spokes from the center of a giant, invisible pyschic wheel that revolves not just in the mind of the artist but in the collective mind of us all?

Do we not each have the responsibility to help this great wheel turn? Are not the pages in our magic books, the canvases we paint, just the tips of its larger spokes coming into view? Through the power of our creativity we can each take a turn at the wheel. Each turn of the wheel is a revolution in the consciousness of the group.